The English Village

1 Much that the modern tourist might hope to find
in an English village – green, inn, old-fashioned
shop and cottages – is shown in this illustration
from Humphry Repton's *Fragments of the Theory and
Practice of Landscape Gardening* of 1816. (Repton,
however, thought that the view from his Essex
cottage could stand much improvement, including
the removal of the green and the cripple.)

RICHARD MUIR

The English Village

with 174 illustrations,
22 in colour

Thames and Hudson

To my parents, and to the other villagers whose roots are in the lovely Nidderdale village of Birstwith

First published in the USA in 1980 by
Thames and Hudson Inc., 500 Fifth Avenue, New York, N.Y. 10110
First paperback edition 1983

Library of Congress Catalog Card Number: 79-67659

Filmset in Great Britain by
BAS Printers Limited, Over Wallop, Hampshire
Color illustrations originated in Switzerland by
Cliché Lux SA, La Chaux de Fonds

Printed and bound in Spain
D.L. TO 1200–1982

Contents

Prologue

SOME PEOPLE thrive on the shifting challenges of the city jungle, but lodged deep in the psyche of most of us is a need for roots and permanence, for constants in a society which has lost touch with its past, and which is distrustful of the future. From the time when the town became more than an overgrown village and began to frown overbearingly across the landscape, the English have contrasted the solid virtues of village life with the graceless alleys, unfeeling buildings and unnatural traumas of the city. Few are blessed with the freedom to choose between the town and the village, for the pell-mell pursuit of employment, efficiency and productivity has drawn most families – eight out of every ten – into the bosom of the town; but for the ever-growing numbers of people who are touched by a sense of unease at the urban industrial future and feel a lack of substance in their lifestyles, the village symbolizes an alternative. It is a place from which strength and reassurance may be drawn, where the past is always present, where neighbourliness is a way of life and the community is so small that no man needs to be a stranger.

Once the unquestioned home of most families, the village has withdrawn from the forefront of English life, but it still offers a different assessment of life's priorities. It remains as proof that buildings need not obliterate a landscape and that co-operation was once an alternative to competition. It has survived foreign invasions, the Black Death, serfdom and countless famines, and if the supreme terrors of the nuclear age should ever strike, doubtless most villages would remain, waiting to succour the survivors.

I am lucky to have spent the first twenty years of my life in the Nidderdale village of Birstwith in Yorkshire, and the last four years on a hill overlooking the village of Great Shelford in the valley of the River Cam, and I always find something interesting in the contrast between the rugged setting of a northern childhood and the softer but older cottages of the mellow south. My first proper job was as a reporter and temporary editor for the *Pateley Bridge and Nidderdale Herald*, and tramping through the snow in an attempt to glean news from vicars and the representatives of the Women's Institute, I began to see the villages that I knew so well as parochial and – for a teenager – boring. Parochial perhaps; but when I later came to survey the testing histories of the people of the village and to explore the remarkable diversity of the different English regions, I found the charge of 'boring' disproven a hundred times over.

2 The traditional village has become an ideal – ageless and unflustered amid the smoke and speed of modernity. In this painting (commissioned for a poster by British Transport Hotels) an archetypal village, with its church and picturesque variety of houses and building materials, sits serenely in its landscape between city and viaduct. The railway has brought commuters to change the village population, but unlike the car (ill. 151) it poses no physical threat.

What is a village? No answer is entirely satisfactory. A settlement with perhaps half a dozen cottages may be judged to be only a hamlet, yet it will be little different from a place with seven or eight dwellings which is rated a village. If we used municipal status as a guide, we would find the 'town' category including many examples of what are to all appearances small and decaying villages, while some 'villages' would clearly be small towns in all but name. We might resort to the elaborate techniques of the economic geographer, and measure the floorspace of shops and assess and grade trading and service functions to draw up a 'settlement hierarchy'. Instead, one might say that a place is a village if it has that indefinable village feeling. Size alone is an insufficient guide: the close network of terraced streets in the delightful town of Lavenham in Suffolk, which grew up and faded with the prosperity of the medieval wool trade, gives it an urban feeling, while Long Melford nearby, with twice the population, has a vast open green that makes it redolent of the village.

The sad historian of the pensive plain.

3 An old villager recounts the destruction of her village while the cottages crumble all around. The illustration comes from the title page of Goldsmith's poem *The Deserted Village*, 1770. He is thought to have been inspired by the case of Newnham in Oxfordshire, which was built as Nuneham Courtenay after the emparking of the original village.

The closer we get to the English village, the curiouser it becomes and the more we find that the sweeping statements of some old historians have been misleading us. First, it is usually safe to assume that the village is older than you think it is, or have been told that it is. The schoolboy's account has the Saxon invaders sweeping across the country like an irresistible wind of change, casting up thousands of new settlements in an almost villageless landscape, whereas we now know that many villages existed before the great migrations, and that in many places the Saxon inhabitants were a minority. When Oliver Goldsmith published *The Deserted Village* in 1770 he thought he was describing a remarkable phenomenon: 'Some of my friends', he says in his dedicatory note to the painter Sir Joshua Reynolds, 'think that the depopulation of villages does not exist.' But when the Vicar of Welton in Lincolnshire invited Dr O. G. S. Crawford to photograph what was thought to be a Roman camp, he unwittingly conspired in the first aerial portrait of a lost village, and since 1925 something like seven thousand lost villages have been found – abandoned for a variety of reasons, including Tudor enclosure for sheep, economic failure and natural disasters. The pace of recent discovery is apparent when we consider that in 1946 the distinguished historian Sir John Clapham wrote, 'deserted villages are singularly rare'.

Secondly, we are finding that the village is much more complex than we thought. In the Middle Ages there was no one set form: although some medieval villages had planned layouts, most grew and shrank rapidly, and there was plenty of experimentation in the siting of the dwellings, the humbler of which needed rebuilding anyway every thirty years or so (see p. 72). We may set off in search of the Saxon nucleus which most villages are supposed to have, and find instead the remains of two or more Saxon villages, with Romano-British village remains also close at hand.

Never really credible is the myth that before the town extended its influence over the countryside, the village was the home of a merry community of milkmaids and yokels whose numb minds encompassed little more than beer and frolics. Although their lives were usually hard, the people were, and are, much more interesting than that, and this book is largely their story. It is a story of pitiful weakness: the villagers were easy prey for whatever rogues history should put in their path, and at times one wonders that they managed to carry on. The explanation of their tenacity and determination to survive lies in family and communal life in one of the world's most beautiful countrysides, and I hope that this side of their story will also shine through the poverty and squalor of old cottage life.

Those who read acknowledgments will realize that without the assistance at the typewriter of the author's wife, books might never come into being. Nina has done more than this, carrying cameras and notebooks through snowbound landscapes, her interest and enthusiasm for the unfamiliar English landscape always a stimulus, while her deficiencies as a navigator have taken us to some fascinating if unexpected places. Her former colleague in the Cambridge University Committee for Aerial Photography, Nicholas Clayton, has suggested subjects for the air photographs and nudged my elbow when some of what I wrote was out-of-date, and members of the department have taken and provided some excellent aerial studies. Former geography lecturers of mine at the University of Aberdeen, Jimmy Coull and Alan Small, revealed the interest and potential of historical geography and, through their writings, Dr W. G. Hoskins and Christopher Taylor have shown how well the landscape story could be told; from time to time I have picked Christopher's brains, and several items from our conversations reappear in these pages. I have gleaned what I could from various experts, but of course any mistakes which may have been made are entirely my own.

It is interesting perhaps that there is no such thing as a 'villageologist' – maybe as well, for it is an awkward word. There are archaeologists, historians, sociologists and geographers who are all in some way or another interested in the village. My own roots are in geography and I have tried to tread the other fields with caution and respect. The village presents many puzzles, particularly with regard to its early history, and clearcut answers are not obtained even when one consults the specialists. And now, more than ever, the village poses far more questions than there are answers. There are good signs that a more 'total' archaeology is beginning to emerge, and this bodes well for our understanding of the village, which is more likely to yield its secrets when the full range of evidence gleaned from old documents, field-walking and excavation is brought to bear.

Many authors will agree that it is the structure of a book that presents the greatest challenge, and I hope that here the wood will stand out from its trees. In a general way the material is arranged in chronological order, but a simple history is not intended. My enthusiasm is for landscape, and the landscape of rural England is largely the product of the (mainly humble) people who experimented on the canvas that nature provided. In the early sections of the book I discuss ways in which the untrained village-dweller or enthusiast can move towards a better understanding of the subject. In its human aspect, the story of the village is in large part the tale of a gritty determination to survive in the face of hardship and oppression, and I devote a special chapter to 'crisis and the village', before going on to look at life in Victorian and Edwardian times, and finally to examine the village's present and future in the light of its past. Some may find the chapter on crisis depressing, but for me the dogged endurance of the people whose lives of hardship so contrasted with the gentle beauties of their stage is a source of inspiration.

One final point: the counties referred to in the text are those that existed before the administrative changes of the last decade. The new counties (which will be found in the index) may offer more in terms of efficiency, but the old ones more closely reflect the traditional regions of England which helped to fashion its beautiful legacy of villages.

Faces of the village

4 The water's edge at Piddinghoe in Sussex. Note the round church tower, a rarity outside East Anglia, which like those eastern towers is built of flint.

5 More hamlet than village, Watendlath in Cumberland takes its name from Norse words meaning 'end of the lake'; the tip of the tarn is seen in the foreground.

6 A mining village, of a sort once common: this scene of terraced brick cottages, lying with unnatural regularity below a slag heap at Willington, Co. Durham, was photographed about 1950. It has since been completely transformed, by levelling of the pit heap and replacement of the cottages.

7 Westmill in Hertfordshire, with its pump house on the green, conforms to the traditional perception of the English village. The medieval church tower is topped by a 'Hertfordshire spike' spirelet.

Introduction: discovering villages

MANY of my readers may themselves be English villagers; others will have left a native village for a life in the town; and it would be surprising if there were even one, English or otherwise, whose forebears were not at one time village-dwellers. It is strange now to think that less than a century and a half ago the majority of the people of this country were to be found living in villages. And the English village is a part of the heritage of much more than just England: many of the people who settled in the New World, in the United States of America, Canada, Australia, New Zealand and many other far-off places were English villagers; much of what they loved there was taken with them and much of what they found oppressive was left behind. The ancestors of Abraham Lincoln lived at Swanton Morley, a Norfolk village, and three Lincoln brothers moved from nearby Hingham to Hingham, Massachusetts, to join their old vicar Robert Peck at the new village which he and his neighbours had founded. Amongst the Friends whose graves lie near the old meeting house in the Buckinghamshire village of Jordans is William Penn, the founder of Pennsylvania; and quite close is a great black barn with timbers bearing the letters R HAR I. Legend tells that the missing letters which time has erased would spell out MAYFLOWER HARWICH.

We hope that this book will stimulate and encourage a number of readers to explore their own village homelands. Some secrets will be surrendered with ease, while others will only be laid bare after diligent detective work. Even apparently ordinary examples have fascinating tales awaiting the teller, and in some cases what had begun as a modest investigation of a place and its past culminates in the publication of a village history. The writings of amateur village historians are numerous: some are poorer and duller than their subjects, most have some merits, and a few of the genre, like Ronald Blythe's *Akenfield* (1969), Rowland Parker's *The Common Stream* (1975), and above all George Ewart Evans's descriptions of Blaxhall, have found themselves, to the surprise of some pundits (and perhaps of their authors), in the upper reaches of the literary hit parade. Whether your interest in the village is passing or intense, some pointers may help in your pursuit.

Where to begin? Well, the village's name itself may contain vital clues concerning its early days. A minority of names are self-explanatory, or nearly so: Salthouse in Norfolk was a depot for the medieval salt industry. Most names appear at first to be meaningless; but it will be noticed that hosts of them end in -ingham, -ington, -chester, -holme, or -stead. Hidden in them there is a wealth of meaning which has become confused as the language of England has changed and evolved. When names are looked at in the light of older tongues, they suddenly come to life, often imparting valuable information about the village in its youth: 'chester' emerges as a Saxon derivative of the Roman word *castra* (camp) and 'holme' is a small island in Old Norse. We must remember that every name that we find had a meaning for the people who gave it, and that village names often describe the features of the settlement or its surroundings that were considered most important at the time of the christening.

Now, if you can trace a name back to its language of origin you have discovered the people who named, and perhaps even founded, the village, and since we know which people were speaking which language at which time, then it is possible roughly to date the period when the name was given. For example, the ending -thwaite comes from an Old Norse word that can mean meadow, suggesting that the name of the pretty village of Hampsthwaite in Nidderdale goes back to a wave of Scandinavian settlement in the Yorkshire Dales, and

history confirms that this settlement took place around the tenth century. Not only does the name tell us which people gave Hampsthwaite its name, and when, but also that around the tenth century the surrounding land was, as it is today, meadowland. Furthermore, the first part of the word suggests a personal name, Hamall, so we might even guess to whom the meadow belonged. Let us be cautious, though, about saying that the Scandinavians founded Hampsthwaite: perhaps they did, but there might have been a village of Saxons there before the Vikings arrived; and the old villagers could have taken flight or been slain by the new colonists, the old Saxon name disappearing with them.

Of course, the amateur village historian will probably not be fluent in Old Welsh, Old English, Old Norse, or any of the other former languages of England and its regions. Fortunately there is no need: experts and place-name societies have provided comprehensive translations, and all that is necessary to obtain an informed if not unambiguous translation of a village name is a visit to the local library. (Some useful works are listed at the end of this book.) Specialists in the field have refined the study of place-names to its limits, and there have even been attempts to trace the Norwegian founders of settlements back not just to Viking Norway but to particular districts of that country by tracing the Norse dialects of the settlers.

The most interesting studies are those which try to discover by linguistic means which villages belonged to the earliest phases of Saxon settlement in England. According to some scholars, a useful clue is contained in the 'ing' element that crops up so often, in names like Hastings, Birmingham or Workington. It comes from the Saxon word *ingas*, which originally meant 'the descendants of' but came to mean 'the people of' or 'the dependants of'. Frequently we find it preceded by a personal name, and followed by 'ham' or 'ton', which denote a home or settlement. Thus Gillingham is 'the home of Gylla's people', and Hastings belongs to Haesta's people. The Saxon invasion, unlike the Norman Conquest, was not a concerted operation: it must have involved many bands of warrior settlers, each band under a particular local leader; and it is easy to assume that the 'ing' names date back to this early period.

For the 'ing' theory to hold water, we would expect to find the *ingas* names most common in the areas which were most exposed to the waves of Saxon invasion, along the coast and the water-courses and routeways used by the invaders to penetrate the interior, and in fact the correlation does exist. Studying England's southern and eastern shores, where the Saxon intruders landed, Kenneth Cameron calculated for each county the number of cases in which a personal name was followed by 'ing'. He found 50 in Sussex, 23 in Kent, 30 in Essex, 36 in Suffolk and 62 in Norfolk. By contrast, in counties lying well away from the invaded shores, he found only 2 cases in Warwickshire, 4 in Cheshire and one in Herefordshire.

Yet while the 'ing' names undoubtedly go back to an early stage in the Saxon settlement, other scholars are beginning to wonder whether they really are the earliest. The cemeteries of pagans – which the Saxons were before the seventh century – were usually located on the margins of village lands; and though early Saxon cemeteries of the fifth and sixth centuries have been found, there is no correlation between them and 'ing' place-names. Recent research by Margaret Gelling seems to indicate that the earliest settlers called their settlement a *wicham*. A few names of this type are found in the south of England (for instance Wickham Bishops in Essex), close to Roman roads which were probably used in the penetration of the interior, and close too to pre-existing British settlements, suggesting friendly contacts. A number of experts believe that place-names ending in -ham, which are common in England, are a little earlier than the 'ing' names, for they show a closer relationship with Roman roads and British settlements.

Another, more tentative, hypothesis is that name-endings such as -ley and -hurst, which refer to woodlands and clearings, reveal a later movement to hive off daughter settlements in the surrounding woodland as the earlier villages became overcrowded.

A smaller number of Saxon village names can be dated by their Christian or pagan associations. The conversion of the Saxon kingdoms began with the landing of Augustine in 597 and went on through the seventh century, so names with Christian links will postdate 597, while pagan names are likely to predate 700. The name of Thundersley in Essex tells of the grove of the thunder god Thunor, while Broxhead may have seen the ritual sacrifice of badgers. Later names include Stokenchurch in Buckinghamshire, which would once have had a log-walled church like that which survives at Greensted in Essex, and Felixkirk in Yorkshire, dedicated to the early missionary, St Felix.

Clearly then, place-names can be an invaluable guide to the early days of the village; but their 'guidance' will occasionally lead the unwary up the garden path! Some name elements are ambiguous: more than nine times out of ten the 'ing' element refers to the settler group, but a few 'ing' names come from the Old Norse *eng* meaning 'a pasture'. Most of the names which end in -ham come from the Old English *ham* which denotes a settlement, but some come from *hamm*, a meadow, and there are six more possible interpretations of -ham names, which are often associated with former Roman sites. The Old English words *ea*, a stream, and *eg*, an island, can both produce names which now end in -ey, so Freshney means 'Fresh River', but Thorney is 'Thorn Island', and Dorney (Buckinghamshire) is 'Bumble-bee Island'.

The languages of England have always been fluid and words that once flowed off the tongue become tongue-twisters to later generations; original meanings are forgotten and invaders sometimes keep the names of the conquered without knowing their significance. In this way, the Celtic *coed* (wood) emerges in Chute Forest in Wiltshire, an unnecessary doubling-up that literally means 'wood wood'. The reader who wishes to translate the name of a particular village may well find that different books offer a choice of meanings: my native village of Birstwith may be 'dwelling in the wood', 'landing place of the fort' or something altogether different. The earliest mention of a name is the most useful, although the early writers took a liberal attitude to the spelling of names, like the Domesday scribes who recorded unfamiliar Old English names in (often poor) Latin. Still, hosts of names are today as they appeared in Domesday nine centuries ago. Very often, an apparently obvious meaning is misleading: the pretty name of Kettlesing near Harrogate may conjure up pictures of the kettle singing on the hob (site of an ancient tea room?) but in fact, so far as one can make out, it refers to a string of lands owned by one long-dead Ketil. Likewise, Killinghall nearby was neither an abattoir nor the scene of a bloody massacre but 'the land of Cylla's people in the river bend'.

Although most names are Old English, place-names present almost as many mysteries as they solve. There seem to be very few names (the River Wye is an exception) which cannot be ascribed to Celtic, Saxon Old English, or one of the languages introduced after the Saxon conquest such as Old Norse, Old Danish and Norman French, so perhaps the considerable Bronze Age population of England spoke a Celtic-like tongue. The profusion of Saxon names overemphasizes the role of the Saxons as village founders and annihilators of the British population: the fact that a village has a Saxon name does not prove that it was not there before the Saxons came along. It is easy to imagine the scene in a Romano-British village when a band of Saxons appears outside the huts. 'What's this place called, then?' demands the Saxon leader, making full use of signs and gestures. The village headman replies with a name as unmanageable to the stiff Teutonic tongue as Welsh names often are to the English. 'To Thunor with that', replies the Saxon, 'I'll call it after myself.' Just as the Saxon villages in eastern England were renamed by Danish settlers, so many villages of British origin will have been renamed by the Saxons. One likes to think that the British villagers survived the Saxon conquest when one finds Saxon and Celtic words combined in a village name like Crickheath in Shropshire, which means 'the heath-covered hill', while the Saxon-named Walworth in Co. Durham is 'the homestead of the Britons'.

While few British village names survive, many topographical features have non-Germanic names, and there must have been many Britons left around to pass on names like crich or crook (hill), pen (hilltop) and avon (water).

Quite a different influence is evident in the place-names of East Anglia, the Midlands and Yorkshire, a region ruled by Scandinavian invaders from the late ninth to the mid-tenth century (see p. 62). In the south and east the newcomers were Danes, but in the north Norwegians coming from the west established settlements. Some of the words used in village names were common to Old Norse (spoken by the Norwegians) and Old Danish, while others such as the Old Norse -gil (hut) and Old Danish -thorpe (an outlying settlement) were peculiar to one language. The most common place-name ending is -by, which simply tells of a settlement. The numerous English -bys and -thorpes suggest quite heavy

Scandinavian settlement in the east, where -toft (homestead) and -holme (small island) are also found. Sometimes the languages of different people are combined, as in Nidderdale, formed of the Scandinavian 'dale' (valley), genitive 'er' (of the) and the Celtic river name Nidd, which means 'brilliant water'.

The Norman conquerors provided us with fewer new names, largely reserving them for their new castles and abbeys. The Normans were not village-dwellers but village-owners, and one can imagine the pride of the Norman gangster-baron who named his new estate Beauchamps, 'beautiful fields' (more often than not smoothed by the English into Beecham). The Normans too wrought some changes in pronunciation: they had difficulty with 'ch' and sometimes softened chester to sester, as in Cirencester. Name twisting carried on long after the Conquest before the spelling of names became standardized, and we do not know who decided that Offord Daneys, in Huntingdonshire, would sound more aristocratic if they changed it to the present Offord Darcy.

Some of the most common English village name elements are set out in the following table. A number have been left out because, like the Old English -bank, -bridge, -brook, -cliff, -cross, -mill, -pool and -ridge and the Old Norse -kirk and Old Danish -bank, the meaning is today as it has always been.

NAME PART	FROM	MEANING
-burgh, -bury	burgh (Old English = OE)	fort, homestead
-by	by (Old Norse = ON)	settlement
-chester, -cester	ceaster (OE), from castra (Latin)	town, camp / camp
-cote, -cot	cot (OE)	cottage
-dean, -den	denn (OE)	pasture
-grove, -grave	graf (OE)	thicket
-ham	ham (OE) / hamm (OE) / etc.	settlement / meadow
-how, -howe	haugr (ON)	hill, mound
-hulme	hulme (Old Danish = OD)	small island
-ing	ingas (OE) / eng (ON)	people of / meadow
Llan or -land	lann (Old Welsh–OW)	enclosure, religious site
-ley or -leigh	leah (OE)	wood, glade
Pen-	penn (OW)	head, hill
-scale or -skill	skali (ON)	hut
-shaw	scaga (OE)	grove
-stead	stede (OE)	place, religious site
-stoke	stoc (OE)	place, religious site
-stow, -stowe	stow (OE)	place, religious site
-thorpe	thorp (OD)	outlying settlement
-toft	toft (OD)	homestead
-wold, -wald	wald (OE)	forest
-wick, -wich	wic (OE)	settlement
-worth	worth (OE)	enclosure, homestead

2 The manor, in classical dress: Winslow House in Buckinghamshire, built about 1700 for Sir William Lowndes, Secretary of the Treasury. Lowndes bought the lordship of the manor, demolished the old house, and had his friend Sir Christopher Wren supervise the building of this imposing brick box (made from the local clay), which rises directly from the village street.

3 The cottage: Watercress Lodge, thatched and secluded, at Ashbury in Berkshire.

The Setting

4 *Opposite, above* The bleak North Sea coast at Aldeburgh in Suffolk, which is now more dependent on tourists than fish.

5 *Opposite* The green at Cavendish in Suffolk, flanked by church, cottages and inn. The plastered and colour-washed cottages have been recently thatched and show characteristic high-pitched East Anglian roofs with geometrical decoration along the ridge. Regional too is the flushwork – patterns made of flint and stone – in the church wall beyond them.

6 *Above* Wordsworth's 'solitary hills' loom above stone houses at Grasmere, Westmorland.

Materials and forms

7 Low thatched roofs and whitened, softly rounded cob walling give Dunsford its distinctly Devonian appearance.

8 *Opposite, above* Sheep graze on the bank of the stream at Hutton-le-Hole in Yorkshire. The cottages behind are built of the local stone; the pantiled roofs could be replacements for older stone-tiled roofs.

9 *Opposite* View from the churchyard at Clare in Suffolk. On the left is a medieval priest's house, later given a famous display of pargetting. Note the variety of window types visible here – the leaded casement of the pargetted house, the original Georgian windows on the upper storey of the house on the right and its more recent larger panes on the ground floor.

Focal points in the villagescape

10 *Above* The church, at Barrington in Cambridgeshire, its tower built of the pale local chalk clunch.

11 *Left* A rare medieval inn, the George at Norton St Philip, Somerset. (The houses on the right reflect the later switch to stone building in this stone-rich county.)

12 *Right* The cross on the green, at Norham in Northumberland. The base is medieval, but as so often the top did not survive, and the present upper part dates from 1870. The salmon on the weathervane refers to the River Tweed nearby.

13 Almshouses in the churchyard at Thaxted, Essex. The range at the left was built as a priest's house, and is now again a single dwelling. The range on the right, of 1714, has nineteenth-century 'Gothick' details. Beyond is an intact tower mill.

14 Stocks and market cross at Ripley, Yorkshire, a village remodelled by aristocratic landlords.

15 Workers' houses and
Congregational Church at
Saltaire, Yorkshire, built
in 1851–76.

16 Canal-side develop-
ment at Stoke Bruerne in
Northamptonshire: grain
warehouse, cottages and
inn serve the Grand
Junction Canal.

17 The irregular lines of roofs and frontages relieve this
attractive cottage terrace at Hambledon in Hampshire of
any sense of monotony. Note the old shop type in the
nearest building.

18 A late medieval house in Abbey Street at Cerne Abbas,
Dorset, displays a jetty and carving above the door. The
house stands on a stone base, above which tiles form
the window-sill of what appears, by the large arches, to
have been a Tudor shop.

19 No two cottage gardeners agree on what constitutes a cottage garden. Here, at Breamore in Hampshire, we have an unusual combination of lilies and potatoes. The house clearly demonstrates brick infill in timber framework.

20 An evocative fragment of cottage life in the Cotswolds village of Great Tew, Oxfordshire, where the geology and climate produce lovely stone cottages and beautiful gardens. The pump is practical, not ornamental.

Until quite recently the life of the village was completely intertwined with the lands which surrounded it, and the next stage in the quest of discovery might be to look at the environment in which past generations of villagers led their working lives. The surrounding landscape will have seen many transformations since the days when the first village foundations were laid, so imagination and information will be needed if one is to reconstruct the setting as it was in the past.

The first question that might be asked is 'Why is the village where it is?' If your village began, like most of those in England, as the home of a small community of pioneer peasant farmers, then you may safely assume that the founders chose the site carefully, looking for a spot that would furnish them and their families with all the resources necessary for a tolerable and self-sufficient life. Some of these resources were more vital than others, so you can imagine the pioneers being tugged at by stronger and weaker attractions, finally settling down at some point of balance between the different pulls. If we were to list these forces in order of importance then we would find that usually access to a reliable source of fresh water from a spring, stream or well would exert the greatest attraction, for nobody wishes to spend the day in hauling buckets of water. Then, in declining order of attraction, might come access to ploughland, meadow grazing land, fuel and building materials and a flattish well-drained site.

One will wonder how these resources of forest, ploughland and meadow were spread out upon the landscape in the days when the village was young, and here the specialist geographer, archaeologist and botanist have some ingenious tricks up their sleeves. Specimens of pollen, snail shells or insect remains may be taken from dateable layers in the soil at a number of sites, on the assumption that if we know what was living and growing in a particular environment at a particular time, then we can deduce what the environment was like. Such intricate techniques are however only brought to bear on important research projects, and the amateur historian might again find place-names a useful source of information.

Although most names may be difficult to date, many will describe the village setting as it once was. In the now drained Fenlands, several village names contain the element 'ey', indicating an island standing above the surrounding marshland: Eye, Ely, Setchey and Tilney are example. The table of name parts above shows that there are many which tell of woodland and others which describe pasture. Sometimes the names even give the species of trees that grew in the ancient forest, as with Boxted (in Essex and Suffolk) and the frequently met Oakley, which indicates a clearing or glade in an oak forest. The name-ending -wade suggests a ford and -grove a thicket, so Iwade in Kent was 'yew tree ford' and Boxgrove in Sussex 'box tree thicket'. A glance at any map will reveal many names that tell of the village in its old surroundings, like Rushmere (Suffolk), Waterden (Norfolk), Alderford (also in Norfolk) and Willow Green (Cheshire).

The explorer still in search of the old village environment might now consider the boundaries of the parish, bearing in mind that these are likely to be very old and that often every effort was made to bring within the village fold as many as possible of the natural resources upon which the community depended (see p. 48). There is a celebrated case in Norfolk of nine parishes which converge on Rymer or Ringmere in order to have access to water in the Brecklands, while in the scarplands south of Lincoln serried ranks of elongated parishes stand shoulder to shoulder, each focusing on a village at a scarp-foot spring, with the lands stretching up to include the grazings of the upland heath and downwards

COLOUR PLATES

21 *Opposite, above* This cottage at Barrington in Cambridgeshire is receiving a new overcoat of thatch, from the piles of straw lying in front of it. Part of the roof has already been trimmed; finishing the roof-ridge will come last (see ill. 84).

22 *Opposite, below* Well-dressing in progress in Tissington, Derbyshire. Petals, mosses and other brightly coloured natural materials decorate the frames which enliven the Midsummer service.

to share the hay meadows, fishing and fowling resources of the valley bottom.

The hobby of village discovery has really taken hold of the amateur historian when he or she begins to study old documents and maps. A surprising amount of recorded material exists to fill in many of the blanks in the past of most villages, and the main problem is to discover documents which may be scattered among parish chests, manorial records, museums and public offices, but the archives of the county record offices are well stocked and the archivists are usually helpful and informative. In some cases, charters which were written before the Norman Conquest describe in detail the boundaries of estates, while an idea of the size, prosperity and activities of the old community can be gained by checking its terse inventory of ploughlands, beasts and human chattels in the Domesday entry (ill. 31). Sketches of fields, houses and mills appear on manorial maps, some of which date from the sixteenth century, while a very clear view of the old open fields and the origins of the post-enclosure fieldscape can be gained from enclosure maps. Any documents relating to an enclosure award made after 1740 are likely to be found in your county record office. Strictly accurate maps of the old countryside are generally lacking before 1801, when the first edition of the Ordnance Survey one-inch-to-the-mile series appeared, in time to record the pre-enclosure state of the lands of many villages. When, usually after 1836, church tithes in kind were commuted into money payments, a large-scale tithe map was drawn, indicating the owners of the parcels of land and sometimes giving the names of many places and landmarks, providing later generations with a detailed view of the mid-nineteenth-century landscape. Three copies of each map were produced, of which one has normally found its way via the parish chest into the county archives.

Last but not least, the modern air photograph provides unique insights into the mysteries of the village setting. Earthworks, foundations, old trackways and field and strip patterns which are invisible to the earthbound eye may stand out quite clearly in the changed tones of growing crops or the shadows cast by a sinking sun. A few features of the ancient landscape, like some Iron Age hut sites, many only be revealed to the expert eye, but many others, like ridge-and-furrow cultivation patterns and some lost villages, stand out in stark simplicity. Half an hour spent studying an air photograph, preferably in conjunction with an old or modern large-scale map, can produce untold riches of information. Most parts of England, with the exception of a few strategic sites and docks, have been photographed several times, and Aerofilms, for instance, will sell copies to interested members of the public.

While deploring the careless use of spades or metal detectors, any sensible historian, geographer or archaeologist will welcome the involvement of the enthusiastic amateur on schemes of local discovery. At the same time, it would be foolish to pretend that there are not pitfalls into which even the quite skilled interpreter can tumble, and this is particularly true where air photographs are concerned. Yesterday's tractor marks, irrigation sprays or muck heaps can produce images which may suggest ancient landscape features, and one must always beware of the unexpected. Recently studying an air photograph of the early Saxon village setting at West Stow in Suffolk, I noted two small parallel marks which seemed to be man-made and might have been related to the ancient settlement. Closer checking showed them to be the start lines of a motorcycle scrambling circuit.

Thousands of fascinating discoveries remain to be made by the observant

9 *Above* Part of a seventeenth-century estate map of Laxton in Nottinghamshire (where a form of open-field farming survives today). In the village narrow plots run back from the houses lining the streets; the church is in the centre; the manor, with its gardens that include a Norman castle motte, is above and left of centre.

10 *Right* The remains of holloways, house platforms and ridge-and-furrow cultivation emerge clearly in this air photograph of the lost village of Quarrendon in Buckinghamshire. Lost village sites are often not completely deserted today; note the working farmstead top left.

35

field-walker. It is one thing (and usually quite easy) to differentiate between natural formations and man-made earthworks, but quite another to identify the features discovered with accuracy. The identifications given on quite recent Ordnance Survey maps may be misleading: not far from my home we have a 'Roman Camp', which is in all probability a paddock, possibly a post-medieval one at that. Lost village sites can often be recognized without too much difficulty, although one should not expect to find ruined walls. Indications of deserted medieval villages come from the gentle valleys or holloways which mark the former streets and the roughly rectangular platforms which may show the former positions of dwellings. Often associated with the lost village is the generally rectangular hollow marking a moated manor, and sometimes one may find a rectangular embanked flat area that may have been a fishpond. A chain of smaller breeding ponds may be found in association with the main one. The mounds of Norman mottes may be imposing or they may be low and undistinguished. Some features will baffle even the expert. The key to good amateur exploration lies in part in knowing when to ask for specialist advice. There are Celtic defence works, medieval lost villages, post-medieval gardens (which constitute some of the most common, elaborate and confusing sites), gun platforms, windmill mounds and a host of other features. Again, one must be ready for the unexpected, and beware lest the search for things ancient cloud one's vision. For some weeks I puzzled over a straight line running across the chalk field by my cottage; enquiries revealed that it was part of an extensive system of tank traps dug during the last war. A linear mark in the growing corn on a nearby hill marks the course of a gas pipeline.

The amateur should not fall into the common trap of thinking that the professionals have already discovered all that is to be found by field-walking. Christopher Taylor's *Fieldwork in Medieval Archaeology* (1974) is an invaluable guide, and Michael Aston and Trevor Rowley's *Landscape Archaeology* (1974) is also useful.

Turning now to your village itself, the first thing to be studied is its layout. It is often very difficult to form a clear picture from ground level, and again maps and air photographs are invaluable for the bird's eye view. Are the dwellings clustered tightly around a green, set out in a line, or scattered loosely like broadcast corn? The pattern is an encyclopaedia of village history if only we can read it, but often this is not easy. The old notion of the 'typical' village with its roads and dwellings centring on an eternal triangle of church, manor and green has given way to the idea that each place is an individual and dynamic entity. Its pattern of growth may be very complicated, embracing a couple of old settlements, growing in one direction while decaying in another, stagnating and then flourishing and expanding. The village is a lively beast. Imagination and an enquiring eye may serve the sleuth better than a formal training in history, and a general impression of the layout may lead on to some useful suggestions. If the village has a green, what does this seem to have been originally? An open space cleared to house a market, an area for common grazing and the keeping of small livestock close to the cottages, the remnants of a broad highway, or a protective enclosure for livestock? If there is younger housing in the village centre, it could well indicate encroachment upon a former green. If the layout has a linear form, then do the houses follow a road, a stream, or perhaps a dry river terrace? If the cottages lining just one side of the street include many old buildings and have elongated allotments stretching back behind them, then the old settlement was probably on only one side of the street. The names of roads and lanes can also be indicative: Mill Lane, Chalkpit Road and Ferry Lane tell you where they went and why.

It is useful to ask whether the village plan seems to lie towards the 'open' or the 'closed' end of the spectrum. In the open village, growth was a somewhat random, spontaneous and piecemeal process, while in the closed village a powerful figure – normally the lord of the manor – kept a close control on development, preventing encroachment on the ploughlands or manor park and checking any spread which might lead the community to support a burdensome number of paupers. Today, planning authorities often decide whether a village shall be open or closed, channelling growth into some places and conserving others.

Related to the question of lordly control is that of deliberate planning. The English village has generally been thought to be a completely natural and unplanned phenomenon, but it has recently been recognized that a great many places were set out according to a preconceived pattern, or planned in part at some stage in their history. At Wharram Percy in Yorkshire the remains of the lost village suggest three cycles of planned growth between the eleventh century and the fourteenth. Traces of planning may be revealed by areas of regularity within a village which otherwise sprawls loosely – a squared-off green, say, or groups of cottages of similar date and design. Model villages, like the eighteenth-century one at Houghton in Norfolk or the nineteenth-century one at Somerleyton in Suffolk (ill. 94), are usually easy to spot, with houses built to a particular design or with distinctive ornamental details. Other planned developments may be harder to detect, and it is only when one notices the regular

11 Appleton le Moors in Yorkshire is a classic example of a linear English village. The air photograph shows the characteristic elongated plots running back from each house and the back lanes which parallel the main street.

12 Farmsteads and cottages cluster loosely around the church and green at Natland in Westmorland.

13 The regular rise and fall of the roofs of the cottages and the outbuildings which join them betray the planned origin of Chippenham in Cambridgeshire.

alternation between high and low roofs on the weatherworn cottages at Chippenham in Cambridgeshire that one realizes this is not a rambling old place, but a model village – built by Lord Orford around 1700.

Some readers will be more interested in the former people of the village than in its buildings, while others will see it as a community of people and homes. To discover the people, one can turn to the record office and the parish chest. As well as describing the bounds of the estate, its homes, lands, trees and beasts, the court rolls of a manor will record the various offences – usually trifling – that the people of the medieval village committed against each other or against their lord (see below, p. 68), how they might be fined or might forfeit their few possessions, and how, as the feudal system decayed, they might studiously ignore the edicts of their local master. In 1896 the Public Record Office published a list of the court rolls in its possession. The parish chest may contain any number of revealing documents, such as registers of baptisms, marriages and burials, which began in 1538, school record books going back to the sixteenth century, deeds of apprenticeship, and settlement certificates, dating from the period after 1662 when any villager with itchy feet was obliged to obtain a statement of his place of origin, to which he could be removed if he looked like becoming a burden elsewhere. Old wills and inventories, diocesan papers, guild records, estate papers – the list of possible documentary sources for the local historian is almost endless, and the interested reader will be helped by David Iredale's booklet, *Discovering Local History* (1973).

In *The Common Stream* (1975) Rowland Parker demonstrated by his study of Foxton in Cambridgeshire that the amateur historian can reconstruct in considerable detail the growth of a village from the medieval period onwards, while in his less acclaimed but superior *Cottage on the Green* he showed how, through the painstaking pursuit and scrutiny of wills, inventories, manorial records and a host of other documents, it is possible to trace the repeated alterations made through the centuries to one medieval cottage, the names, families and occupations of the different inhabitants, and even the household items that they possessed and how they treated each other.

Lest we become too obsessed with rich but dusty documents, let us recall W. G. Hoskins' salutary advice that some of the historian's best friends are his boots and a map. The amateur is likely to have as good a pair of eyes as the professors of history or geography (probably better), and even if one's interest in the village is but mild, any country journey can be enlivened by scanning the passing scene for clues to its history, its peoples and its problems. Rare indeed is the village that does not have an enthralling tale to tell to those who care to listen.

Some aspiring students of the village may be lucky enough to have a nearby university or Workers' Educational Association branch that offers courses in local history under expert guidance. My own Great Shelford has been subjected to scrutiny by guided amateurs from the WEA, and the result is a published guide of great quality and perception. The preservation of our cherished but threatened rural landscape cannot be achieved by narrow specialists or professors alone. It relies on the support and determination of the public at large. Never was the destruction greater or the need for a general involvement in conservation so high.

14 The process of renaming still goes on (as does the erosion of eccentricity); the villagers of Exton in Rutland cannot remember how Pudding Bag Lane got its name.

1 · The village and its origins

SOME VILLAGES have a history which extends back over more than two thousand years, and still stand rooted to the very spot where Iron Age farmers built their huts centuries before the birth of Christ. Their changing dwellings have echoed to the lilting speech of Celtic families, the drawling vowels of the Saxon peasant and the imperious bark of the Norman lord.

Half a century ago, when fewer conflicting facts were known, simple standard versions of history and prehistory could flourish. According to them, the prehistoric and British people farmed the uplands because they lacked the equipment to farm the heavy valley soils. They lived in dispersed farmsteads and villages were scarce or nonexistent. Then along came the Saxons with their heavy plough and communal farming tradition to establish dense networks of agricultural villages where none had previously existed.

How much of this picture of the past can survive is a matter of opinion. For example, recent years have seen great advances in the techniques of pollen analysis (see p. 33), and its evidence suggests that a fair amount of the English native forest was removed in Neolithic times, thousands of years before the Saxon invasion. (In addition to deliberate clearance, shoots would have been nibbled out by the browsing livestock of herding communities.) Systems of ancient fields which are only visible from the air and which were once thought to belong to the Dark Ages now often appear to date from the Bronze Age, or even before. Saxon parishes are found to share their boundaries with the land units of Romano-British villas, and some villages stand on the sites of such villas, which the Saxons were thought to have despised and avoided. The hill fort site at South Cadbury in Somerset was occupied by prehistoric people of the Neolithic, Bronze and Iron Ages, and refortified by both Romano-British and Saxon defenders.

Most recent research seems to support theories of continuity rather than revolution in the countryside. We think of the countryside as being conservative, but we have perhaps not realized just how conservative, and how deep are the roots of our past. The richest evidence of pre-Saxon settlement may well be confined to upland areas, but two millennia of ploughing could easily have erased the traces of ancient farms and villages in the valleys.

The first thing that we find recorded about many villages is a soulless inventory of people and assets which appears in the Domesday Book of 1086. But by this time many settlements were already old, and it is clear that, for the history of the village, there is nothing so difficult as a beginning. Experts debate whether this beginning is found in the flimsy shelters of Stone Age fisher folk, in the farmsteads and hamlets of the Iron Age farmers, in the Roman villa, or in the jumbled huts of the Saxon invader. What is certain is that by the tenth century AD a vast number, perhaps a majority, of the villages that exist today had been established, along with many more which have perished, and that – with few exceptions – they came to be known by Saxon names. What is controversial is the proportion of those villages that stood directly on the sites of older Celtic villages and farmsteads, or were built in the ruins of Romano-British villas. The persistence of many village sites once chosen does not assist the archaeologist searching for clues to origins: we can hardly excavate in a family sitting room to see if, beneath the debris of the Saxon age, there lies the buried junk of a British family!

When we attempt to peer back beyond the Iron Age, into the Bronze and Stone Ages that preceded it, the evidence becomes scanty and conjecture takes

15 The existence of an old village at the prehistoric temple of Avebury in Wiltshire exemplifies continuity in the landscape, but note that the church shuns a location inside the pagan ring. Medieval villagers made various attempts to destroy the stones, and the crushed remains of a barber were found during the twentieth-century raising of one of the giant sarsens.

over from fact: the village, like most else from those periods, finds testimony only in a few material scraps which may be ambiguous or unrepresentative. The ancestor of the English village, in the form of the (perhaps temporary) settlements of the handful of relatives who shared their lives and fortunes as members of a hunting clan, must be as old as the first immigrants, for it is difficult to imagine the hunter and his dependants living alone. At the same time, the hunting and gathering life will sustain only the sparsest of populations, so the 'villages' that existed could not have been large. Traces have been found at Star Carr, near Pickering in Yorkshire, of a settlement comprising a small group of families who lived on a swampy lakeside some time around 7500 BC. They built themselves a rough landing stage above which they huddled on a platform of brushwood, and their household refuse includes the remains of fish and deer; but of their dwellings and society nothing is certain.

Immigrants introduced farming to Britain around 4000 BC. With these people of the Neolithic or New Stone Age, we know more about their death than their life, since their most permanent constructions were long mounds of earth with which they covered their tombs. Their dwellings must have been built of perishable materials, and by far the best British survival of a Neolithic village occurs not in England, but at Skara Brae in Orkney. Timber was not available there, and so the houses are unlikely to be typical of the villages of forested Neolithic England. While still in use, Skara Brae was overwhelmed by a sandstorm; it lay preserved and entombed until 1850, when a storm stripped away the enveloping dune to reveal a small cluster of circular stone-walled huts with stone-built cupboards, hearth and beds – the roofs of hide or some other perishable material having long since disappeared.

Otherwise, the nature of Neolithic settlement is largely a closed book. We can be sure that where timber was at hand, it would have provided the most practical building material. The main evidence for ancient timber buildings comes from post holes found in the subsoil, and the relative scarcity of such finds does not necessarily indicate an absence of people or of building ability: structures built on raised earth or turf foundations would have left no trace, while erosion over a period of four or five thousand years could have stripped more than a foot of subsoil from many slopes, removing any signs of post holes that may have existed. The scale of construction that was possible is shown by the traces found at Mount Pleasant in Dorset of an enormous wooden ceremonial building over 100 feet (more than 30 metres) in diameter, comprising 180 massive posts, erected around 2500 BC. Recent excavations in Ireland have unearthed the remains of Neolithic houses with strong post-built timber walls.

One reason for the shortage of Neolithic village sites may simply be that while the farmers made great inroads into the natural forest, they practised not settled farming but nomadic livestock rearing, accompanied by a shifting form of cultivation based on clearings in the forest which were briefly farmed and then deserted. The strange 'causewayed camps', concentric ditches surrounding many chalkland hilltops, reveal no permanent habitation, and may have been places for meeting, feasting and perhaps trading among the wandering farming families.

The evidence of Bronze Age settlement, which began in the third millennium BC, is concentrated in the chalky and sandy uplands of southern England, where the light soils and the relatively thin vegetation cover must have been attractive to the primitive farmer. Such evidence as exists suggests a dispersed pattern of settlement, with each unit – the homestead of a single or extended family – consisting of a roughly rectangular enclosure, banked, ditched, palisaded or perhaps protected by a thorn hedge. Within the enclosure, which would hardly have excluded an army but could have kept animals or unruly neighbours at bay, were set one or more circular huts, about 20 feet (6 metres) in diameter, with a thatched roof supported by posts and containing a centrally placed hearth. Also within the enclosure there may have been working areas and underground pits for the storage of grain.

Where the remains of several huts are discovered within a single enclosure, such as the nine unearthed at Thorny Down in Wiltshire, it is tempting to think that we have the remains of a very early village. The evidence is not conclusive, for timber buildings will rot and new ones may be erected nearby, so that instead of the remains being those of several contemporaneous dwellings they may represent the rebuilding and slight repositioning of a single dwelling. At Itford Hill in Sussex, on a site radiocarbon-dated to 1089 BC, six possible enclosures and two unenclosed huts may have co-existed, of which Professor Barry Cunliffe writes: 'It is tempting to interpret the overall plan in terms of a central establishment for a patriarch around which about six other family units have clustered, giving rise to a substantial hamlet.'

The animal bones unearthed in domestic refuse, seeds embedded in pottery, and field outlines visible from the air as crop marks enable us to know more about the economy of the Bronze Age than we do about the homes and settlements. The inhabitants of the Late Bronze Age were mixed farmers who ploughed the lighter upland soils with ox-drawn ploughs, raising barley and wheat in small, squarish, banked fields, and grazing sheep, cattle and goats on the surrounding downlands. The light soils were not particularly fertile, and to produce reasonable crops it would have been necessary to turn the livestock on to the arable fields after the grain harvest.

On Dartmoor in Devon, between the blanket bog of the upland surfaces and the former dense forests of the lower slopes, remains have been found of both isolated farmsteads, associated with mixed systems of farming, and two types of substantial village, the one with the dwellings enclosed in a surrounding wall, the other unenclosed. The settlement at Stanton Down contained no less than 68 huts. Both types of village were associated with a livestock-raising way of life, which may have been combined with a little gardening, as suggested by the presence of small walled plots. For the rest of England, good evidence of Bronze Age huts has been found at Grassington in Yorkshire and at Mam Tor in Derbyshire.

The Iron Age was marked by waves of Celtic immigration which began in the eighth century BC and pulsed intermittently for seven or eight hundred years. This movement brought a quickening in the rate of technological improvement, a denser pattern of settlement and the expansion of the farmed area.

Dispersed family homesteads seem to have remained the norm, though villages did exist. Traces of at least ten huts have been found at Hay Cliff Hill in Dorset and a similar number of circular huts, stone-walled and enclosed in an outer wall, existed at Bodrifty in Cornwall. On a marshy site at Glastonbury in Somerset almost a hundred circular wattle huts stood within a defensive palisade, perhaps ten to twenty of them in use at any one time.

In the Celtic period there were many refinements in society, including the development of a British coinage; population increased and expanded, and improved strains of grain and livestock were developed. British towns, functioning chiefly as tribal capitals and supporting mints and craftsmen, had appeared by the time of the Roman invasion in the mid-first century BC; but the village of substance seems to have been the exception rather than the rule. Looking at the Celtic rural landscape, with arable fields on the lighter soils, scattered circular hut farmsteads and a sprinkling of small enclosed villages, the Bronze Age farmer of the preceding millennium might have seen little that was strange or revolutionary.

We have not discovered quite enough to describe the 'typical' Iron Age village, and probably the term 'kindred hamlet' would be more accurate for most settlements. The truth might not be stretched too far if we imagined two or more large circular wooden-walled huts with conical thatched roofs, providing shelter for the brothers, cousins and in-laws of the extended family. Outside the huts there are working and cooking areas, and pens for the domestic animals. Fowls peck around and pigs root and grunt in the nearby thicket, and while the men farm the nearby fields of wheat and barley, tend the cattle and sheep on more distant pastures, or set off for some hunting, the women might be gardening or weaving plaid designs in homespun woollen cloth, stained muddy shades of brown, red, purple, yellow and green with natural dyes; or they might extract grain from buried storage pots and grind it in stone querns, or make cheese – all with half an eye on the fire, which needs a regular stoking with sticks gathered by the children.

Each hamlet held its lands and produce in common, but tribute in grain and livestock was demanded by the local chieftain, who might have built his hut within a nearby hillfort. It has been suggested that some hamlets were inhabited by freemen, and others by bondsmen, and that the amount of tribute depended upon the status of the community. When the tribal and provincial rivalries which forever rumbled up and down the country smouldered close to home, the community would be tempted to repair the palisade surrounding its huts and

16 Imagination has played a part in the reconstruction of an Iron Age village at Cockley Cley in Norfolk, with its moat and gate, but the defensive aura is surely authentic.

look to the defences of the hillfort. Excavations reveal many examples of the periodic repair and improvement of fortifications, sure indications of breaks in the fragile peace of Celtic England.

Much is uncertain about rural life in Iron Age England, and the written observations of Roman writers are sometimes contradicted by archaeological evidence. In AD 87, Plutarch observed that there was nothing worth taking from the British, who had a sparse existence and were poor, while just under a hundred years later Dio Cassius suggested that before the Roman conquest the British tribes lived on gruel made from bark and roots. There were considerable variations within England: the Catuvellauni arrived in south-western districts only a little ahead of the Romans and seem to have been more efficient crop farmers than other Celtic tribes, while in the hillier north and west livestock rearing was much more important than cropping. Everywhere, farmsteads seem to have been more numerous than villages; a high proportion of the land of England was farmed and a fair density of people was supported. In many of the more productive parts of the countryside, such as south-east Northamptonshire, a farmstead may be found to each one-third of a square mile (one square kilometre) of land.

Recently, at least two attempts have been made in England to reconstruct working Iron Age hamlets, one at Butser Hill in Hampshire and the other for a BBC television series. Such experiments have the advantage that they take the problems of day-to-day life from the realm of the armchair historian to the field of practical trial and error, but they must always be somewhat artificial. It is impossible, for example, to discover the role that hunting played, since guinea-pig Celts can hardly practise skills on the prize beasts of surrounding farms, while rabbits, which were by no means unwelcome to one twentieth-century 'Celtic' community, were introduced to England only in the early Middle Ages. One aspect of Iron Age village life which impressed itself forcibly upon the participants was mud – in the shoes, in the food, in fact everywhere.

At Cockley Cley in Norfolk we can see an ambitious re-creation of an Iceni village of around A D 60, on the site of a real village which was destroyed by the Romans following the revolt of Boudicca. The reconstruction relies upon evidence from Classical writers and contemporary villages unearthed in Denmark, and much is inevitably speculative. The village is defended by a flimsy but spear-proof palisade, a moat and a drawbridge. The moat is fed by a fresh stream bubbling from the chalk, which must have attracted the original settlers, and while the defences are not strong they might have kept out small raiding bands from the rival Trinovantes tribe to the south, who would have been pelted by the slingstones of the village defenders as they advanced towards the moat.

Within the defences are a variety of buildings: a circular hut for the chieftain, with wattle walls and a conical thatched roof, which has a large ash tree providing a central support; a long house for the half-a-dozen élite families of the village, with a sleeping area containing beds covered in skins and furs, a cooking area with baked clay vessels and space under the same roof for the wintering of cattle. The weaker peasant members of the warrior community are housed in smaller and more squalid huts. Other buildings include a chariot house for the lightweight carts which carried the village spearmen to the scene of battle, a corn store, with shelter for the rat-proof clay vessels in which grain was stored, and a smoke house, used to preserve the carcases of the surplus cattle which the village could not feed over the winter. The brutal turbulence of Celtic life is suggested by the lookout platform perched high in a tree, and the (fanciful) snake pit in which enemies of the village might be thrown to the adders which abounded in the dry heathlands round about. Serious archaeologists express grave doubts about the authenticity of much that appears at Cockley Cley; but while many of the details may be over-ambitious, when viewed from a distance the palisade and towering gate defences must recreate the forbidding atmosphere of a defended Iron Age village.

The farmstead and the small village were two elements in the settlement of the Celtic countryside; the hillfort was a third. Crowning so many English hilltops, the hillfort is the most prominent survival of the Late Bronze and Iron Age past – a witness to an insecure and divided society. Though the hillforts were almost certainly built primarily as defensive nuclei for surrounding populations and therefore had strategic rather than local significance, excavations at several sites have revealed signs of permanent occupation: although only one-eighth of the 52-acre (21-hectare) interior of the massive hillfort at Hod Hill in Dorset has been excavated, traces of almost fifty huts were discovered. Several hillforts in

17 An impression of the village in Hod Hill fort, Dorset, crowded with circular huts, based on excavation of part of the interior.

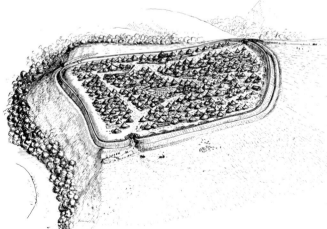

Wales and the Welsh borderlands have produced evidence of rectangular buildings set out in planned fashion along streets, in such numbers as to suggest that the forts enclosed not villages but small towns. It could be argued that if a hillfort was available local populations may have decided that they might as well settle within its defended area as outside. Nevertheless, the amount of central direction necessary to co-ordinate the building of such massive defences, together with the planned layout of their interiors, suggests that the hillforts were the bases of a strong ruling authority, perhaps local capitals which would also have attracted craftsmen and traders, and it has been suggested that they contained the germs of the feudal society of the Middle Ages. But they were an evolutionary blind alley as far as the English village is concerned.

The greatest contributions to the English heritage made by the Romans during their four-hundred-year occupation were the town and the road, though both were to fall into partial or total disuse in the uneasy years of Saxon harassment surrounding the Roman withdrawal in the early fifth century. In the countryside the Romans established villas – large, well equipped commercial farms which provided elegant accommodation for the Roman or Romanized British farmer, his family and workforce. In that its community included such specialists as joiners and masons, the villa in economic terms was not too unlike a small English village of the late medieval period.

A number of different settlement forms were thus present in Roman England: the town, either a planned military and economic foundation or a reorganized and expanded British settlement; the villas, dispersed among the choicest farmlands; the British farmsteads; and the scatter, denser than was once thought, of British villages, with some hillforts probably being abandoned if they represented threats to Roman control. So long as the countryside was at peace, the villages would have been little affected by changes in political control, though the better conditions for trade resulting from the peace imposed by the Romans – improved communications, town growth and garrison demand for food – may have led villagers to develop more commercial forms of farming.

A few people are so self-assured, in need of challenge, or simply footloose that they will migrate at the drop of a hat, but most migrants and certainly most mass migrations need a strong stimulus before a homeland and kinfolk are deserted for an unfamiliar destination. Often both 'push' forces and 'pull' factors are involved. A number of causes for the Saxon migration have been suggested; and it was probably a combination of domestic problems and the lure of greener pastures that drew the Angles, the Saxons and the Jutes from their homelands in Jutland, the north German forests, the marshes of the Elbe estuary and the windswept Frisian islands to new lands beyond the North Sea horizon.

These new lands were not entirely unknown: Saxon pirates had made a nuisance of themselves by AD 200, discovering the rich pickings to be had from coastal villas, churches and towns and causing fortresses to be built at vulnerable spots like Brancaster in Norfolk. The first Saxon settlers, it now seems, arrived in the fourth century. No period is perhaps more important to our understanding of the development of the English landscape, and none more controversial, than the three dark centuries that followed. A leading landscape archaeologist recently remarked to me that if he could travel in a time machine he was confident he could recognize the landscapes of the Bronze Age or the Iron Age, but, he said, 'I haven't a clue what early Saxon England looked like!' A clearer picture of these 'early English' people, their arrival and home-making will only be provided by the development of a more total archaeology, in which the evidence of each specialist field – documentary history, landscape archaeology, site excavation, and the typological study of pottery, brooches and household goods – is able to make a full and integrated contribution.

Revolution and continuity are concepts which vie with each other throughout history, and the nature of the Saxon conquest provides a fierce battleground for them. In the past, the fact that few Celtic words have found their way into the English language and that there are so many villages with Saxon names suggested an evolving scene in which the fearsome Saxon hordes fell upon a confused and disunited British population, exterminating the countryfolk or driving them into the bleak fastnesses of the uplands of Wales and the West Country; thereafter, the theory went, the Saxons populated the countryside with their villages to create a completely new pattern of settlement. More recently, accumulating archaeological evidence of many kinds has created a different picture, with great variation from place to place.

Key evidence comes from Saxon pottery, which has been the subject of intensive study by Dr J. N. L. Myres. The story that it seems to tell can be matched up with early documents and with excavations of settlement sites, and the result is to refute the version of history that has been taught for decades. The first Saxons settled in England as mercenaries in the mid-fourth century, when the country was still ruled by the Romans. They were employed to defend this outpost of the empire, perhaps against raids by their fellow Saxons or perhaps against the northern and western peoples of the British Isles. In return for their service they may have been given grants of land, and the first Saxon village in England could date from this period. In and around Cambridge, they seem to have mixed and married with their Romano-British neighbours, and some graves from this period contain a mixture of Saxon and Roman grave goods.

With their empire on the Continent under severe pressure from barbarians, the Romans withdrew their legions from England about AD 410, and while it is possible that Roman expeditionary forces may have briefly returned, Britain was cast adrift on an uncertain sea. The controlled settlement of Saxon communities seems to have continued under the British kings who succeeded the Romans. By about 450 the settlement may have greatly exceeded what the authorities intended, amounting in some places to outright domination, and in various regions an armed struggle for the control of land will have broken out. The Venerable Bede, a Saxon cleric and historian writing shortly after 700, looked back and summed up that troubled period: 'as bands of the aforesaid nations eagerly flocked into the island, the people of the newcomers began to increase so much that they became a source of terror to the very natives who had invited them.'

The bloody accounts of Saxon conquest given by Bede and – much closer to the events – by Gildas, the heartbroken Celtic monk who saw the collapse of the Romanized and (partly) Christian society which he cherished, may give us a jaundiced picture of events. Certainly the warfare between Saxon and Briton was, in certain places and at certain times, both bitter and considerable. It was also far from being one-sided, and after the great British victory at Mount Badon, attributed to King Arthur, which probably took place about 500, several decades of relative peace, and in many places British supremacy, followed. It was not until 685 (in Bede's lifetime) that the Saxons gained Carlisle in the north-west, and they never settled the extreme south-west.

The vast majority of Saxons and Britons were peasant farmers who could only survive by working hard and long on their lands, and it is impossible to believe that they lived in a state of perpetual warfare. In countless valleys, estates and villages a *modus vivendi* must have been established, allowing both parties to get on with the essential task of feeding a family. Intermarriage must have taken place, and war-making may have been left to a warrior élite in each society. We might even question whether the British peasant preferred to be ruled by often unstable and vicious native 'tyrant' kings.

So the Germanic conquest of England was not concerted, and it did not occur at a stroke. It was a largely disorganized and piecemeal process involving bands of warrior farmers and petty leaders (see pp. 13–14), who may in many cases have been discharged legionaries. Incoming Saxons were perhaps not always unwelcome, or always strong enough to seize the lands of their choice. Some of the British were certainly killed, some put to flight in the first shocks of encounter. Many were enslaved, then absorbed into mixed village communities. Quite possibly, sufficient British country people survived to form the bulk of the population in old, reconstructed and new villages. The village of Piercebridge in Co. Durham stands within the walls of a Roman fort, and, as has been said, the name of nearby Walworth means 'the settlement of the Britons'.

When a new village was founded, why was that particular site chosen? Some settlements grew up at 'geographical events' – bridging points on rivers, springlines, gaps in chains of hills. But generally it is pointless to look at a modern farming landscape and expect to find the features and resources which influenced the early settlers standing out in bold relief. We must try to imagine the landscape as it was before drainage removed the marshes and further clearance of forest laid bare the land. In the south-east Midlands, for example, the marshy river floodplains and poorly drained clay soils would have been avoided, while the well-drained gravels of the river terraces overlooking the floodplain would have exerted a powerful attraction. As we have seen (p. 33), the most useful features would have acted like a series of magnets, drawing the village-builders this way and that. Ploughlands and hay meadows offered the chance of greatest productivity and demanded the most intensive work; even dry chalkland or marsh might have a contribution to make to the settlers' economy. With self-sufficiency an essential consideration, pioneers would have looked for a site with reasonable access to woodlands and common pasture, and – an indispensable feature – a good supply of drinking water. In Norfolk nine parishes near Thetford in the parched Brecklands converged on an area of heathland and on the lake of Ringmere for water; while seven parishes took a share in marshland commons near Tilney Smeeth. Thus villagers tried to incorporate and make use of as wide a range of local resources as possible: ploughland for the grain harvest, meadowland for hay, upland pasture for summer grazing, marshland for fishing, fowling and reed-gathering, and the forest for timber and the foraging herds of swine. When parish boundaries were marked out to delimit the areas of support for the village church, in some places as early as the seventh century, it now seems that in perhaps a majority of cases they perpetuated land units which are sometimes pre-Roman and may even be pre-Celtic, giving formal ecclesiastical (and thus legal) recognition to boundaries of great antiquity. The form of a few parishes was affected by ecclesiastical

wheeling and dealing, but in general they represent cells of village-centred self-support. The elongated form of parishes in the Lincolnshire scarplands is no accident: the villages tend to be sited where springs issue at the foot of the scarp, and their lands extend downwards to include the meadows of the river floodplain (and the fishing in the river), and upwards to include common pasture on the heath.

This is not to say that mistakes were never made, in the choice of a site or the alignment of a street. Dozens of examples of abandoned early villages have been revealed by the airborne camera. J. B. Mitchell has likened the actions of the first settlers to those of a picnic party, 'trying first this then that side of a bay, first one side of a hedge then the other, and in the end putting up with much that is not ideal rather than move yet once again'.

The air traveller, looking down on almost any part of flat lowland England, cannot fail to be impressed by the remarkable regularity of settlement, with villages at intervals of about a mile, or 1.6 kilometres. J. K. St Joseph, Professor of Aerial Photographic Studies at the University of Cambridge, has calculated that in eastern Northamptonshire the average distance between villages is 1.2 miles (1.9 kilometres); in western Huntingdonshire it is 0.95 miles (1.52 kilometres). The distances between settlements remains consistent in hilly areas where the villages are confined to valleys: a number of valleys converge near Salisbury in Wiltshire, and the villages which line their sides are spaced at intervals of 0.89 miles, 0.90 miles, 0.94 miles and 0.99 miles (1.43, 1.45, 1.51 and 1.59 kilometres).

The distribution of villages is so even that some scholars have been tempted to see the working of a grand plan, while others – geographers of the old school of 'environmental determinism' or of the younger mathematically inclined breed – seem to see remorseless geographical or economic forces at work, grinding away at the settlement pattern until just the right density of villages had been achieved.

18 Piercebridge, Co. Durham, lies neatly within the defences of a Roman fort which stood on the northern bank of the River Tees. The villagers still come and go through the Roman entrances; Roman roads crossed in the foreground field and the Roman baths lay where the road swings to cross the bridge.

The 'grand plan' thesis is not very attractive: it does not fit in with the 'disorganized spontaneity' which seems to have characterized the Saxon settlement, and it would have been most difficult to formulate and enforce among a people who lacked accurate maps or surveying techniques. Equally, while environmental forces may set limits to the number of agriculturalists that a given area will support, these controls do not extend to directing people where to live when choices of several sites are available. The numerous successful mother-and-daughter settlements, such as Great and Little Shelford in Cambridgeshire or the Gransdens on the Cambridgeshire-Huntingdonshire boundary, show that proximity and survival can go hand in hand. Few villages began as marketing centres, but through the centuries many of them gained commercial roles; and the forces of economic competition may have put the weaker of a pair of closely located markets out of business. Still, a village may lose its commercial role and remain useful as a place to live in: the market trade of Hoxne in Suffolk was captured by its medieval rival Ely, but Hoxne survives.

The taking-in of farmland from the waste proceeded outwards from each village nucleus and it is not unreasonable to imagine a colonization which involved the establishment of the earliest villages at fairly regular intervals close to the main routeways used in the penetration of the interior (see p. 14). Subsequently there must have been a hiving-off of daughter villages and surplus population, and a movement of later immigrant communities into the voids between existing villages.

The tendency of Saxon villages to consist of closely clustered dwellings is no more than a tendency, and a later Saxon one at that. Numerous examples can be found where the arrangement of dwellings was quite loose. Always the layout was carefully adjusted to the natural features of the chosen site: the bumps, curves and damp hollows, the stream or spring, and the existing tracks or slopes which suggested streets were more important than any preconceived plan. It is often the case that while the Saxons chose a site and established the directions of some streets, their original layout became lost in a later village of gradually accumulating buildings and slowly adapting form, with some planned growth taking place in the medieval period.

Classroom geography often reduces villages to a few stereotypes – the 'green village', the 'nucleated village' or the 'street village'. Real villages defy these crude generalizations and there is no such thing as a typical village plan. While Saxon settlers might sketch an outline on the canvas of the village setting, the full elaboration of theme was the product of centuries of later evolution. Often a point is reached where the form and nature of the original settlement is lost in a maze of later experiment and modification.

Now overlooked by a large chemical plant, Duxford in the Cam valley is pretty in parts but unremarkable. Its only claim to national fame came during the last great war when the airfield, which now houses a valuable collection of historic aircraft, was the base of the legless Battle of Britain ace Douglas Bader. As with most other villages, the story of Duxford's origins and development is only revealed by the careful study of its landscape and relevant historical documents. At first glance, the village seems to be rather formless, although strangely it has two parish churches.

The key to Duxford is provided by two streets, named St John's Street and St Peter's Street after the two churches. They run parallel, about a quarter of a mile (400 metres) apart, and they head towards ancient fords across the River Cam.

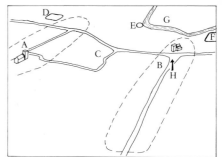

The remains of a village green, now much built upon, lie to the south of the northern street of the pair. The church of St John, to the north, was mainly built during the twelfth and thirteenth centuries, but a fragment of Saxon carving incorporated over the doorway hints at an earlier foundation. St Peter's also dates from the twelfth and thirteenth centuries, but an earlier Norman window remains in the chancel.

There can be no doubt that in Duxford we are seeing the product of the joining together of two villages which were separate in the Saxon period. Each had its church, and each took its alignment from a track which ran down to a ford across the river. From the eleventh century onwards the villages were collectively known as Duxford, and the amalgamation was consolidated as buildings were constructed along Chapel Street which links the components. In due course, the fords became insignificant while the connection with Cambridge, about 7 miles (11 kilometres) to the north, was intensified by travel and trade. The village then took on a north-south orientation to replace the earlier double east-west orientation as dwellings were set up along the road leading out to the market and university town.

Thus far it may seem that a little detective work has disclosed the main secrets in the Duxford saga, but not so. Rather than being one village composed of two nuclei, Duxford on deeper inspection appears to be what Christopher Taylor has named a 'polyfocal settlement'. More than two original nuclei are involved; the vanished green may belong to a third element that went to make up our composite village; while the manorial history of the area is quite confusing. Instead of there being two or three manors listed in Domesday Book we find four, and there is a possibility of another deserted settlement in the parish. Standing by the river and between the two churches is Temple Farm, a sixteenth-century timber-framed building. Its name indicates its origin back beyond the

19, 20 Duxford, Cambridgeshire, from the air. A site of northern village with (now redundant) church of St John; B site of southern village with church of St Peter; C remains of old green; D, F moated manor sites (F is just out of the picture to the right); E site of Templars' manor; G River Cam, H viewpoint in ill. 21.

21 The view along St Peter's Street in Duxford as seen from the ground. The jetty house in the foreground is of the sixteenth century while the church tower has a parapet and spire which have been added to the plainly Norman original.

sixteenth century, in a manor house of the Knights Templar, and this will have been another important component of the early village.

Given that the village lands appear to have been shared by up to five different manors, the origins of Duxford probably involve more than the two or three church/street and green nuclei already mentioned. Possibly the complex village is the product of the merging of a number of originally dispersed settlements which were later represented by Domesday manors and then enlarged to form the two or three components which, with the Templars' manor, eventually composed a unified Duxford. So much for the myth of the 'typical village'.

The hut dwellings of the early Saxon villagers rotted to dust within a relatively short period, and most of what we know of them comes from the groundplans disclosed by aerial photography and from the stained mud in the holes that once held posts destroyed long ago. A number of Saxon hut sites have been found – at Crossgates near Scarborough in Yorkshire, at Bygrave in Hertfordshire, Sandtun in Kent and St Neots in Huntingdonshire. A substantial excavation undertaken at Sutton Courtenay, Oxfordshire, after the First World War exposed an apparently squalid settlement including some three dozen rectangular one-storeyed wooden huts, formerly identified as dwellings but now thought to be sheds serving dwellings as yet undiscovered. Two weaving sheds and a pottery workshop were found, but the household goods unearthed were few and poor in quality.

It would be wrong to draw too many conclusions from the example of one settlement, and that a failure. In Germany, a Saxon village of the ninth century was excavated at Warendorf to reveal very substantial rectangular houses up to 90 feet (27 metres) in length, as well as some barns and humbler dwellings. Conclusive evidence for the existence of such long houses in Saxon England remains to be discovered.

More light on the English experience came in the late 1940s when the remains of a very early Saxon settlement, which had been entombed by drifting sand, were discovered at West Stow in Suffolk. The area – near a contemporary British village – was excavated in 1965–72. No fewer than eighty buildings were

22 Much expert care has gone towards the reconstruction of the early Saxon village of sunken-floored huts and halls at West Stow in Suffolk. Walls are of split vertical log planks and a framework of rafters can be seen on the hall which is still to be thatched.

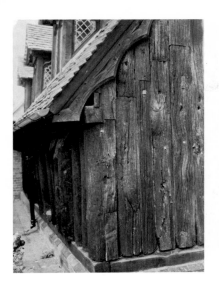

discovered, all dating from before the gradual desertion of the village early in the seventh century. The archaeologists divided them into 'huts' and 'halls'. The huts had floors sunk into the ground and were covered by sloping poles on which thatch was spread, giving a tent-like appearance. The halls were floored and walled with oak and their pitched roofs were of woven hazel, lying on rafters of ash and thatched with straw or sedge. They were substantial buildings, with the oak posts of the walls braced with tie-beams and the gaps between the posts sealed with wooden planks. The posts and planks seem to have been skilfully jointed together, as no traces of wattle and mud infilling were found. The halls appear to have been the focal points for extended family units, and the surrounding buildings probably served for storage, workshops and living quarters. The discovery of large quantities of bones of domestic animals – cattle, sheep and pigs – and of such animals as deer, along with grain seeds, suggest that the inhabitants of West Stow engaged in mixed farming, spiced with hunting and fishing excursions.

Wooden buildings lack the permanence of stone and are more vulnerable to fire and weather, but they should not be regarded as 'inferior' to stone structures. At Cheddar in Somerset and Yeavering in Northumberland evidence has been found of ambitious wooden palaces. The small church at Greensted in Essex has a nave solidly built of vertically-split wooden logs, and St Martin's at Canterbury may have late Saxon timbers in its roof. Very recently an astonishing radiocarbon date of AD 1026 was obtained for the manor barn at Belchamp St Paul in Essex. If a Saxon timber barn has survived the passage of time, we can confidently expect that houses containing original Saxon timber work must still lie undiscovered in the English countryside.

With the exception of Greensted, the Saxon churches that we see today are of stone. The range from the remarkably early (seventh-century) and large church at Brixworth in Northamptonshire, with arches made of Roman bricks from an abandoned fort nearby, to the tall towers of Earls Barton in Northamptonshire and Barton-on-Humber in Lincolnshire, both built about the year 1000, and decorated with stone strips and arcades in patterns which must refer to timber construction.

23 *Above left* The church at Greensted-juxta-Ongar in Essex retains its Saxon log walls – sadly undatable by the carbon-14 method owing to their impregnation with a wood preservative.

24 *Above* The carbon-14 method gives an early eleventh-century date for this upright post (supporting later timberwork) in an Essex barn at Belchamp St Paul, substantiating the beliefs of the remarkable self-taught student of timber building, Cecil Hewitt.

The Saxon village community had neither the wealth nor the means of transport to construct their dwellings with anything but the natural local materials. Reeds or straw for thatching were widely available, and by the time of the Norman Conquest the technique of building known as cruck framing had evolved (ill. 68). Most common in the north and west, it provided a stronger structure than tent-like dwellings or those based on posts and tie beams. A curving oak tree was split to form the two sloping sides of an 'A', with the split logs joined at the top and spread out at the bottom. A strengthening beam formed the bar of the 'A'. Two such 'A' frames, connected by beams at the roofridge and sides, provided the framework for a sturdy building. The gaps between the beams were filled with wattle of woven branches and then 'daubed' with a mixture of mud and cow hair to form a weather-proof wall. The one disadvantage to cruck framing was that the height of the building was limited by the length of the framing timber: taller buildings demanded more elaborate methods. At least one leading expert believes that cruck building was characteristic of Roman Britain, and displaced from the eastern counties by invaders who brought other techniques of timber building. He also thinks that the solid but simple reconstructed huts at West Stow are poor representatives of what may have been elaborate and ornate timber homes. The glories of medieval carpentry may have derived from skills which were well developed in the Dark Ages.

The Saxon period was one of slow but steady progress. In most places the expanding population relied on more than just the subsistence of the pioneer. Defensive settlements blossomed into commercial centres and new trading towns were set up at the royal behest. During the tenth century, for perhaps the first time since the Saxons had overrun the land, England became again a land of *towns* and villages, and trade began to involve goods other than the bare essential of salt and iron. Even so, the Saxon towns depended heavily upon the fruits of their own lands and the life of the townsman was often combined with that of the farmer, while the whole superstructure of towns rested upon the solid base of village farming. It remained exceptional not to be a villager.

We have looked at the Saxon village in terms of its site, its form and its buildings, but a village is nothing if not a community, so what of its people?

Most nights, the newly established Saxon villager must have slept soundly: as a farmer, he was wedded to a lifestyle which demanded hard work in return for mere survival. Sometimes, huddled with his family beneath skins in his tent-like hut, he may have woken to the sound of rain dripping through the straw and brushwood thatch, or trickling through the doorway, to form puddles on the sunken earth floor. Outside, the night must have been of a blackness seldom seen in England today, unrelieved by flashing headlights or the rosy glow above a distant town. Our farmer knew no maps; and the lands far beyond his shimmering wheatfields, beyond the common pasture and beyond the encircling forest waste, were only sensed by him in myth and legend, from the epic tales of a conquering grandfather and the stories told by village folk crouched round a fire, with heads fuddled by ale and mead.

A crash and a scream may have echoed from the distant forest, and the Saxon's thoughts turned to outlaws, wolves and boars, and then, more darkly, to his own bloodthirsty pagan deities, to the older gods of the British and to the Christ of the

Celtic monks of the legendary western mountains, to the ghosts of a people dispossessed and the true intentions of neighbours who are learning the Saxon language and customs but who whisper and murmur in an older tongue.

As unease set it, the problems of survival grew in the mind: what would happen if the crops failed and the seedcorn was eaten, and what if the roving warbands of rival leaders hungrily passed this way? Could enough game be caught to support his family? Society had no net to catch the failing household, and the great men did not give their help without conditions. Plague and famine were part of life and were probably accepted with resignation. From skeletons found in cemeteries villagers' physiques can be guessed, and the richness or stringency of the environments in which they lived. War wounds were not uncommon, and bones distorted by arthritis and rheumatism were the price of hard-weather toil, while the teeth of older people were often fiercely worn down by the chewing of gritty flour.

The free, democratic and resourceful peasant of England before the Norman Conquest is a potent symbol of romance, but when we look at the Saxon village community in its developed form we find a society which is based not upon equality and independence but upon class and obligation. If we search for the origin of this system, the answers to important questions remain elusive. Too little is known about the early history of the Saxons in England, but even less is known about them in their north-west German homelands at the time of the migrations. There is much to suggest that the Saxons responded to the new conditions that they met, adapting old ways to suit new circumstances.

Some scholars believe that the 'invasion' was accomplished by bands of the free followers of local leaders. In their view it was only later that society separated out into rigid classes, ranging from that of the privileged aristocrat to the slave, the heavy burden of obligation increasing with each step down the social ladder. Another theory sees the feudal manor, with its cowed village population, as the direct descendant of the Roman villa and of its servile workforce. Certainly some ecclesiastical parishes of the Christian Saxon era and the boundaries described in a number of Saxon land charters would seem to coincide with estate units worked by Roman villas.

Whatever divisions may have existed among the immigrant Saxons, the reasons for their intensification in England are not hard to imagine. No sooner had the colonists settled their affairs with the native Britons than their leaders set about fighting one other, and no sooner had these self-inflicted wounds begun to heal than, in the ninth century, England was beset by attacks from the Danes. To survive during such tumultuous times a man needed a protector. The freeman, in 'commending' himself to a local notable, had begun to sacrifice his freedom. At first the association was a personal one which the freeman could end at will, but before long he and his lands were considered to be linked to the lord for all time. Unpredictable crop failures and famine, and the high taxation taken to raise the protection money or *Danegeld* needed to buy off Danish invasion, also helped to break the freeman, for when a powerful patron saved the day rescue came at the price of independence. In the centuries following the Saxons' settlement in England ties of kinship and tribe were superseded by bonds which tied families and their lands to a patron: in the tenth century a law obliged every man to have a lord who would answer for him before the law.

Let us go, then, and meet the people of an established Saxon village. They are introduced to us by a number of ancient manuscripts; and a fairly clear picture of

25 Top people feast in the hall. Saxon artists were masters of delicate linework and this sketch may date from just before the Norman Conquest.

26–28 *Opposite* Men at work, from an early eleventh-century Anglo-Saxon manuscript. Peasant ploughmen coax a four-ox plough team while a sower follows close behind. *Centre* Three peasants wield scythes, and a fourth works with a pitchfork; the man on the left sharpens his scythe with a whetstone, while the one on the right, who has just done the same, seems to be catching his breath before resuming work. *Bottom* As the harvest comes in, Saxon peasants are hard at work in threshing the grain with flails and winnowing the grain and chaff.

the West Midlands country community is given in a discourse on estate management written at the beginning of the eleventh century, the *Rules of Individual People*, which sets out the rights and duties of various classes. The people that we meet there have been given their social slots by master or by birth; they are intensely aware of their own particular positions in village society and, while forced by the dictates of survival and lord to work as a community, they are jealous of their small privileges and as resentful of any person who attempts to step beyond his station as was the servant household of the Victorian great house.

Although his lofty hall would remind us more of a barn than of a mansion, the *thegn* was the owner of a considerable estate of perhaps 600 acres (some 240 hectares). He was bound to his superior – a king, a bishop or an earl – for military service, the upkeep of fortifications and the building of bridges. Below him came the *geneat*, who normally owned more than 30 acres (12 hectares), for which he owed his lord service in the form of messenger duties and the lighter kinds of manual work. Also free, but of a lower social status, was the *cotsaeta* or cottar, the holder of perhaps 5 acres (2 hectares); he was obliged to perform at least one day of labour each week on the lord's lands in addition to a host of lesser and more specialized services. The most arduous life must have been led by the *gebur*, whose holding of around 30 acres (12 hectares) and grant of two oxen, one cow, six sheep and 7 acres (3 hectares) of sown land from the lord was his only at the cost of two or three days of labour each week and a multiplicity of special duties and payments. As Professor Bruce Lyon has remarked, the *gebur* would need many strong sons to help him before he could cover his obligations and find the time to work on his own lands. With his wearisome bonds of dependence and servitude, the Saxon *gebur* led a life that was little different from that of the villein of the later Middle Ages.

PRINCIPIVM IANI SANCIT TROPICVS CAPRICORNVS
IANVARIVS HABET DIES XXXI LUNA XXX
IIII AXXIX VIIII VRE KALENDARUM GES CONCIDITUR AGNUS.

AUGUSTU MENSEM LEO FERVIDUS IGNE P VRIT
AGUSTUS HABET DIES XXX LUNA XXIX
VIII Q C AUGS MACHABEUS MERITO TRADUNTUR SEPE KALENDE.

TERMINAT ARCITENENS medio sua sig a decembri
DECEBER HABET DIES XXXI LUNA XXX
XIII O D DUE PRIMA DIES MENSIS KASIARUM CONTINET ALMUM.

Living in many villages, and of comparable status to the *gebur*, were the more specialized rural workers, such as the swineherds and the beekeeper. The *folgere* was a free peasant who did not have a landholding and worked exclusively at a task such as shepherding or cheese-making; each *folgere* had his own duties and received his own particular payment. Unfree, and at the bottom of the social hierarchy, were the bondsmen and bondswomen, slaves who were allowed to work a mere strip of land and who were kept alive on a subsistence handout of food, 12 pounds (5.5 kilograms) of corn at harvest, a couple of sheep carcases and a cow being granted each year. (If Norman feudalism was to make life more onerous for the village community as a whole, at least it may have alleviated the conditions of the slave. The Normans were not accustomed to the full-blown slavery of Saxon society and the records suggest that, following the Conquest, slaves were elevated into the ranks of the cottars.) Finally, standing slightly apart in this hierarchy, came the *gerefa* or reeve, who was part foreman, part estate manager, and intermediary between the lord and the peasant workforce, an organizer of labour and distributor of tasks.

The day dawns differently in the hall of the lord and the huts of the peasants. For the lord it is a day of sport and perhaps of travel, for the peasants a day of toil – different tasks for different stations but hard work for all, with the beckoning Sunday and the distant prospect of an ale-swilling Saint's Day to relieve the monotony. With only a creaking board and grimy sheepskin between their bodies and the cold earth of the hut floor, a cottar and his family rise stiffly at the first hint of dawn. He prepares for a day cultivating the land, with urgency if the ground is his own, but with a grumbling reluctance if the day is one set aside for work on the lands of his lord. His first task on a frosty November morning is to harness a ploughteam of oxen which stand steaming and drowsy in their pen, two beasts of his own and two pairs borrowed from neighbours in age-old custom (see p. 61). Then, stumbling along with the awkward, heavy, iron-shod wooden plough, the cottar and his team make their way towards the strip of land that is earmarked for ploughing, picking a clumsy zig-zag course through the labyrinth of strips and headlands in the patchwork field landscape of ridges, furrows and drains.

At first the cottar's thoughts are for his feet. They are most likely bare, chilled and deadened by the frozen earth; experience suggests that they will warm as ploughing gets under way and to wrap them in rags is to invite the growth of balls of heavy mud that will catch in the furrow and lurch the plough from its straight course. Peering forward over the straining shoulders of the leading oxen and throwing his weight against a plough which seems to have a life of its own, the ploughman has long hours for thought. Let us not imagine that he is a mindless yokel, for even an Einstein would find it hard to escape a life of mundane toil if born into the ranks of the cottars. His thoughts are not of promotion and 'success': success for him is a lofty rick and enough food for the family. Nor are they of travel, for he will never venture further than the nearest market; or of wealth, for coins seldom enter his household and what the family needs, by and large, the family makes or barters for. He thinks of the programme of jobs to be done, obligations to be met, of the wild birds and beasts which fill the woodland, and of how to catch them. His world is the world of the village and the field, and there is enough of interest there to fill his mind.

At noon his son arrives, as the sons of ploughmen had for centuries past and as they would for a thousand years to come, with a bundle of bread and cheese and a jug of ale. As they meet on the headland, the cottar swings his team into a turn, giving a slow curve to the last few yards of the furrow, and while he eats, the oxen cough and blow. By the time the sun reaches the western treetops, man and beasts are exhausted. An acre (less than half a hectare) has been ploughed. With the rolling step of the furrow still in his feet, the man returns to the smoking village hollow, to pen the oxen with water and hay. As dusk settles, and with a few nagging little tasks completed in the fading light, he heads for the welcoming hearth.

While the cottar was in the fields, his children, who will never see a school, have spent the day performing the petty but essential tasks which have occupied peasant children for countless generations – gathering firewood, searching for eggs, ratting, bird scaring, stonepicking and, perhaps, scouring twig and thorn for tufts of wool from passing sheep.

Wool gathered and shorn will find its way into the coarse weaves of peasant clothing, a tweed-thick mantle and tunic like heavy flannel for the father and similar but longer and hooded garments for his wife. The *thegn* dresses in much the same style, but his tunic is of softer cloth, with leather or golden thread in the cuff, while his wife has under-garments of soft linen, woven from foreign flax.

The *thegn* in his hall offers spit-roasted game, mead and wheaten bread to his guests and principal retainers. The cottar family nearby, squatting around their hearth in the heavy gloom, eat rye bread, gruel, thin ale and ewe's-milk cheese, with mutton stew on special occasions. In the dying glow of the embers, the man, huddling in his cloak, tinkers with a broken harness, while his wife darns his only tunic with homespun wool. Both will sleep early and well: he has the aching legs and forearms of the ploughman; she is tired from the daily round of water carrying, spinning, sand-scouring the iron cooking pot, and has an arm that throbs from the grinding of grain in the circling quern stone whose monotonous revolutions so resemble the days in her life.

This scene seems far removed from the life of the modern village, but in many ways it is only a century away. Similar thoughts filled the head of the nineteenth-century ploughman, who while more solidly housed, was hardly better fed than his distant ancestor. Both were tied to a master, spent rainy winter days among the communal chatter, air-choking chaff and clattering flails of the threshing floor, and struggled to work with frozen limbs and half-empty stomachs. Though separated by a thousand years of linguistic evolution, they shared words of country dialect that are not heard in the modern city and could communicate with enthusiastic vigour on a host of country topics which are unknown to urban man.

While we can roughly sketch the lifestyle of a Saxon peasant family, great variations existed from region to region, from class to class and even from manor to manor. The author of *The Rules of Individual People* was at pains to point out to his readers that 'The customs of estates are various. Nor do we apply these regulations, which we have described, to all districts.' And duties entailed rewards:

> There are many common rights: in some districts are due winter provision, Easter provision, a harvest feast for reaping the corn, a drinking feast for ploughing, food for making the rick, at wood-carrying a log for each load, at corn-carrying food on completion of the rick, and many things which I cannot recount.

For the Saxon peasant, as for his lord, land was everything. The amount of land that a man owned gave him his status in the community; it determined whether his family would be well-fed or starving, and it was his only source of wealth. Rather than the field being the servant of the village, the village was the servant of the land, and it existed because it suited the communal farming methods of the peasant and the manor.

Saxon farming is often associated with strip cultivation in open fields. It seems unlikely that this system was imported to England by the Saxons, for at the time of the migrations they were working small rectangular fields similar to those found in Romano-British England. At first the new settlers may have followed a pattern of farming which was to survive for centuries in the English uplands and Scotland, based on an infield and an outfield: the infield, close to the settlement, was in permanent cultivation, while the more distant lands – the outfield – were farmed from time to time. The life of a village was no longer than the fertility of the infield, and when that land was worn out the village community would uproot themselves and settle elsewhere. Eventually, perhaps in response to the growth of population and land shortage, a more intensive manner of farming was developed.

After a few seasons of grain cropping, even the best lands become worn out. Not having recourse to the rather dubious modern chemical stimulants, the Saxons could only renew the fertility of their fields by allowing each portion of land to lie fallow for a season. A two-field system was commonly operated in England outside the Danelaw (see below, p. 62): village land was divided into two fields, one of which was cropped while the other lay fallow. Such a system is wasteful, since each field only produces crops every other year. It was then discovered that an alternation of crops, such as oats followed by wheat, is less exhausting to the ground than repeated cultivation of the same crop, and this prepared the way for the three-field system of farming, where a field lies fallow only every three years. The terms 'two-field' and 'three-field' are still used, but it now seems that as the system evolved it was blocks of strips which rotated rather than whole fields. This system served England well and continued in a general way until the late eighteenth century, when the innovators of the Agricultural Revolution introduced winter root crops and clover into the rotation as substitutes for the regular fallowing. The three-field system now survives only on the Laxton lands in Nottinghamshire, where a medieval rotation of spring corn–fallow–winter corn continues to produce good results.

Experienced farmers, with an eye for the little signposts to fertility contained in the soil texture, colour and vegetation cover, the Saxons laid out their fields to take account of soil quality, slopes and the demands of their farming methods. So good was their choice and positioning of the ploughlands that a great many Saxon field boundaries have been retained to this day.

Once set out, the village open fields were divided into lanky strips, each about ten times as long as it was broad. The length of the strips was commonly a furlong – a 'furrow long' (220 yards, or 201 metres), possibly the distance that a team of oxen could draw a plough without pausing to rest. Their width was usually about 22 yards (20 metres). Each team of six or eight oxen dragged a heavy plough which was capable of digging a deep furrow, so removing the need for double or cross ploughing which had determined the rectangular shape of the older fields. The plough team would probably work for a long morning, and, as we have seen, before being released to graze in the afternoon they could be expected to plough an acre (0.4 hectares), the area of a strip. It was expedient to

waste as little time as possible in turning the plough, hence the elongated shape of the strip, and at the end of each group of strips there was a headland upon which the plough was turned for the return journey. By controlling the direction of the plough, which would throw soil to one side, ridges were built up running parallel to the direction of the strip – usually four ridges to each strip – and these corrugations helped the drainage of the land. Where open-field land has been turned into pasture, usually during the enclosures of the Middle Ages, the remains of these ridges may still be seen, particularly when the sun is low (ill. 99). In some parts of the Continent, notably in Poland, ridge-and-furrow cultivation in open fields is practised today.

The ploughland was not communal property, but in order that everyone should share proportionately in the good land and the poor, each family's land consisted of strips that were dispersed throughout the open fields. It is not known whether a redistribution of strips to maintain equality of holding was made in England, as it was in the lands of Russian peasant communities before the nineteenth century. Men held shares in the meadow proportional to their share in the arable lands. Beyond the privately owned ploughlands and meadowlands were the often extensive areas of communal pasture – the 'common', fragments of which still survive in communal ownership.

Although the ploughland was privately owned, its division into strips in two or three vast village fields ensured that decisions about its use were taken communally. Furthermore, much of the work on the land could only be carried out efficiently by the co-operative efforts of the farming people, particularly at the most exhausting seasons of ploughtime and harvest.

As we have seen, six or eight oxen were needed to pull the heavy plough. The peasant, owning perhaps 30 acres (12 hectares) of land, would only have been able to support a couple of oxen, so the formation of a team to plough just one strip of land would have required the pooled resources of three or four families. Although people collaborated, the village was not a haven of socialism and there were always individuals, like the greedy fourteenth-century peasant in *Piers*

29 *Above left* A strip-like pattern of land tenure survives in the Great Field of Braunton in North Devon – a tiny and slightly altered relic of the beautiful patchwork landscape of medieval open-field farming.

30 *Above* Long evening shadows reveal the ridges and furrows of the former open-field farming at Little Willicote in Warwickshire. Note the 'reversed S' form of the strips in the top centre field, probably formed as the team was swung at the approach to the headland.

Plowman, who would nibble at the edges of a neighbour's strip: 'if I went to the plough I pinched so narrowly that I would steal a foot of land or a furrow.'

Now we begin to see why the village was so tightly interlocked with the developing Saxon way of life. After the Enclosure Acts of the eighteenth and nineteenth centuries provided farmers with packages of land in compact blocks, the temptation to desert the village farmhouse and build anew in the centre of a compact landholding was often great. If, however, one's landholding consisted of a large number of widely dispersed strips, there was no great advantage in living on any one of them. Further, the obligation to carry out regular work on the lands of the lord and the need for co-operative ventures with one's neighbours meant that there was no better place to live than in the village itself, at the very hub of the local economy. The peasant in the village was relatively secure from danger, close to his church and to his neighbours and centrally placed in relation to the scattered lands upon which he worked.

Time spent in travel was time wasted in a community that was never far removed from the threat of famine, nor embarrassed by surplus, and tasks that were most demanding of time and labour were sensibly located close to the village. Near its heart there were the cottage garden plots, surrounded by the zones of meadowland and ploughland; furthest away were the common grazing lands, where stock could be left with the minimum of supervision.

What we have said is generally true of the greater part of agrarian England, but it by no means fits the whole country. Local differences in landscape, soil and custom have always existed, and they combine to produce the regionalisms which are the delight and the strength of England, now growing and being nurtured after decades of centralization and neglect.

In Cornwall and some remoter parts of the west, the Saxon village and open-field farming did not displace the older Celtic patterns to any great degree, and the landscape remained essentially one of hamlets, farmstead and small fields. Kentish peasants, too, were as likely to have been dwellers in farmsteads or hamlets, and villages were less the rule there than in the Midlands. Perhaps the relative calm of Kent during the early Saxon settlement removed the need for defensive villages, while Kentish involvement with Continental trade reduced the overbearing importance of arable farming.

In the windswept hilly country of the north, the peasant was often more stockman than ploughman, and the thin population and the sheep- and cattle-herding lifestyle favoured scattered farmstead and hamlet settlements rather than villages. Around some hamlets a form of farming which resembled the Scottish 'run rig' one-field system seems to have been used, with land being taken in from the surrounding pasture and cropped until the thin upland soils were exhausted, then allowed to revert to pasture while another field was taken in.

There were social differences, too. In 886, just ten years after the first Danish settlement in England, a treaty was drawn up between Alfred and the Danes which gave the invaders the territory bounded on the south and south-east by the Thames estuary and the Roman road known as Watling Street (the modern A5). The area adminstered under Danish law – Danelaw – covered East Anglia, the five Danish boroughs around Leicester, Nottingham, Derby, Stamford and Lincoln, and the kingdom of Northumbria (most of present-day Yorkshire). Soon in the north a westward movement of Danes up the river valleys met and overlapped with an eastward movement by Norwegians coming from the west coast. Scandinavian rule lasted only about fifty years, though it was renewed briefly after 1016 when the Dane Canute became king of all England. But the influence of Scandinavian law and custom persisted for centuries. Instead of feudal villeins, the inhabitants tended to be free peasant landowners; their land was divided up according to Scandinavian, not Saxon, units, and their monetary system and laws long remained different from those of Anglo-Saxon England.

Although the English nation is composed of an intricate mixture of immigrant races, it is with the Saxons, among the least known and understood of their ancestors, that most English men and women feel the greatest sense of kinship. The Saxon period began with dimly-glimpsed settlements that looked less like an English village of today than like an African village of thatched huts and storerooms. It ended – to the limited extent that it did end – at the Norman Conquest, with the establishment of a stratified and partly town-dwelling society, which was soon converted to a rigid feudalism.

Research always tends to throw up more questions than it solves, and the more we learn about the English village, the greater an enigma it becomes. Had this chapter been written a couple of decades ago, the reader would have had a straightforward account of the village's origins. Today, views of the early stages are in turmoil, with evidence that conflicts and with almost as many arguments and nuances of interpretations as there are researchers. The Saxon settlers, it seems, did not wipe bare the slate of English settlement and mark out a new pattern of 'nucleated' villages of closely clustered huts. The nineteenth century was an age of nationalism, and we have been tempted to see different types of settlement as the products of different national cultures. That the Saxon leaders gradually established political control of England is not in question, but it is doubtful whether the new political order was at once accompanied by revolutionary changes in the countryside. For centuries the Saxon peasant and the older inhabitants of England probably lived side by side (if not always cheek by jowl), and the Saxon language gradually gained predominance. Slowly, the village became tied to its fields and more permanent, the community were reluctant to desert the church which they had built, and lords began to regulate affairs.

When we turn to the village itself we find not a settlement fossilized from its moment of birth, but a place which is lively and dynamic with a population which, as it grows, experiments with the plan and responds to changing needs and ideas by changing the orientation of the village, abandoning bits of street here and throwing out lines of growth there. A new word is entering the language of the archaeologist and historian: villages are often found to be 'polyfocal', spanning the remains of two or more earlier settlements.

While the village begins to present itself as a dynamic and changeable place, it is set in a human landscape which is more conservative than we thought. Continuity seems to be the key, with the successive invasions being absorbed into a lifestyle that changes at its own slow pace. One does not win over the English countryside in a frantic assault but should listen to its needs and compromise.

2 · In the Middle Ages

THERE IS a popular belief that the Middle Ages were a period of near stagnation whose torpor ended in the blinding flashes of the Renaissance and Reformation. For the people of the village, the period was exceptionally hard: the bonds of feudalism formed in the Saxon age became tighter and all-embracing as the system was refined, formalized and expanded under the hard-headed and wolfish Norman conquerors. Yet surprisingly, when oppression was most severe and life for the peasant reached the depths of austerity, the rural population grew rapidly, pressing up against and often beyond the bounds of the economically productive farmland. Before the Middle Ages were ended and the peasants able to glimpse an age when the chains of servitude would rest more lightly upon their shoulders, this surging growth of population had been checked by the hammer blows of pestilence. Hosts of villages never regained the levels of population which they had supported at the beginning of the fourteenth century, and for a few villages, the plague brought total extinction.

For the village itself, the Middle Ages were a formative period of great vitality. Each community, consciously or unwittingly, was engaged in an experiment with its environment. Homes were seldom so costly or so permanent as to endow the village with an inflexible skeleton or rigid plan. Dwellings could be removed and new ones set up on a fresh site as circumstances required. During the fourteenth century, the original village of Horton in Northamptonshire seems to have been abandoned as the villagers deserted a hillslope site for a lower one aligned along a river valley. (The move was to prove unfortunate, for at some time a little before 1676 the whole village was destroyed during the creation of a park by the owners of the nearby hall.) While the crude huts of the medieval peasants had little hold on the community, the church was the most splendid stone building that could be afforded, and it would not be demolished. Wherever we notice a church which stands in isolation we have good reason to suspect that the original village has moved. Caxton in Cambridgeshire is a case in point: the present village can be found aligned along the Old North Road, but its church is some quarter of a mile (400 metres) away. Around the church are the holloways which mark out the pattern of former streets and lanes, while fragments of medieval pottery are scattered in the fields all round. In this case documents survive which suggest when the move took place. About 1247 the lord of the manor of Caxton obtained a charter granting him the right to hold a weekly market, and it must surely be then that he chose to move the village to its present location, where the market would be on the route of travellers moving north and south along the bustling highway.

Horton and Caxton are by no means unusual. For far too long the study of history has been dominated by the preoccupation with documents. Inspired by the example of Professor Hoskins, a new generation of landscape historians are also studying history where it was made – in the towns and countryside. The more one looks, the more it becomes apparent that most villages have experienced several stages of experimental adjustment to their surroundings. New streets are thrown out, while others may wither, and quite frequently the whole settlement moves, leaving the church behind to slumber in isolation.

Before the sturdy crop-necked Conqueror had stamped out the dying twitches of rebellion, he sent out his clerks to draw up his bank statement so that he might know the extent of his winnings, how severely he could levy his taxes and how his favours had been bestowed. In the soulless lists of the Domesday Book, we have an inventory of the people and assets of England surveyed in 1086. It is

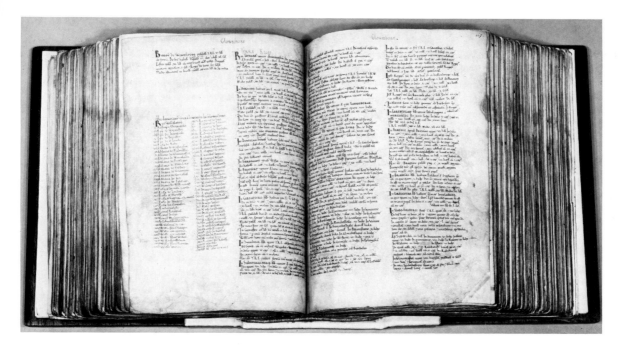

not a complete catalogue of villages: some which archaeology has shown to have existed at the time are missing, and confusion can result from the many cases where the village and the manor did not coincide. The lands of Wallington in Hertfordshire were divided between five major landholders, and those of Harpswell in Lincolnshire between three, while Marnhull in Dorset has three separate focus points. What was intended in the Domesday Book was a list of taxable assets. In each case the catalogue of lands begins with those held directly by the King. All entries follow the same overall pattern, recording (1) who held the land before the Conquest, (2) a description of the land, with the number and status of the inhabitants, number of ploughs, mills, etc., and the proportion of land held directly by the lord ('in demesne'), and (3) the value of the land in the time of Edward the Confessor ('T.R.E.', *Tempus regis Edwardi*) and now – that is, in 1086.

The timeworn pages tell of a land of peasants upon which the ranks of churchmen, soldiers, merchants and great lords were but a thin veneer. Could we gather together a representative couple of thousand men of Domesday England we would find about 760 *villeins*, men who, like the Saxon *gebur*, were tenants of holdings up to some 30 acres (12 hectares) of land; almost as numerous would be the 620 or so cottars or *bordars*, whose rented lands were considerably smaller. Standing more proudly there might be 240 free tenants. The 180 cowering slaves were the only group who might expect some improvement upon their Saxon status. All of these people are in some way or other tied to the 70 lords of the manor. While some of the peasants live in small towns, we would have caught only about 60 burgesses in our net.

The Normans did not invent feudalism, but they did extend and regularize it, tidying up some local customs and improving its efficiency as a means of separating the humble majority from what little wealth they had, creating an inhuman system which was unhindered by ties of blood or culture which may

31 Part of Domesday Book relating to Gloucestershire. On the far left is a list of landowners, headed by the King and the Archbishop of York; few of the names seem Saxon. The entry for Barton in the next column tells, amongst other things, that in the time of King Edward the Confessor it rendered 1,000 loaves of 'dogs' bread' (to feed the royal hunting dogs). The entry for Marshfield, in the far right column, is typical: 'There are 14 hides. In demesne 5 ploughs, 26 villeins, 13 bordars with 30 ploughs, 18 slaves. The priest has one of these hides. In King Edward's time worth £35, now £47.'

have linked the Saxon lord to his lesser neighbours. The feudal ladder reached upwards from the humblest cottar to his king, and each rung was marked by the exchange of protection for services. The people of the village would probably have been happy to do without the protection if they could forget the services: for them it was a way of life which put the fruits of their labour into the coffers of their lord. Even so, feudal law and the hardening of manorial custom into local law gave the peasant a minimal protection against his master and other lords. The lord was prohibited by law from killing or maiming his bond-tenants, and after Magna Carta he was at least nominally prevented from arbitrarily fining them. They could however be sold along with estates with no more to-do than would be involved in selling a horse, field or tree. One of many of its kind, a charter of around 1205 describes how Robert the Chaplain, who leased the manor of 'Ginges' in Essex, released to the Abbess and convent of Barking all his rights to the bondage, chattels and family of Edward son of Hamelin. What Edward son of Hamelin thought of the arrangement we are not told and it is unlikely that the other parties involved much cared. What an abbess and her nuns were thinking of in dealing in human beings, we might well ask, but ecclesiastical foundations controlled much of the land of England, and they were not noted for any special leniency. Cistercian monks (who were noted farmers) moved and rebuilt at least three villages in Leicestershire and several others elsewhere that interfered with their agricultural grand designs. But though they could be sold, the lowest ranks in the hierarchy under the Normans were still better off than Saxon slaves: they were entitled to protection by their lord and to various formalized privileges.

In addition to the various regular and special labours which the people of the village were obliged to perform on their lord's lands or demesne, they had to make periodic payments in cash or kind – perhaps a few eggs at Easter, a hen or a load of sticks from time to time, sixpence here and a bushel of wheat there, and their best beast when they died. Regular sums were extorted from the villagers or the village at any excuse, and though these dues had fine names, like tithingpence, lardsilver, recognizance and aid or tallage, in effect they simply moved the lord's burden of taxation on to the less fleshy shoulders of his tenants. These obligations were listed meticulously, and many manuscripts survive to

32 A harvest wagon of about 1340 (from the *Luttrell Psalter*). Efficient wagons for heavy haulage seem not to have developed until the sixteenth century. With few spokes and studded wheel rims, this cart will have given a rough and uncertain ride. The use of three horses to pull and three chaps to push implies difficult ground as well – in fact, up the margin of the manuscript.

bring the days of drudgery to life. In 1183 Bishop Pudsey of Durham made a survey of his lands and dues which is known as the Bolden Book, after a village near Sunderland. We learn that at Stanhope there were twenty villeins who farmed between ten and fifteen acres (4–6 hectares) – an oxgang – each. Each paid two shillings rent and was obliged to give the Bishop sixteen days of labour on his demesne every year. Each also had to give up four days to carting the Bishop's corn, the villeins providing the carts themselves; in the autumn each was to prepare four strips of seedland and to spend two days in mowing, haymaking or carting the corn. On those days the lord would provide food. Elsewhere on the manor, which lay in hunting country, the type of service depended upon local circumstances. The villagers at Heighington must provide ropes for deer enclosures, and those of Usworth, Binchester and Lanchester were obliged to care for greyhounds. Stanhope too lay within the bounds of the Great Hunt and the tenants there were also expected to prepare the kitchen, larder and kennels, spread rushes and bracken on the floor of the hall and chapel and generally make themselves useful around the temporary village which was set up during the hunting season.

33, 34 Farming just before the Black Death (from the *Luttrell Psalter*). *Above* This harvest scene with women on their knees could still have been seen five hundred years later; costumes changed, but even the knot used to tie the sheaves was probably the same (compare ills. 119, 134). *Below* Gloved ploughman and assistant guide an ox team pulling quite a sophisticated plough, with iron coulter and share and wooden mouldboard.

Women were sometimes tenants in their own right, particularly after outbreaks of the plague left many vacant tenancies. Long before the Black Death, Juliana Strapel was a free tenant on the Essex manor of Ingatestone. In 1275 she was obliged to provide an annual rent of 5s. 9d., a ploughshare and 11d. for lardsilver. She had to provide the demesne with two days of ploughing and one-and-a-half days each of weeding and harrowing; she was expected to turn up for haymaking at Hanleigh for as long as the job took, reap an acre at the grain harvest, produce a man to perform three other 'boon' works (feudal obligations) and help in nut gathering. Like all the other tenants of Ingatestone she will have grumbled her way reluctantly to perform her boon works, but probably she did not consider herself to be too badly treated. Other tenants will have had more swingeing rents to meet, and there were far dirtier tasks than nut gathering.

As well as the rents, dues and boon works, the peasants were fined by the manor court at almost every turn; they paid to use the lord's mill, or were fined for keeping hand querns at home; they paid to marry outside the manor or were fined for not paying; they were fined if they joined the clergy without the lord's permission and even if they followed the spirit of the Bible and gave shelter to strangers. The ecclesiastical lords were as skilled at fining as the layman, and the Church invariably took a tithe from the peasant when he was alive and a 'mortuary' of his second-best beast when he died, the best having already been snapped up by the lord of the manor.

The numerous manor court rolls that survive provide a monotonous catalogue of the ways in which the people of the village were fined for their follies. Here are samples from Tooting, south of London, and from three Cambridgeshire villages.

Tooting, 1247:

> William Jordan is in mercy [of the court] because he ploughed the lord's land badly. Arthur is his pledge. Fine 6d.

Foxton, 1324:

> It is found on the evidence of Brother Robert that Alice Barley would not allow the lady's bailiff to take a lamb which she had seized from Hugo de Banns, so she is fined 3s. 4d. for contempt. And Robert Barley is fined 12d. for contempt of the lady and Brother Robert in obstructing him from doing his duty.

Cottenham, 1442:

> William Warde stopped a certain ditch in Cottenham which was a boundary between Henry Arneburgh and William le Wode and planted willows in the midst of the bottom of the same ditch appropriating the same ditch to himself where it was the boundary between the fee of the lord bishop of Ely and the fee of the lord abbot.

All this is rather tame stuff; rely on a Fen Tiger to add some spice. Landbeach, 1435:

> John Frerer . . . kept a foreign woman in the lord's bakehouse at the lord's expense for how long they know not.
>
> Item that the same John sent a cartload of the lord's turves value 6d. to the house of John de Waldseef at Westwyk where Milsent his concubine was staying.

After meeting their burdensome bills of bondage, it is not surprising that the villagers had little left to purchase luxuries or even essentials: their lifestyles were based on a make do and mend, do-it-yourself sufficiency. Within most villages there were people who combined peasant farming with the practice of special crafts – as bee-keepers, shepherds, wood-turners, smiths or potters – but much of their industry went to the service of the lord. After a hard day in the fields, the people of the village, depending upon their sex, might like their forefathers bend their aching fingers to harness-mending, tool-making, knitting, or the weaving of coarse, itchy cloth from homespun wool or flax. Flat loaves of heavy wheat or rye bread were baked, the 'oven' sometimes no more than a heated flat stone; and brewing in a warm corner of the hut there might be a tub of weak ale made from home-grown malt and barley. When archaeologists explore the foundations of medieval peasants' huts they find no riches, but crude stone loom-weights, home-made needles and combs of bone, fragments of leather harness and of flimsy rough-stitched shoes or drinking vessels from the horns of a village ox. Only a very few essentials like salt, iron and tar entered the hut from the world beyond.

Occasionally the frustrations of the village people would explode: usually these revolts were small-scale and local, as when in the fourteenth century a mob of Yorkshire villagers who were tired of the Abbot of Fountains stealing their common lands for sheep pasture set upon and beat up his shepherds. With co-ordinated planning, England was the peasants' for the taking, but no means existed by which they could organize a country-wide uprising; they were confused and mystified by the Church, and once under arms they began to worry about the state of their crops and families. When in the reign of Henry VIII the nucleus of the Pilgrimage of Grace formed up on Market Weighton common in Yorkshire, under a brown velvet banner bearing the Five Wounds of Christ, to defend the Catholic faith and seek general redress, their purpose was as ill-fated as that of the men of Kent and Essex who had joined ranks in the Peasants' Revolt a hundred and fifty years earlier. Led by Wat Tyler, those rebels arrived in the capital in 1381 with great force and clamour, having burned many of the manor rolls which bore the details of their bondage, then scurried back to their lands after forcing a worthless charter from Richard II. Soon Richard appeared in Essex at the head of a powerful army, meeting the peasant deputies at Waltham and proclaiming, 'Villeins you were and villeins you are; in bondage you shall abide, and that not your old bondage, but one incomparably worse.' (Before too long, however, events were to prove him wrong.)

Faced with adversity and oppression, the people of the village did not abandon all hope and effort; they multiplied, set up new villages and pressed the frontiers of farming to their limits, sometimes ploughing land that has never been ploughed since. At the time of the Conquest, the population of England may have numbered around 1¾ millions: less than three hundred years later it had swelled to at least 3¾ million souls, and some put the population peak of around 1250 at about 5 million. It is clear that the villages of the thirteenth century were bursting at the seams. The techniques of reclaiming fenland and heathland and the basics of scientific farming were not properly developed until the eighteenth century, and although the records of the Domesday Book are seldom as clear as we would like, there is plenty there to show that already by 1086 the limits of practicable ploughlands had almost been reached. More land could only be won by extending the village fields at the expense of the forest or by doing as the

English did during the First and Second World Wars, driving the plough into lands that were thin and poor and scarce able to reward the ploughman for very long.

Almost every village had its population problem. For a while relief could be found by taking in clearings from the waste or uncultivated land which lay at the edges of the village fields, a process known as 'assarting'. These assarts were seldom divided into strips, so the old village lands became surrounded by a fringe of fields of quite a modern aspect. The lord viewed the changes with mixed feelings, for while he was unlikely to disapprove of a move which would increase his tenantry and income, he valued the forest too: accordingly, assarting needed full lordly sanction, often in the form of a charter. From such charters we learn how around 1225 Mabel, Abbess of Barking in Essex, confirmed to the convent's steward John de Geyton the right for life to the assarts made at Writtle Park and Hanley Wood. Christopher Taylor has compiled some records of clearance in Dorset: they tell, for example, how in 1257 'Adam de Warner, the reeve of Marnhull, occupied in Todber one acre [0.4 hectares] of land enclosed by a hedge', and how in 1302 'Walter atte Wodeseyned gives to the Lady Queen 12 pence for a perch and a half encroachment opposite his gate.'

The word 'waste' is misleading: it was not without reluctance that the forest was cleared from lands which were often ill-suited for farming. The waste provided the lord of the manor with his sport, hunting (all but the royal game of stag and boar); it was a storehouse of building materials and firewood, and a rich larder of beechmasts and acorns for the village swine. One could not take a single tree without permission. Rowland Parker's search through the court rolls of Chatteris manor in Cambridgeshire reveals that 'Sir William de la Haye cut down a certain willow tree reserved for this manor, due to the negligence of the reeve; the value of the tree was 6*d*. which shall be paid by the reeve.' Though the word 'forest' comes from the medieval Latin *forestem silvam*, meaning the wood (*silva*) 'outside', or not enclosed, it was counted as a part of the resources of the village, and was the only safety valve for many over-expanding populations.

During the Middle Ages, and until the last century in many places, the woodland was a carefully managed and controlled resource, with timber being coppiced (repeatedly cut at ground level to produce long, slender branches), pollarded and felled according to various systems of rotation. While the greatest deforestation of England probably took place during the Neolithic period, at the height of the medieval population boom it is likely that many of the woods were reduced, as assarting nibbled away at their margins. But Nature bided her time, till a worsening climate combined with the exhaustion of the marginal soils to put farming on the run. Population was probably already falling before the Black Death began its rampages, killing perhaps one-fifth of the people of England in 1348–49. After this, in most places there was land for all. (The impact of the pestilence will be described in detail in Chapter 5.) Historians have seen in the plague the cause of the decay of feudalism, with the labour shortage which the catastrophe caused forcing landlords to offer generous terms to the peasantry and to compete with each other for the privilege of employing what had become a scarce resource. Certainly the pestilence had an effect upon the conditions of the survivors: in 1350 the medieval chronicler Knighton grumbled that at harvest one could not 'hire a labourer for less than 8*d*., plus food; a reaper for 12*d*., plus food. For which reason, many crops rotted in the field for lack of labourers.' He also commented on the effect on priests and chaplains:

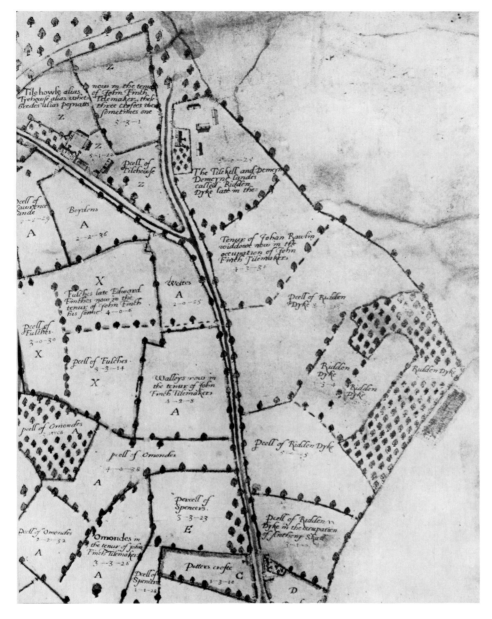

35 This map of Ingatestone in Essex, made in 1600/1601, clearly shows a large triangular area of assarting lying to the right of the road. The words 'Ridden Dyke' refer to lands cleared of woodland. The clearance is shown by a surviving charter to have been made by John de Geyton, steward of the convent of Barking, about 1225.

there was hardly anyone who would accept a benefice for up to £20 or 20 marks; but within a short while there flocked into orders a great multitude whose wives had died of plague, among whom were many unlettered men, the merest laymen, who could only read after a fashion, let alone understand.

The cornerstone of feudalism was the power and the right of the lord of the manor to extract labour from his peasants. If wages and money rents were substituted for labour services and payments in kind, then the lord was left as little more than a glorified employer and rent collector. The feudal system did not disappear in a forest of revolutionary peasant banners: it gradually disintegrated.

There is plenty of evidence that the commutation of labour services was well under way before the Black Death came to buttress the rising wages against which the landlords were on the whole impotent. By the middle of the fifteenth century, labour service had largely died out, and with it villeinage. The villages which emerged from the shadows of the Middle Ages were peopled by the families of hired labourers and tenant farmers. The tenant farmer was usually a 'copyholder', that is he held a copy of his land title which was taken from the manor rolls, and paid an annual rent to the lord of the manor. Unlike the freeholder who was often his neighbour, he had no freedom of tenure, but so long as labour was valuable and the manor relied on its ploughlands, his holding was secure.

Once bound by heavy chains of duty and obedience, the peasants now often ignored the commands of the manor courts. Those who were in bondage either walked away or bought their freedom, so that in the sixteenth century only one man in a hundred was a serf, and serfdom had disappeared by the seventeenth century. Most lords cut their losses by exchanging strips with their tenants in order to create a compact manor farm out of the tangle of rented and manor strips, but a considerable number discovered the profits to be made from sheep, and this created severe problems (as we shall see) for dozens of village communities, just as sheep were to displace the families of crofters in the Scottish Highlands two or three centuries later.

The appearance of the medieval village remains something of a mystery. As most villages have undergone several rebuildings since the Middle Ages, much of the best information comes from the lost medieval villages, which, with the use of air photography techniques, have recently been found to be exceedingly numerous. The fact that medieval cottages – as opposed to mansions – have not survived intact suggests that they were not very substantial places at the best of times. In parts of Lincolnshire and Yorkshire it seems that chalk – a deplorable building stone – was used, and elsewhere turf, cob (basically mud) and wattle and daub provided the walls. Roofs were of straw, reed or bracken thatch. Because the homes were so insubstantial, the medieval village was probably a fluid place, which could easily be altered: evidence from Wharram Percy in Yorkshire, the most thoroughly excavated lost village, shows that cottages were largely rebuilt about every thirty years. Even the best-built peasant home had but footings of stone and a stone-tiled floor. It was not until the great rebuilding began in the sixteenth century that the peasant housewife was provided with a home to be proud of.

There are sufficient lost village remains to show us that medieval settlements were just as diverse as those of today. Frequently, the village was surrounded by an earthen embankment, which separated the domestic and backyard animals from the animals or crops in the open fields all around. A ditch for draining the site, or a back lane, or sometimes both, often followed the line of the bank. At Great Stretton in Leicestershire the village had the form of a fat 'L', with roads following the outer sides of the 'L'. The moated manor house and its fishpond stood at one end and the church of St Giles in the angle, while the fifteen or so crofts and their yards were scattered around in an apparently haphazard manner. At Cestersover, Warwickshire, the homes and yards lined both sides of a street: from the old nucleus of the moated manor and medieval chapel at the northern end, the street was subsequently extended southwards, possibly in a planned form, over some former open field farmland. At Wormleighton, also in

Warwickshire, the homesteads seem to have been in two clusters which were separated by a fine chain of fishponds; one small cluster to the south-east faced the church, while a larger cluster of homes lined a narrow green some 400 metres (¼ mile) to the north-west, with the moated manor house lying behind. In some cases the homesteads would face directly onto the street, while in others each house would stand back within its own tenement or plot of land.

In many medieval villages, the layout of homesteads was quite jumbled, with the existing pattern of streets or roads providing the only visible controls on how the settlement should grow. Other villages, on the contrary, show considerable signs of planning. In Scandinavia, some were laid out according to a 'sun division': peasants owned cottage plots which were related in size to their holdings in the village fields, and these plots all radiated off the street or green. Within the fields, the strips were distributed so that neighbours in the village were neighbours on the land as well. There is some evidence that this pattern was repeated in north-east England, where there was considerable Danish influence: if so, it would reveal quite comprehensive village planning early in the Middle Ages.

The village of Kimbolton in Huntingdonshire was set out along the approach road to the castle and, in order to ensure the collection of market tolls, the road was displaced to run through the market place. Medieval prosperity seems to have led to a scheme to extend the village in planned form across the River Kym (we can guess this from field-walking, names and documents), but the area set aside for growth was not in fact developed until recently. Finally, some villages had an area of planned growth attached onto or built into an otherwise unplanned layout, as at South Cave in Yorkshire, where a market area was introduced.

36 In this illustration of about 1340, which may have been drawn from life, a peasant woman pauses from spinning to feed her hen and its lively brood. Note that the hen is shown to be tethered: no farmers now would bother with such a task, but for today's battery broilers this would have seemed the Golden Age!

In decacordo pfalterio: cum cantico

37 Lost village and fishponds at Wormleighton in Warwickshire (see also p. 132). A main fish pond, B chain of fish breeding tanks, C position of the green which was flanked by cottages, D site of the moated manor, E hedgerows planted just after destruction of the village, F more recent canal. Traces of ridge and furrow which would predate the main pond seem to be visible within its embankments.

38 Lost village earthworks at Great Stretton in Leicestershire. Holloways reveal the former street pattern; the moated enclosure of a manor lies top left, the church at the centre.

39 The cross-country road diverts at Kimbolton in Huntingdonshire to run through the main street and market, between the church (with a spire, right) and the castle (left, remodelled by Vanbrugh after 1700).

3 · Relics in the landscape

ONLY a minority of villages – the model creations of the eighteenth and nineteenth centuries – were built in the calculated pursuit of prettiness. Nevertheless a great many villages that we see today, with buildings of many ages and relics, some long disused, of the old way of life, have much to please the eye and quicken the sense of history. The old cottage homes, and the tales they tell about the lives of past generations, will be the theme of the next chapter. Here we shall be looking at the equally picturesque and revealing public features that have formed part of the religious, social, working and household lives of communities past and present. Some of these ancient survivors, like the church and the green, are today almost as valued and protected by the villagers as ever they were, while the pumps and stocks, mills and lock-ups that have escaped the vandalism of past decades may now be deliberately preserved as valuable mementoes of a life that has passed.

One of the oldest surviving features in the village landscape, the green exists in a bewildering variety of forms. Some greens are vast and imposing, like those at Long Melford in Suffolk, Old Buckenham in Norfolk, or the 40 green acres (16 hectares) at Shipbourne in Kent, while others are so small that they have been almost devoured by recent road widening. There are triangular greens, like those at Writtle in Essex and Nun Monkton in Yorkshire, neat rectangles like that at Milburn in the Lake District, and a wealth of other shapes and sizes. Some greens have become split up by the encroachment of cottages, like the one which has become seven or more smaller open spaces as homes have advanced at Barrington in Cambridgeshire (ill. 150); and others, like the former pair at Great Shelford nearby, have disappeared completely.

It was commonly thought that greens had their origin as central enclosures into which the villagers could drive their livestock for protection against raiders and predators. This was the case with the numerous green villages of the Anglo-Scottish border zone, where raiding was a way of life before the Act of Union in 1707: once the cattle were safely folded, the gaps between the surrounding cottages were sealed by gates known as lydgates. The origins of most greens are lost in the mists of time, but as our understanding of medieval archaeology increases it begins to appear that many, perhaps a majority, were introduced into existing villages during the Middle Ages. Where their history is known it reveals a wide variety of uses, suggesting that perhaps there always were several reasons why a village should want a green. Landbeach in Cambridgeshire has one of the very few medieval greens that can be dated: Corpus Christi College, Cambridge, had acquired the manor of the Chamberlain family in 1359, and in 1439 created the green out of the lands of a holding which had fallen vacant. At Whittlesford in the same county, the present green is part of the remains of the old manor garden; village tradition wrongly claims that the original green was seized and built upon by the squire: in fact the land concerned was simply unused, and awarded to the squire during the enclosure of the village fields. The green at Titchmarsh in Northamptonshire, with its puzzling bumps and hollows, appears to have been formerly part of the gardens of a mansion. Recent research in some Norfolk villages has shown that several greens were formed from areas of damp pasture which were unsuited to arable farming. It seems that increasing population growth during the twelfth century put pressure on the agricultural resources of some settlements, and there was a drift of settlers from older village centres. Homes were built around the pockets of pasture, which provided valuable grazing for domestic animals and were thus converted into greens. One

of the reasons why the English village so fascinates is that the more we discover, the more the simple explanations go out of the window and the village emerges in all its variety, complexity and mystery.

If some of the oldest greens may have originated as defended enclosures, others began as broad thoroughfares running through the heart of the village, providing ample space for roads and paths, common grazing close to the huts or cottages for the raising of small livestock, and space for community structures such as the smithy and pound, sometimes the church, and later the stocks. Other greens are clearly younger than their village and were deliberately created, often by a lord seeking space for a market. At East Witton in Yorkshire the owners, the Cistercian monks of Jervaulx Abbey, founded a new village planned around an elongated market green beside the straggling old village, obtaining the right to hold a market and fair in 1307. Sometimes a powerful owner seems to have carved out a market green in the heart of an older green-less village, probably demolishing several huts in the process, as seems to have happened at Castle Rising in Norfolk and at Quainton in Buckinghamshire, where the base and stump of an old market cross can be found standing at the top of the tussocky triangular green. Finally, some greens are clearly no older than the planned model villages that have surrounded them for the last hundred or two hundred years (ill. 94).

Whatever its origins, the green was always a useful place providing space for trading, dancing and boisterous celebration, and long after the medieval age had passed communities preserved their greens against cottage encroachment after enclosure had carved up the other common village lands. The many village greens that remain today are jealously guarded.

40 At Long Melford, Suffolk, the vista at the end of the vast green is closed by the Elizabethan almshouses and, rising behind them, the Perpendicular church, with its proud tower and large windows, built from the profits of the wool trade.

41 Maypole and green – a 'typical' combination in fact rarely seen today – at Ickwell in Bedfordshire. The green here is immense: we are looking at only half its extent.

42 At Appleby, Westmorland, the green takes the form of a broad grassy highway lined with houses, a planned layout dating back to about 1110.

43 This circular pond and communal pump are in the charming Oxfordshire village of Wroxton.

44 The view across the green from the bishop's palace at Lyddington in Leicestershire. The stump of a medieval market cross stands on a mound, framed by ironstone cottages the colour of gingerbread.

The village pond, less frequently met with than the green, is another feature which may have a variety of origins. Ponds are often found in connection with lost villages, as at Wormleighton in Warwickshire (ill. 37), which suggests they may have been widespread among medieval villages. Some, shrunken and reed-grown, are the remains of the ponds which supplied the village watermill with its head of water; others may have been dug as a watering place for livestock; and others still are the remains of village and manorial fishponds. The latter, generally of a rectangular form, were most conveniently built when a small stream was available for damming, and a sluice was often provided to allow the escape of surplus water. Chains of ponds sometimes existed with a number of chambers used for fish-breeding or the separation of different species: the air photograph of Wormleighton reveals a fine linked series of pools. (Most old village fishponds have run dry through lack of maintenance or the lowering of watertables due to drainage and increased human consumption.) Sometimes the catch was reserved for the lord of the manor, but often the villagers took their share of a source of protein that was much needed by a community which could seldom afford to eat meat and saw the bulk of the livestock slaughtered in autumn for lack of winter fodder.

The fresh water essential to a village's survival was in many cases provided by a stream, which the villagers shared with their cattle, ducks and geese regardless of hygiene. Rising springs, which bubble to the surface where an upper layer of pervious rock such as chalk or gravel meets a lower impervious layer such as clay or shale, provided a purer water supply, and spring points were favourite village sites. Some springs, like St Winifred's Well at Woolston in Shropshire, were thought to be holy; Stevington in Bedfordshire has a holy well beside the church; Derbyshire is famous for the Ascension Day custom of 'dressing the wells' with Biblical pictures formed by pressing flowers, beans and pebbles into clay, and five wells at Tissington are dressed in this way (pl. 22). If surface water was not available in the vicinity, then the villagers were obliged to dig for it. Wells are not particularly common survivals: with their deep shafts they are a danger to children and animals, and might be filled in when a village pump or piped water became available. More frequently seen is the cast-iron village pump, which superseded many wells in the eighteenth and nineteenth centuries. Victorian benefactors loved to erect monuments to their own patronage, and an elaborate pumphouse or the canopy for a well often provided the excuse for a display of largesse.

The most ubiquitous of all surviving medieval buildings are parish churches. Ten thousand out of an estimated total of seventeen thousand parish churches were standing by the time of the Reformation; eight thousand of them had been built by 1400. Some two hundred and fifty churches have substantial Saxon remains. An unknown number stand on prehistoric mounds or the sites of pagan rituals: Edlesborough in Buckinghamshire was built on an older and quite probably pre-Christian mound, and Rudston in Yorkshire has a pagan monolith in the churchyard. The great quantity of medieval churches is testimony to the hold of religion on the medieval mind: while a man and his family might tolerate a home of sticks and mud, their church must be of the best and most durable construction that the community and its masters could afford. Even if the services in the tortured Latin of the half-educated priest were completely unintelligible, the unaccustomed spaciousness of the building was more than compensation. The brilliant stained glass, wall-paintings or mouldings picked

45 The village pump at Monks Eleigh in Suffolk tells its own tale. It was cast by Ransomes & Sims of Ipswich, famous makers of farm machinery.

out in bright colours, and the carving in oak and stone offered a passport from the peasant world of dirt and toil to another of style, colour and ritual. In the good times, the church was a place of communal rejoicing and thanksgiving, and in the worst, a place of sanctuary from the mob or host.

Strangely though, when the church was more genuinely the focus of communal life, the building and its setting were treated with less reverence than in later, less devout ages. The churchyard was often the place for a Sunday market, with all the clamour which the event entailed, while dancing and the drinking of prodigious quantities of ale took place there on fair and feast days. The church itself was a meeting place for traders, tithe collection and other communal affairs.

The greater part of the cost of the church was normally borne willingly by the manorial lord or lords, who, despite all the contradictions of the feudal age, were generally God-fearing men. In the Middle Ages East Anglia, with its vigorous woollen textile industry, was by far the leading manufacturing region, and places like Lavenham, Long Melford and Clare which are today little more than villages were leading industrial towns. In these and many similar towns the wealthy wool and cloth merchants created vast palatial churches for the glory of God and the salvation of their souls. In some cases the village church was the foundation of an abbey, which furnished it with priests and collected the tithes. Few opportunities to improve, embellish or extend the building to accommodate a growing village congregation were missed, and in consequence most churches incorporate the additions of many ages.

The rocks of scores of English regions are displayed in their parish churches. Even in the chalklands, rather than resort to the timber, wattle and daub of their domestic buildings, the parishes footed the heavy bill for hauling good stone from quarries like the ones at Barnack in Northamptonshire, or experimented with the hard flints yielded from the local chalk. In Norfolk a tradition of round towers – which could be made entirely of flint, without dressed stone or brick for the cornerstones – developed.

The way in which architectural styles changed with the passing centuries is well known. Saxon churches are often tall and narrow, with slender window slits (which were usually unglazed), and occasionally decorative carving. All the major Saxon churches have perished, so it is hard to form a judgment of their architectural and sculptural quality. Norman churches, broader and heavier in their proportions, with round arches decorated with ornament that grows progressively richer as we pass from the eleventh to the twelfth century, are more numerous. Towards the end of the twelfth century these Romanesque riches were subdued by the new discipline of Gothic: pointed arches, lancet windows, a multiplication of mouldings giving a lightness and verticality unattainable in Norman buildings. But, as with Romanesque, the Gothic style became increasingly complex and lavish, the austerity of Early English giving way by about 1300 to the flowing lines of the Decorated style, with its broad windows full of tracery, its foliage carving and fondness for spatial elaboration. From the early fourteenth century we possess sculpture in stone and wood that expresses delight in nature, superb technical accomplishment and material prosperity. The various parts of the country are distinguished by favourite architectural features – tall spires in Lincolnshire and Northamptonshire, for example, or the characteristic tracery known as 'Kentish' in the south-east.

The last Gothic style, the Perpendicular, evolved in the years around the

46 *Above* Anglo-Saxon: the tower of Earls Barton church, Northampton- shire, decorated with strips recalling timber- framing.

47 *Above right* Norman: Christ in Majesty, on the tympanum of Barfreston church, Kent.

48 In its secluded setting, the little-known church at Cranwich in Norfolk, with its thatched roof, Saxon round tower and circular churchyard, is one of the loveliest in the whole country.

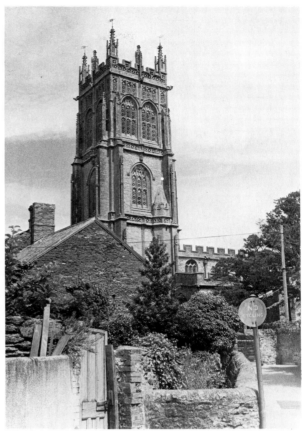

appearance of the Black Death in 1348, and it was once fashionable to make a connection between the two, attributing the reduction of ornament and the move towards standardization to the loss of so many craftsmen in the plague. This now seems too facile, since the change in style had begun long before 1348. What was lost in the details was made up in the effect of the whole: interiors, with their large windows lighter than they had ever been before, now became grids of panelling and glass; wooden roofs burst forth in angels and brightly coloured bosses; on the exteriors the towers (generally now without spires) rose higher and higher until in the Cotswolds, East Anglia and Somerset they reached a perfection that makes them in many ways the culmination of medieval design.

Most parish churches go back to a Norman original, if not to a Saxon one. With the years they tended to be rebuilt in whole or part, and by the end of the medieval period almost every English village had a building that was to be big enough for its needs until the present day.

With the Reformation comes a sharp change in architectural style and an equally sharp decline in the number of churches built. Renaissance forms are taken up, though there are relatively few village examples to compare with those of the cities. Brick, already used in the early sixteenth century, becomes widespread.

In the early nineteenth century the Gothic style was revived. A wave of new church building swept the country (though again its effects were little felt in the

49 *Above left* Early English variations on the pointed arch at Raunds in Northamptonshire, a region of spires and fine building stone.

50 *Above* Somerset Perpendicular: the lacy tower of North Petherton, built of the local red and blue lias, one of the best in a county renowned for its pinnacled and traceried late medieval towers.

villages, except where a patron might pay for a wholly new church), and a programme of energetic restoration commenced, which was usually necessary, after eighteenth-century neglect, but not always sympathetic. Stained glass which had been smashed, along with other images, as part of the excesses which accompanied the adoption of a Protestant religion in the sixteenth century, and Puritanism under Cromwell, was often replaced by the Victorians, who also might enrich the chancel and make it more 'holy' by the use of chancel rails, choir stalls, coloured tiles on the floor, and a reredos behind the altar.

The difficulty of moving heavy cartloads of building stone over long distances and the readiness of the people of one parish to mimic the church-building successes of neighbouring parishes ensured the development of regional styles. In Somerset and Devon, wealthy patrons instructed their builders to incorporate the triumphs of nearby churches in their new creations; in Cambridgeshire towers turned octagonal to echo the grandeur of Ely Cathedral; while at Walberswick in Suffolk a rare contract survives in which the local masons, Adam Powle and Richard Russel, are instructed to model the west door and windows on those of nearby Halesworth Church, while the tower should be like the one at Tunstall. (Seventeenth-century decline of the port community later caused the abandonment of part of the noble church.)

The normal situation for the village church was in the heart of the community which it served, often on an elevated piece of ground, although in a few cases the manorial lord put his own convenience above that of the congregation, building the church in his own backyard, or, in the case of Wyke Champflower in Somerset, right onto his house. When in the 1720s the old village of Houghton fell to emparking by Prime Minister Sir Robert Walpole, the Norfolk villagers were shunted into a new custom-built village nearby, and their medieval church of St Martin left stranded in the park. In Norfolk there are a number of churches

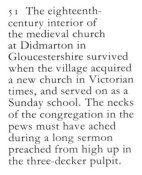

51 The eighteenth-century interior of the medieval church at Didmarton in Gloucestershire survived when the village acquired a new church in Victorian times, and served on as a Sunday school. The necks of the congregation in the pews must have ached during a long sermon preached from high up in the three-decker pulpit.

52, 53 Accessories of death: a rare medieval lych gate, at Ashwell in Hertfordshire, and a churchyard at Wilmington in Sussex whose yew tree is said to be nine hundred years old. The lovely tombstone is dated 1771. It is sad that so many fine and interesting stones have been cleared wholesale in recent years in a misguided quest for churchyard 'tidiness'.

which stand quite isolated from any village, and though some are on the sites of deserted medieval villages, others constitute one of the mysteries of the English landscape. The village of Swaffham Prior in Cambridgeshire, on the other hand, has two churches sharing the same churchyard: local feudal rivalries seem to have been involved but the details are obscure.

In the churchyard, headstones did not become common until well after the Reformation, and before then a single cross sufficed for all the occupants. Two other features which are frequently found in association with the church are the yew tree and the lych gate. There are various explanations on offer for the yew: its evergreen foliage has long been seen as a symbol of immortality; many may result from an instruction by Edward I that yews be planted to shelter the church from storms; and there is also a tradition that yews were planted to ensure a regular supply of bow wood for the fearsome English longbow. The lych gate, whose name derives from the Old English word *lich* (corpse), was placed at the entrance to the holy ground to provide shelter for the coffin-bearers awaiting escort by the priest. Many of the lych gates found in villages today are Victorian or younger, although a few medieval examples have withstood the vandalism of the Reformation and the ravages of the weather: such are those, for instance, which still stand at Beckenham in Kent and Ashwell in Hertfordshire.

The price of salvation was fixed at a tithe, one-tenth of all wood, corn, milk and eggs and of the increase in livestock. Tithes in goods were introduced in 794 in Mercia and during the ninth century in the rest of England, and continued to

54 A cathedral of agriculture: the tithe-barn at Great Coxwell, Berkshire, built by Cistercian monks not long after 1204. High stone bases support massive oak posts: on these countless people have carved their initials – one as early as 1472.

be collected until 1836, after which they were commuted into a cash payment which survived until 1936. The tithes supported the rector of the parish, or the monastery which provided the clergy, and they paid for the upkeep of part of the church fabric. A large barn was needed in which to store the tithes: the size of these barns may give an indication of the former productivity of a parish. Some were in a poor condition by the close of the Middle Ages, when superiors had difficulty in cajoling the peasantry to maintain the structure of church and barn. The exhortations that appear in court rolls would not have been so numerous if they had been observed. Barns which did survive were often taken over by later farmers, trimmed down and renovated, but some interiors survive. As we have seen, a barn at Belchamp St Paul in Essex may have been built before the Norman Conquest (ill. 24), and later medieval examples include noble structures at Bredon in Worcestershire and Great Coxwell in Berkshire.

Although some villages were owned by manors centred elsewhere and some supported several manors, the manor house is a quite frequent feature of the village scene. The house was normally built in, or close to, the settlement and was for centuries the most imposing private dwelling, until rivals appeared in the form of the vicarage of the proud parson and the home of the successful farmer or of the prosperous immigrant. The magnificence of the manor, or the lack of it, were related to the fortunes of the lord, the richness of the manor lands and the ability to avoid gambling and speculation; also, sometimes, the degree of readiness to rack-rent the tenantry and engross their lands, amalgamating them into larger units and forcing out the smaller tenants.

The manor house had its origins in the hall of the Saxon noble. Its face was changed with each upturn in wealth, and the rectangular moat which had once offered a vestige of security became, in many parts of England, a symbol of gentility. In the Saxon hall, the closest approach to privacy involved the partitioning of a section of the floorspace for sleeping quarters. Refinements came gradually. In the years which followed the Conquest, the kitchen was moved from the open yard into a covered building which was often detached from the living quarters: warmed by a central hearth without a chimney, the hall was quite smoky enough. Further partitioning of the hall space created separate chambers and extensions were added, often including a private chapel. Earth floors became tiled, wooden ceilings were introduced, and chimneys made their appearance. The oldest occupied home in England is a Norman building which was rediscovered as the well-preserved nucleus of a larger house at Hemingford Grey in Huntingdonshire, but early houses are very rare.

In areas where good stone could be obtained, the security and status of the lord were often underlined by his possession of the only stone building in the village apart from the church. In other places, increasing wealth was charted by extensions to the timber hall, which gained cross-wings to provide an 'L'- or 'H'-shaped plan, and during the Tudor period brick came into fashion, often replacing wattle and daub as an infilling for the wooden studwork. Much of the wealth of the manor was invested in its house: many experienced several reconstructions, culminating in the addition of a stately Georgian façade to mask the twists and slopes of the old timber building that lurked behind. Some became veritable stately homes. Where prosperity was less, or less prudently managed, the house remained compact, a mere farmstead with only the coat of arms above the doorway to proclaim the former glory.

55, 56 The two faces of Adlington Hall, Lancashire. The range with geometrical timber-framing, both decorative and functional, was plainly intended for proud display. Tastes changed, and in the eighteenth century a new brick range was added at right angles to present a classical, symmetrical front to the world.

59 This magnificent dovecote at Willington in Bedfordshire was built in the 1530s by the *nouveau riche* Lord John Gostwick, using materials from two dissolved priories. Each of the two doors leads to a high chamber lined with pigeonholes.

57, 58 Watermills. Weatherboarding and jutting sack hoists often betray a former mill, such as this one (*above*) at Houghton in Huntingdonshire.

Below A medieval mill, with its stream – set with eel-traps – pond, race, and overshot waterwheel (from the *Luttrell Psalter*, *c*. 1340).

60, 61 Windmills. *Above* A medieval post mill (also from the *Luttrell Psalter*), guarded by the miller's dog. The miller himself is taking a sack of grain from a woman's shoulder. The small mounds on which medieval mills stood often survive. *Right* The Union Smock Mill of 1814 at Cranbrook in Kent.

Sometimes rivalling the manor as the building with the least popular inmates was the dovecote. The lord had a monopoly in the business of dove rearing, and while the birds provided him with meat and fertile droppings, they ravaged the crops of all and sundry. Various designs were used, massive stone towers in the early Middle Ages and lighter wooden or brick-built houses later. A strangely pyramidal roof on a village house may betray a former dovecote. Where less severely modified, the structure can be detected by its lack of openings other than the small holes to admit the birds, which are placed high above the reach of vermin.

A less permanent structure, which nevertheless furnished the lord with a steady trickle of fines, was the village pound – an enclosure, often sited on the green, for livestock which strayed onto neighbouring plots in the days of the open fields. Pounds were usually built of perishable rails and hurdles, and few have survived, except for a handful built of stone or brick, as at Elsdon in Northumberland and Swaffham Prior in Cambridgeshire.

Wherever grain was grown, few villages were without a mill. Here the task of grinding the villagers' grain into flour was performed, and while the job could be done cheaply if less efficiently at home, using hand querns, the community was normally obliged to patronize the lord's mill, where some of the grain would be taken in return for services rendered. With the provision and maintenance of the mill machinery a costly undertaking, lordly patronage was usually necessary.

The two forms of power available in the Middle Ages were wind and water, the fashionable 'renewable' resources of the modern age: both were harnessed to revolve the heavy grit millstones, giving rise to two quite distinctive village buildings, the windmill and the watermill. Windmills stood on the highest and most exposed sites, while watermills were low-placed, tied to their supply of water power. In both cases, the mill builders sought to be as close as possible to the peasant growers of grain.

Watermills were common throughout England wherever there were streams to be harnessed and grain to be milled: they almost certainly eixted in Roman times, and the Domesday Book records more than five thousand. In all medieval watermills a flow of water which was normally regulated by sluice gates was used to rotate a paddlewheel of elm. Where the undershot principle was used, the water flowed under the wheel, while the more efficient breastshot and overshot principles used wheels set at a lower level than the incoming flow. From the revolving axle of the wheel, power passed to the millstones via an ingenious system of interlocking cogwheels. In more advanced mills, subsidiary gearwheels diverted energy to hoist sacks and sift flour. In the eighteenth century the wooden wheels and machinery of the watermills began to be replaced by cast iron, and then the decline of village mills set in, with the centralization of milling in towns where steam or electrical power was used to crush the grain between steel rollers. A few village mills survive with their machinery still intact; others have been converted into private dwellings whose former use is proclaimed by the silted remnants of the millstream and pond or rusting lock gates.

The role of water and the wheel was duplicated by the wind and sails in the windmill which, according to legend, was introduced to England by returning Crusaders. Early illustrations indicate that medieval windmills were small wooden structures. Not surprisingly, since windmills are exposed to the forces of the weather that they seek to harness, no medieval examples survive, but several existing mills stand on the sites of medieval predecessors. Two of the oldest

62 Guildhall and church at Thaxted, Essex, before the scene was overrun with cars.

survivors are the smock mill of 1650 at Lacey Green, Buckinghamshire, and the post mill of 1665 at Outwood in Surrey. In all windmills the sails must be able to be turned to catch the wind from any quarter, and varying solutions to this problem produced the three types of mill that are still seen today. The earliest is the post mill, in which the whole structure revolved around a central post. From it the rarer smock mill developed, with a revolving upper part standing on a wooden base whose spreading planked sides resemble the shape of a rustic smock. Most substantial is the tower mill (pl. 13), which evolved during the eighteenth century: the machinery is housed on various levels in a tall brick tower, and the sails are borne on a domed cap, so that although a storm might sweep away the sails and cap, the body of the mill was safe. Where the tower was very lofty, a gallery might be built around it giving the miller access to his sails, which were spread with canvas and could be furled according to the strength of the wind, just as on a sailing boat.

Not all the windmills and watermills which grace the English landscape were built for milling flour. The medieval watermills of the Forest of Dean drove hammers used to beat out the ore body in the old Sussex iron industry; in woollen industry areas they drove underwater hammers for the process of fulling, which cleansed and firmed the cloth; in the Fenlands, windmills were equipped with water-scooping wheels to transfer water from one drainage level to another.

A fair number of villages boast the remains of a medieval guildhall or moot hall. A guildhall is usually a relic of former glory: perhaps the most splendid survival is to be found at Thaxted in Essex, where the timbered building perched high on its oaken struts was the market, exhibition and conference hall of a thriving guild of cutlers. Smaller guild and moot halls are found in several villages with humbler pasts, like Whittlesford in Cambridgeshire, West

Wycombe in Buckinghamshire, or Steeple Bumpstead in Essex. They were usually connected with a village society concerned with maintaining the church. A restored moot hall where the ground level is shared by several medieval shops can be seen in John Bunyan's village of Elstow in Bedfordshire.

Some large villages, like Dedham in Essex and Long Melford in Suffolk, supported fine grammar schools; before the Elementary Education Act of 1870 made public funds available for primary schooling the community had to rely upon private donations, usually in the nineteenth century channelled through the church into parish schools, or 'National Schools'. Until the sixteenth century the endowments of the wealthy were normally showered upon the church itself, which offered some prospects of salvation in return for past favours. During the eighteenth century, the activities of bodies such as the Society for the Promotion of Christian Knowledge produced schools in many villages, and by the start of the next century, perhaps half of the villages of England had a school of one kind or another. Even so, the enthusiasm for education was far from universal: the squirearchy by and large favoured minimal standards of education to prevent their labourers from aspiring to demands considered above their station, while the half-starved families of farm labourers relied upon the pennies which could be earned from child labour at bird-scaring or stone gathering. Both before and after the 1870 Act, absenteeism was high during the key weeks of the farming calendar (see p. 161). Today, the village school is more needed than ever it was for the preservation of the community, and the cost-conscious local authorities which close down schools as their enrolment falls below 'critical levels' could find no better way of sabotaging the villages which lie within their care.

Although many publicans would have us believe otherwise, very few village inns are medieval establishments. Peasants in the Middle Ages consumed ale in large quantities, but most of it was brewed at home. Many villages supported two or three alewives, often widows, who specialized in the brewing of ale for sale, and were fined when their standards fell below those of the appointed village ale taster. This fellow held one of the rare feudal offices for which there was any competition, and one which long outlived the feudal era. In the seventeenth and eighteenth centuries, in some localities, it was customary for the ale taster to wear leather britches. A puddle of ale was poured onto a seat and the taster, with all the dignity befitting his noble service, sat in it. When he rose thirty minutes later, any spoiling of the ale by the addition of sugar would be indicated by his britches sticking to the bench.

The alewives of the fifteenth-century village operated from ordinary cottages: specialization came later, when many ale mistresses gave way to licensed innkeepers who dispensed food and lodgings as well as ale. The grand old inns which can truly boast a history spanning three to five centuries are usually found in villages which had some former importance or lay upon coaching roads (pl. 11). Their noble frontages are often pierced by wide carriageways which admitted the coach to the security of the inn yard and stables at the rear. Many of the handsome regular façades of these hostelries were added in the Georgian era, and it is often interesting to peer round to the rear of the building in search of the old timber-framed inn behind. The grander inns of the eighteenth century displayed signs rather than the posts or box bushes which identified their humbler brethren. The average real 'olde worlde' village ale house was a rather seedy place. Before the licensing laws restricted the number of inns there was fierce competition between many poorly-furnished inns and ale houses, a sizeable village having perhaps more than a dozen. Until 1872, beer could be sold at all hours of the night or day.

A more sombre side of village life might be represented by surviving stocks or the lock-up. Although stocks, which combined incarceration with public humiliation, and often imprisoned helpless strangers, were used in the medieval period, the somewhat rare surviving examples need not all be particularly old: many stocks were still used at the beginning of the last century. Good examples can be found by the market cross in Ripley, Yorkshire (pl. 14), mounted on wheels at Colne in Lancashire, and with whipping posts at Aldbury in Hertfordshire, Ninfield in Sussex and Meldreth in Cambridgeshire. The set at Feock in Cornwall is, like much else in the county, distinctly odd: it has holes for seven legs – three-and-a-half pairs. Lock-ups were poky places where the village constables secured prisoners awaiting conveyance to proper gaols. They come in a variety of forms (two of which can be seen at Litlington in Cambridgeshire and Steeple Bumpstead in Essex), and often resemble a reinforced privy with small barred windows, though Harrold in Bedfordshire and Castle Cary in Somerset have more spacious lock-ups in stone. Like the stocks, they were in use into the nineteenth century, and indeed several were not built until the 1830s and 1840s.

The list of relics in the village landscape is by no means complete. Beside some villages there are the ruins of a fort or earthworks, an abbey or priory, sometimes a castle; but structures such as these were not *of* the village, and their associations were more than local. On the other hand, one may come across an old fire engine house, a communal bakehouse (ill. 136), a toll house, an open-air cider press, or any of a number of other fragments of a former way of life based on local self-sufficiency; and it is to this way of life that we shall now turn.

63 Mischief a-plenty in the Early Victorian village school. Young children of mixed ages (only elementary schooling was provided) are on hand to distract the boy reading from his primer under the stern supervision of the 'dame'.

4 · The villager at home

THE VILLAGE is known and admired both as a close-knit rural community and as a collection of homes and buildings. The special appeal of cottage dwellings usually lies in the way they combine in rambling and unregimented clusters to create charming and often evocative vistas, rather than in the intentional or ornate prettiness of a particular building. Most settlements contain houses of different ages, styles, sizes and shapes, and an appreciation of the village as a whole is enhanced by an understanding of each individual.

Charming or unremarkable, the dwellings are little mines of information. They tell us about the affluence and poverty of the villagers and their changing lifestyles, and they contain clues to the local geology and past transport conditions. Their style illustrates how architectural fashions have been diffused from urban centres to rural backwaters, and how the now-forgotten masons and carpenters of the English regions chose to adopt, modify or ignore these fashions, often producing local designs of their own making.

Apart from the squire, many parsons, and any wealthy newcomers, the village populations, depending upon the period and local circumstances, existed in conditions which ranged from unadorned sufficiency to outright poverty. Their homes, whether paid for by the occupants themselves or by their employers and masters, were, after the medieval period, often built well, but seldom at unnecessary expense. They were constructed of materials which could be obtained and brought to the site at a reasonable cost, and they were built by local craftsmen, with the prospective occupants and their friends once playing a large part in the operation. With all this in mind, it becomes clear why each village dwelling speaks of the level of prosperity, the availability of transport, and local building traditions and preferences as they existed in the area at the time when it was built. Also, since only a very small proportion of older village dwellings have survived without considerable alterations, they reflect too the changes in well-being, lifestyle and building methods that have taken place over the years.

In the fifteenth century, in areas lacking good building stone, the practical choice for a house would be oak framing, wattle and daub and thatch; in the later nineteenth century, it would be for bricks and a roof made of slates brought from Wales. But while the Victorian age did see great developments in machine production and transportation, their effect on building in the country was far slower than is generally supposed: bricks were still being made commercially by hand from local clay near the end of the century.

Anyone attempting to date the buildings in a village without recourse to documents is likely to face an almost impossible task, for most of them will be the accumulation of generations of change and adaption. Our fifteenth-century timber-framed dwelling may have been repartitioned and extended in the following century to provide more rooms and storage space. Two, three or four centuries later, its thatched roof may have been replaced by one of pantiles or slate, and larger-paned windows installed to replaced the earlier leaded frames in the Georgian or Victorian era. The plaster covering, either original or added in the seventeenth or eighteenth century, when timber framing was out of favour, may have been removed in the nineteenth or twentieth century, and the timber framing emphasized with a coat of black stain. Factory-made bow windows may have been forced into the long-suffering structure in recent years, to complete the 'period' look. Modern owners seeking authenticity might remove the bow windows, revert to leaded casements and strip the Victorian blacking from the timbers.

As in the English countryside in general, many things in the village are older than they appear to be. Take a stroll along Abbey Street in the Cam valley village of Ickleton: you are walking along a branch of the prehistoric Icknield Way, which runs from East Anglia to Wessex, and the street takes its name from a medieval priory, abandoned four centuries ago. With the exception of the odd cottage which looks seventeenth-century, but is in fact fifteenth-century, the street appears to be lined by typical nineteenth-century brick-walled and slate- or tile-roofed cottages. Enter one of these, and things may not quite appear to be as they ought; the walls are thicker and not so level as you would expect, and the new plasterboard ceiling is masking an older uneven ceiling supported by twisted sixteenth-century beams. Bits at a time, the whole street has been affected by generations of 'improvement'. During the last two centuries, the fifteenth- and sixteenth-century cottages have had brick walls built to encase the original walls of timber, wattle and daub, they have been raised to give extra height and had damp-courses knocked in to keep the walls dry. Slate roofs have replaced thatch, and fireplaces have been provided for every room. The Victorian landlord who paid for most of the improvements must have taken pride in his well-lit and easily maintained renovated cottages. Ironically, if preserved in their earlier state they might be worth five or even ten thousand pounds more today.

Much is made of the way in which English villages appear to belong to the surrounding landscape, a harmonious and almost organic part of their setting. The effect is produced partly by the piecemeal growth of the village, with each new building usually being adapted to the contours and features of its particular

64 Abbey Street in Ickleton, Cambridgeshire. The old timber-framed buildings on the left have been encased in brick. The cottage just beyond the ladder is extremely old and consists of an aisled hall with a two-storey cross-wing added about 1500.

95

65, 66 Change at Pembridge in Herefordshire: views from different directions on Main Street taken in 1950 and 1979 record the 'restoration' of a timber-framed building by the removal of plaster, creating the magpie look. The little brick cottage between the timbered houses has disappeared. Had a photograph been taken at the dawn of the camera age it might have shown some thatched roofs and the cottages painted black.

site, rather than conforming to the rigid geometry of a plan, and partly by the need in past ages to use the locally available building materials. The straw thatch of the East Anglian cottage is a natural product of the surrounding wheatfields, while the Carboniferous limestone of the Pennines village matches the winding walls and bare scars of the landscape, changing its mood with the quickly changing light and weather, sometimes sparkling and sometimes stark. Even in the midst of the Fenlands, where most buildings postdate the eighteenth- and nineteenth-century drainage of the landscape, the austere and box-like brick and slate dwellings are in keeping with the bare and uncurving environment. Having said all this, it is easy to be misled by the stereotype and imagine the typical village without the occasionally incongruous and overbearing houses of the Victorian middle classes – professionals and successful businessmen – and the pinchpenny contempt for people and setting of so many council housing estates.

To begin the story of housebuilding at – or near – the beginning is to talk about timber, as this was the material normally used throughout England, with the exception of some near desolate upland areas, where centuries of grazing had denuded the landscape, and where stone could be easily collected or quarried. Still, we cannot assume that surviving timber-framed houses give a representative picture of the medieval village home. Apart from the regular modification of buildings to fit changing needs and fancies, the wealthier a man the more substantial would be his house and the more likely it is to survive. When we admire the solid and often imposing timber-framed houses in Lavenham, Suffolk, we are seeing not so much of the homes of a peasant community as structures built for public, commercial and private uses by weavers, merchants and shopkeepers grown rich upon a booming wool trade. Elsewhere, such houses were the homes of the lord of the manor or of the yeoman farmer who had emerged from the feudal age a few steps ahead of his fellows.

Over much of feudal England, the average villein lived in a hut not vastly different from those of the early Saxon village at West Stow (see pp. 52–53), consisting of a pole or ridge tree propped up at either end by posts, and against which sloping poles were laid to provide a tent-like framework, which would be thatched using brushwood, heather, straw or reed. Lacking windows or chimney, such huts gave a minimal shelter and would have been in constant need of repair. At least one medieval village is said to have been swept away in a Yorkshire gale.

The destruction of a mere village might not have seemed worth recording by the Norman scribes, but when a storm struck the capital, as happened in 1091, the event was worthy of note, and though one would expect the houses in the city to be more strongly built than those of the village, we learn – in a somewhat highly coloured account – that

winds, blowing from all quarters in a way marvellous to relate, began on 17 October to blow so violently that they shattered more than 600 houses in London; churches were reduced to heaps, as also houses . . . The fury of the wind lifted up the roof of the Church of St Mary, which is called at Bow, and crushed two men there. Rafters and beams were carried through the air, and of these rafters four of twenty-six feet [eight metres] in length, when they fell in the public street, were driven with such force into the ground that they scarcely stood out four feet [just over one metre], and as they could in no way be pulled out, orders were given to cut them off level with the ground.

Inhabitants of the Scottish borders in the Middle Ages are said to have been little troubled when their houses were destroyed by the English, saying, 'We can rebuild them cheaply enough, for we have only to require three days to do so, provided we have five or six poles and boughs to cover them.' Medieval English peasant homes need not have been much more substantial.

As the Middle Ages waned, the more prosperous and enterprising families aspired to more comfortable dwellings. There are many variations in the techniques of timber-framed building, but the basic distinction is between the box frame method, most common in the south and east, and the cruck frame building of the north and west. Whichever system was employed, the object was to produce a strong framework which would support the thatch and hopefully withstand the worst excesses of the English climate. For this main structure, the wood chosen was oak, with its strength, durability and weather resistance. The infilling of the spaces between the main trusses, to form a solid wall, presented few problems. The trusses were strengthened by diagonal braces, and lighter upright oak studs provided a framework to which 'wattle' (woven hazel or blackthorn branches) could be nailed to carry the plaster-like 'daub' of mud or a stronger mixture of mud with straw and horse or cow hair (ill. 72).

The post-and-truss method of box framing involves the use of strong vertical posts at each corner of the house. Horizontal tie beams connect the tops of the posts at each gable end, and the gable ends are linked by horizontal timbers known as wall plates at the eaves, and sills at the base of the house. In the better-built houses, the sills and the bases of the trusses rest on a firm rubble foundation. The strongly jointed uprights, tie beams, wall plates and sills form a solid box structure to support the roof. In the roof, the principal rafters (heavy oak beams) slope upwards to the horizontal ridge tree running along the top. Additional

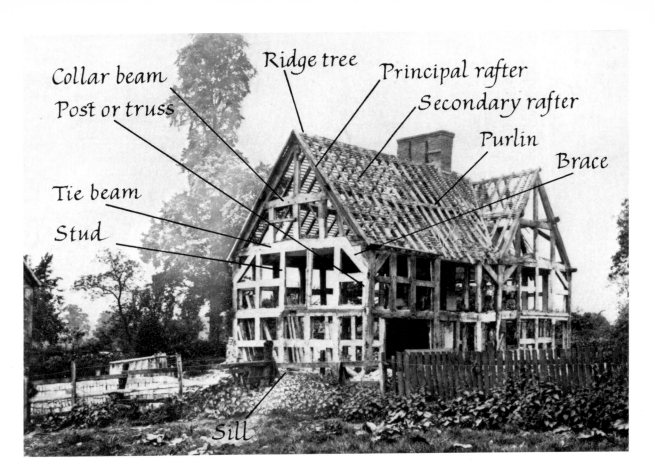

Collar beam

Post or truss

Ridge tree

Principal rafter

Secondary rafter

Purlin

Brace

Tie beam

Stud

Sill

67 The component elements of a large timber-framed house exposed. Many of those used in this sixteenth-century building at Wigginshall near Sutton Coldfield are particularly massive, and the 'strong box' concept is plainly displayed.

68 This cruck frame at Didbrook in Gloucestershire may date back to the fourteenth century; the inward curve of the cruck blades is unusual.

strength is provided by purlins running parallel to the ridge tree, and common rafters running parallel to the principal rafters. In some houses, the corner posts consist of inverted oak trunks with the spreading root bole providing a wider support for the tie beams and wall plates.

A familiar variation on the post-and-truss house is that with a jetty or projecting upper storey. Many timber-framed houses were built as single-storey buildings in which the smoke from the hearth circulated amongst the rafters before escaping through a smoke hole (ills. 87, 88). Later houses were built as two-storey buildings with overhanging upper floors. The reason for the jetty is disputed. In the cramped streets of a medieval town, it would allow a little more floorspace than was available at street level, but it is also found in village houses fronting quite broad streets and with ample building space to the rear. One explanation is that the jetty is a response to a shortage of oak timber long enough to allow the corner posts to run the full height to the roof, while another suggestion is that the weight of the upper storey bearing down on the floor timbers of the jetty countered the upward thrust from the weight of furniture or supplies placed on the floors of the upper rooms.

The technique of cruck framing has already been described (p. 54). The bracing of the cruck frame with horizontal tie beams, wall plates and sills is similar to the methods employed in the box frame house. Because there are no joints between the corner posts and the rafters at each gable end, the cruck frame construction is even stronger. The disadvantages of the method were the wasteful demand for timber, a whole tree being needed to provide each pair of crucks, and the limiting of the height and width of the building by the size of available crucks.

The oldest timber-framed houses were constructed on their sites by the occupants and a few helpers, but as the houses became more sophisticated there

69 *Below left* Tiers of fifteenth-century jetties overlook the narrow street which leads up to the church at Thaxted in Essex. The guildhall shown in ill. 62 can be seen jutting out at the end of this row.

70 *Below* The old vicarage at Prestbury in Cheshire exemplifies the timber style of the West Midlands. Some think that the heavy framing timbers reflect the frequent use of weighty roofs of stone tiles, but here mature timbers were clearly to hand and much of the work is more decorative than functional.

was a greater reliance upon the local carpenter. The basic frame of a house was built in the workshop and the components were often stamped with guide numbers, and then hauled to the site, where the frame was swiftly erected, after which the lighter studwork, infilling and roofing were added. From start to finish, a stout and durable house might take but three months to build. Green timber is easier to work than seasoned, and likely to be supplied anyway when there is rapid turn-over; and the interesting curves of old timber houses have often been produced by the later warping of fresh cut timbers.

Historians have portrayed the utilization of the English woodland from the Conquest onwards as being quite parasitic. Recent researchers, such as O. Rackham, have shown that woodland resources were carefully husbanded, cropped and conserved by builders, smelters and boatwrights alike. Without this systematic management of the remaining forests the demand for timber would never have been met. On Rackham's calculations, a typical timber-framed Suffolk farmhouse might contain timber from more than 300 trees, half of these being quite young and less than 9 inches (23 centimetres) in diameter. The degeneration of English woodlands came largely with a fall in the demand for special timber during the nineteenth century and the desire by landowners for a more rapid return on investment, which caused a deterioration in the crafts of woodmanship and the management of standard, coppiced and pollarded trees. The cost of timber remained quite high but relatively stable from the medieval period until the nineteenth century and on the whole the owners and managers of forests were able to satisfy constructional and industrial demands. During the fourteenth century, a good oak tree was worth around £75 in modern prices.

The availability of timber varied from place to place, but in well-populated areas there was a reliance on slimmer, younger trees which were felled in rotation. In the north-west, where the density of population was low, more mature trees survived to provide the heavy timbers which are common in the medieval and Elizabethan houses of the region. In the West Midlands, the curving timbers of the black poplar were admirably suited to the arches of the cruck-framing technique, though this was only a local and minor rival to the oak and is now a rare and threatened species of tree. Even the sallow and hazel trees which contributed the wattle infilling were cropped in a systematic manner from underwood coppices.

It has been suggested that the reduction of population by the Black Death may have reduced pressure on woodland, but this is difficult to establish. Generally, the increasing dependence upon young timber taken from managed woods and cut on short fifteen- or twenty-year rotations is evidenced by the use of numerous slender studs and a strict economy in the use of heavy timbers. In Lancashire and Cheshire, such economy was less imperative and wood continued to be used liberally, the elaborate geometrical bracing designs employed being as much decorative as functional. Cecil Hewitt, consultant for Essex County Council, has discovered how timber buildings can be dated from the expert study of the types of joint which were current at particular periods. Frequently the new joints developed by the master joiners employed on cathedral construction were later copied by village carpenters. Often obscured by the wall fillings, the work of the medieval joiner is displayed to advantage in many ancient barns.

Only when the frame embodied a high standard of timber, carpentry and carving was the structure intended for display, and though modern villagers have discovered that they can add thousands of pounds to the value of their

cottages by exposing the original studwork, the general tendency was for the frame to be given a protective coating of plaster and limewash. In the Georgian era, timber framing was unfashionable, as was the lack of symmetry in the older houses, and many quite decorative frames still lie undiscovered beneath a levelled plaster façade. The Victorians, with a penchant for the Gothic, decided that they approved of timber framing, and many frames not intended for the public gaze were revealed and artificially blackened to produce the favoured magpie contrast with whitewashed plaster. The latest fashion, influenced by a better understanding of the past, is to remove the stain, and display the ancient timbers in their natural grey-brown hues. At least one modern supplier provides wall paints which mimic the traditional colour washes based on natural dyes such as madder and ochre. While the blackening of the timbers was encouraged by municipal gas companies with tar-like by-products to dispose of, we cannot be sure that the 'natural' look is authentic either. There is pictorial evidence that originally some timber-framed buildings were brightly painted, with ox-blood-reddened timbers and blue-washed walls.

Infilling the frame – whether the preference was for a 'clam staff' of close-set hazel wands or a wickerwork wattle, a daub of mud plaster or a stronger brew including reinforcing fibres – presented no technical problems, though the regular need for running repairs was irksome. When bricks reappeared on the English scene, they often replaced the older infillings, usually being set between the studwork in an attractive herringbone pattern which helped the shedding of water. When specialist plasterers took over the task of house finishing, they sometimes demonstrated their skills by forming patterns in the wet plaster (see pl. 9). Overlapping rings and woven patterns were common, while this art of 'pargetting', which was most popular in the seventeenth century, also produced some strikingly decorative reliefs of curving floral designs, still preserved and commonly seen in Hertfordshire and the south-west of East Anglia. Pargetting was still occasionally practised early in this century. Some owners avoided the need for regular attention to inaccessible plasterwork by hanging their walls, or at least the upper parts of them, with weatherboarding or tiles.

Timber-framed buildings of English oak were strong, warm and homely. Were it not for the escalating costs of oak timber, there is no reason to suppose that timber-framing would not still be a standard form of English rural architecture.

71 *Above left* This fine old farmhouse in the Cambridgeshire village of Whittlesford goes back to the fifteenth century; the gabled cross wing is a seventeenth-century addition. Shaped brackets support the jetty timbers and a former smokehole in the gable is implied (compare ill. 87; the chimneys are much later). The timbers may always have been plastered.

72 *Above* The original wattle which held a thick coat of mud daub is exposed in this timber-framed building.

Building in stone was never cheap, and the cost of transport, in the era of hideous communications before the turnpike age, introduced by legislation in 1663, and the coming of the canal and then the railway in the following centuries, was more to be considered than the cost of quarrying. Except in the construction of churches and very occasionally the homes of the wealthy, building stone came from local quarries and travelled but a short distance to the site. Consequently, abrupt changes occur in the village landscape as one enters the range of a local quarry, perhaps nowhere more striking than in the swift passage from the brick clay of Bedfordshire to the threshold of the Northamptonshire ironstone quarries.

Away from the deforested sheep-scoured slopes of upland England, where there was no alternative material, stone building began as a defensive exercise by nobles who had reason to fear each other or the community in general, and they often continued it as a concession to prestige rather than comfort. In the counties of the Scottish marches, massive defensive stone farmhouses were built up to the sixteenth century. Elsewhere in England where stone or brick building is now the norm, earlier generations of buildings were often of timber. The Yorkshire Dales are famed for their stone village houses, but most of those date from the seventeenth- and eighteenth-century building boom: before that, rough stone sod-thatched dwellings rubbed shoulders with others of timber. Only later did wood shortages and improvements in quarrying and transport conditions give stone a predominance over timber in many parts of England (see pl. 11).

Generally speaking, the homes of small lords or well-to-do farmers were not built in stone before the middle of the sixteenth century, and even in areas such as Gloucestershire, which are rich in building stone, timber-framing was used or combined with stone until the seventeenth century. Where good stone was not available, design went directly from timber to brick, although flints, either used whole or 'knapped', were until quite recently a substitute for stone or brick in the chalklands. In some areas noted for their stone buildings, the advance of the cheap factory brick is now checked by planning policies, which require at least a facing in the traditional materials.

Stone buildings are colder than those of timber, but more resistant to fire, and unless a poor stone like the clunch of the chalklands is used, or the construction is poor (as with many Norman rubble-filled walls), they are virtually indestructible. They are also much more difficult to date, although as a general rule the more carefully dressed and smoothed the stone the more recent the building is likely to be.

Stone varies greatly in its colour, texture, and in the ease with which it can be worked. Where the native stone was an ancient, uncompromising coarse-grained material like the granite and schist of the south-west, it was used in rugged uneven chunks. Even where the stone was a 'freestone', capable of being sawn to give a smooth-faced ashlar surface, the extra cost was often foregone, and the stone laid as coursed rubble, which gives a pleasing texture to many village buildings in the oolitic limestone belt running diagonally between the highland and lowland zones of England, from the Tees in the north-east to the Exe in the south-west. Stone building is particularly effective in the landscape when its colours are echoed in nearby exposed cliffs or ploughed fields. The red sandstones of South Devon and golden limestone of the Cotswolds are renowned, while in Northamptonshire local masons realized the attraction of incorporating rows of brown iron-stained stones amongst the yellower courses.

Mud, used either in great dollops, as in the West Country 'cob', or baked by sun or kiln into bricks, is probably the commonest village building material. Cob, a mixture of puddled clay and various combinations of chopped straw, gravel and cow hair, is most frequently seen in villages in Somerset, Devon and Cornwall. The cob is built up in horizontal layers to form walls up to 3 feet (a metre) thick, and these walls are warm and perfectly sound when a good rubble foundation, an overhanging roof and a regular coating of limewash and grit are provided. Cob-built cottages are easily recognized by their bulky appearance and the rounding of projecting edges and corners as protection against the weather and friction from passing animals (pl. 7). The 'clay lump' of Norfolk is a close relative of West Country cob, and the 'wichert' of Buckinghamshire is a mixture of chalk and clay.

Bricks and clay tiles were used in England by the Romans, but subsequently the art of making them seems to have been lost. Newly-made bricks reappear in the late twelfth century, at Polstead Church in Suffolk and Little Coggeshall Abbey in Essex, and in both cases they seem almost certainly to be of local manufacture. While bricks were often imported from Flanders, it has recently become clear that far more were made in England, and also that they were used earlier, than had been thought. The town of Hull was rebuilt in brick from about 1300 onwards. During the fifteenth century, growing prosperity in counties poor in stone but rich in clay led to a great development in the native brickmaking industry. In general, bricks, like many other working-class staples such as tea and potatoes, began as a luxury, and their popularity diffused downward through society. They were used for churches, and for the houses and castles of the powerful, before appearing in the house of the yeoman in the form of a fireproof chimney-stack. By 1600 they were being used to build entire farmhouses in the south-east of England, and in the century that followed they were adopted elsewhere, though they did not reach some parts of Yorkshire and Lancashire until after the improvement in transport at the end of the eighteenth century.

Major buildings apart, bricks were at first generally used as a substitute for wattle and daub, being set in the spaces between the studwork of timber-framed buildings. As the craftsmen gained confidence and experience, it was realized that the timber frame could be dispensed with altogether, and during the eighteenth century brick became widely used in the homes of all classes. The traditional techniques of building in timber still exerted an influence, and there were even rare attempts to replicate the jetty house. In due course, the material became commonplace, and while Tudor aristocrats were proud of their brick mansions, by the early nineteenth century it was fashionable in some areas to conceal the brickwork under a layer of stucco.

Local brickmaking industries developed wherever suitable clays could be dug, and differences in the mineral composition of these clays and in the method of firing produced differences in colour, ranging from the whitish bricks of Cambridgeshire through various shades of pink, amber and red to the blue-black bricks of Staffordshire. Sun-baked bricks remained in use until the present century, and competed for a long time with the kiln-baked product. Early bricks were often long and narrow and of a purplish red colour. They tended to be quite small until a tax was levied in 1784 on each brick, and the industry naturally gravitated towards producing larger sizes.

73 Collyweston in
Northamptonshire is
famous for its nearby
quarries, where the stone
was left exposed to the
frost and could then be
split into narrow slabs
used for roofing tiles. The
village displays its wares.

74 *Above right* The circular
lock-up at Castle Cary in
Somerset, with its finely
worked roof reminiscent
of the later police helmet,
dates from 1779. The
local builder charged £23.

75 *Right* Chalk clunch
is one of the poorest
building stones: the
angles of these cottages at
Uffington in Berkshire
have been reinforced with
brick.

76 *Above* The Cotswold oolite, easily sawn as a freestone, has been given an ashlar surface in this manor house at Mickleton in Gloucestershire.

77 *Right* The hard igneous and metamorphic rocks of the Lake District defy chisel and saw, and are laid as rubble in this seventeenth-century cottage at Matterdale. The dry stonework and whitened walls are traditional in the area and in parts of the Scottish Borders.

78 *Right* Brick-making in
Norfolk in 1888: the clay
is laboriously packed into
moulds.

79 The noble timber-
framed house at Great
Coggeshall, Essex, built
by Thomas Paycocke, a
wealthy clothier, about
1500. Bricks were later
used for infill; later still a
Georgian plaster façade
was added. The building
was restored in 1905.

Various methods of laying bricks were employed, depending upon the relationship between 'stretchers', laid lengthways, and 'headers', laid with the long axis at right angles to the wall. When the bricks were used as an infill in wooden studwork, the attractive herringbone pattern was popular. In the sixteenth century the English bond was favoured, with courses of stretchers alternating with courses of headers, or of alternate headers and stretchers. In the eighteenth century the most popular bond was the Flemish, in which each course consists of alternating headers and stretchers.

Although houses of cob, of stone, and even cruck-framed designs were still being built in the nineteenth century, after 1880 brick was produced mechanically on a large scale (especially around Peterborough, in Bedfordshire and in north Wales), and its price fell, so that it became a fairly universal material throughout England. There is little doubt that the occupants of the four-square brick and slate village cottages considered their new homes to be great

80 *Above* Toseland Hall in Cambridgeshire was built completely of brick in the symmetrical style of about 1600. The apparently archaic timber-framed outbuilding to the left is contemporary.

81 *Far left* A fireproof brick chimney on the end of a cottage at Badley in Suffolk.

82 *Left* Only the pediment relieves the austere symmetry of this mid-Georgian brick house at Hadleigh in Suffolk.

107

improvements upon the timber-framed or cob-walled homes which they replaced or supplemented, but from the aesthetic point of view late nineteenth-century brick usually has to try much harder to appeal. While the older hand-made bricks have weathered and mellowed into the most attractive shades and textures, the hard uncompromising machine-made product used in cottages whose box-like symmetry conforms to a standard plan often rests uneasily in the village landscape.

From the court rolls of Mincinbury Manor in Hertfordshire, we learn that in 1505 'Richard Kyne has not yet repaired his house as bidden at the last court', while two years later 'Willima Fepe and William Barr permit their houses to be ruinous in roof, woodwork and plaster, therefore they are bidden to repair them'. Clearly the worried landlord and the apathetic tenant are figures of long historical standing. Probably more houses have decayed through a failure to maintain the roof than from any other cause, since weakness there will produce damage and decay throughout the structure. Because of their importance roofs have been replaced more frequently than walls, and there are many slate-roofed villages which were thatched until about a century ago. Traditional roofing materials include thatch made of rye, wheat straw and reed, and tiles of clay and stone.

Thatched roofs were almost universal until the sixteenth century, and there are still around 50,000 thatched houses in England, providing work for 800 thatchers. Although bracken, rye straw, gorse and brushwood were used in the past, today roofs are thatched in Norfolk reed or wheat longstraw, which is sometimes combed with an iron-toothed rake and known as combed wheat reed or Devon reed. Reed is expensive and not easy to obtain outside East Anglia, where ancient reed beds are harvested for thatching at the Wicken Fen conservation area. Straw suitable for thatching comes from one of the long-strawed varieties of wheat which are not commonly grown; they are desirable not so much for the length of the straw as for its springiness when dry and its supple nature when dampened. Stan Arbon, an experienced Cambridgeshire thatcher, grows the long-strawed French variety called 'Bouquet' on his smallholding and reaps it with an old-fashioned combine harvester, as the modern machine damages the straw.

There are variations in the techniques of thatching from craftsman to craftsman and from region to region: the high-pitched and gabled roofs of East Anglia contrast with the lower roofs of the West Country, where the thatch usually continues around to cover the gable end and produce a pie crust effect. Beginning at the bottom of the roof, bundles of straw 'yealms' are secured with hooks driven into the rafters, and to each other by staple-like 'spars' made by twisting and bending a split branch of hazel. The yealms are laid in overlapping courses, with the greatest thicknesses at the most vulnerable places, the ridge, the gable ends and the corners. Often a thick reinforcing top layer of yealms is laid to cover the ridge and bound down with a network of long hazel 'sways', arranged in a design of repeated lozenges. When the covering of yealms is complete, the straw can be shaved to produce a neat appearance (pl. 21); a well thatched roof does not need much in the way of finishing. A decorative design of scallops or points may be cut into the thick layer of yealms covering the ridge, a difficult technique, since the thatcher must imagine the effect as seen from ground level. A modern refinement consists in covering the thatched roof with wire netting as protection against bird damage.

Although the combine harvester, as well as ruining the straw as far as thatching is concerned, has deprived the thatcher of much autumn work in thatching the wheat ricks, the art of thatching is far from dead, and the arrival in the village of affluent commuters ensures a steady custom. The well thatched roof has no superior in terms of insulation, but it has always been vulnerable to fire and requires higher insurance premiums. The life of a thatched roof ranges from fifteen to thirty years in the case of wheat straw, while advocates of reed claim a life of sixty years, though no roof can last longer than the hazel spars and sways, which can only be relied upon to give around twenty years of good service. Clearly a thatched roof is both a pleasure and a liability. Deeply disturbed by the rate at which the thatched roofs in the county are being replaced by tile, in 1979 Essex County Councillors intensified their conservational campaign and extended their tally of listed buildings.

In the past thatch, especially in combination with timber-framing, was a cause for real concern, and in the days before the organization of an efficient public fire brigade fire could spread through town or village in no time. When fire struck the Fenland village of Eye in 1848 only the church and one cottage survived. Even today the owner of a thatched village house is wise to stand on guard on Guy Fawkes night. Previously, hooked poles were stored in public places – frequently the village church – to assist the rapid removal of burning thatch.

There was little available in the way of compensation for unfortunates like George Furman, a small farmer in the village of Springfield, who lost his hall, parlour, buttery, bedrooms and shed. In 1654 he petitioned the county justices of Essex, saying

> A sudden sadd and lamentable fyer which consumed and burned downe ye sayd Dwelling house and all ye wearinge apparrell of your sayd Peticioner his wiefe and children except such as was upon theire backs and all theire howshold stuffe whatsoever theire Corne butter Cheese & poultry and other thinges to the valew of 103 *li.* 6s. 11d. besydes the sayd Dwelling howse ye rebuildinge of which will cost neare 40 *li.* to the utter undoeinge of your poore Peticioner and his famely.

While sympathizing with George Furman, we are grateful to him because he tells us that the value of his moderate size village house was £40. When we calculate this against the rural wages of the time, it appears that housing was considerably cheaper in 1654 than it is today.

83 *Above left* Thatched ricks are a rare sight today. These belong to the Cambridgeshire thatcher Stan Arbon, and their long unbattered straw is destined for the roofs of nearby villages.

84 *Above* A prodigious amount of straw is needed to thatch this characteristically high-pitched East Anglian roof in the Cambridgeshire village of Meldreth. The extra thickness on the ridge will be cut with a neat geometrical edge.

85 Slate-hanging is displayed in this basically fourteenth-century building at Dunster in Somerset. Such weather-resistant walls are common in humbler cottages in rain-blasted Cornwall where local slate quarries stood close by.

Certain kinds of sandstone and mudstone have formed in such a way that they can easily be split along the bedding plane between the different layers of sediment in the rock. Slate, a mudstone baked and hardened deep inside the earth, is the most widely used roofing stone, although sandstone is also used where weather resistant and easily split varieties are to be found. Local quarries were for centuries exploited to provide roofing slates in parts of Cornwall and the Lake District; when the canals and railways made most of England accessible to the Welsh quarries in the later nineteenth century, slate roofing became a national building style, with the sombre roof as characteristic of the period as the brick walls supporting it. In the north of England, slate often replaced older roofs of massive sandstone flags.

Even in areas where quarries could provide stone roofing tiles, it was not until the seventeenth and eighteenth centuries that many villagers were able to afford such a roof, and by this time tiles of baked clay were often a cheaper alternative. Like bricks before them, they were first imported from the Netherlands. With the establishment of a number of local English industries, clay tiles were widely adopted as replacements for thatch, with interlocking 'S' shapes being popular. Flat tiles, often with decoratively curved ends, were also used to protect exposed walls, with the tile shell usually covering only the upper storey. 'Mathematical tiles' interlock to give the effect of a fine brick wall. Many local manufacturers existed, producing a variety of designs, and the owner of an old tile-roofed house may have difficulty finding matched and interlocking replacements.

Very few homes had glass windows before the sixteenth century, and rooms were poorly lit by the light which filtered in through shutters, wickerwork screens, strips of translucent horn or skins hung over narrow window openings. Glass windows began as valuable status symbols, the small, thick, square or diamond-shaped panes set in lead casings, as with the stained glass in a church. Though such windows could not give an undistorted view of the outside world, their ability to admit light without draughts must have been greatly prized. These early window panes were made from blobs of glass which were spun and flattened while in their molten state. Only fairly small discs of glass could be made by this method; they were cut to provide small panes, and the familiar 'bottle glass' panes come from the centre of the disc, where a lens formed at the end of the rod. Somewhat larger panes of 'crown glass' made by the same method, in which curving swirls can sometimes be seen, were used throughout the eighteenth and part of the nineteenth centuries. They are held by slim wooden glazing bars, and usually appear in vertically-opening sashes. Humble houses might have horizontally sliding sashes, or casements. During the nineteenth century it became possible to produce large sheets of clear rolled glass, or plate glass, and its use gradually filtered down from the manor house and rectory to the labourer's cottage in the course of the century.

Windows can provide valuable clues to the dating of a house, although they can be deceptive. Windows divided by vertical stone or wooden mullions are associated with Tudor architecture, but they are a feature of many farmsteads in the north of England which were rebuilt in the seventeenth century. In this as in many other cases, designs adopted in the fashionable south-east only gradually found their way northward and westward. Styles might also be set which were deliberately backward-looking: the *cottage orné* of the Regency, the mid-Victorian estate cottage and the interwar house might all have 'olde English' leaded casements, and a reaction against plate glass led 'progressive' Victorian architects to revive the multiple glazing bars of the eighteenth century. So, while characteristic windows were used in different periods, the amateur village historian must always be on the lookout for changes, the slow diffusion of styles across the country, and the mimicking of older manners.

In many villages, householders have added and removed windows quite freely, and discontinuities in the surrounding brickwork often showed where an opening has been blocked up or altered. A window tax, levied between 1695 and 1851, resulted in the bricking up of some windows, and tended to keep the overall number down. From the late sixteenth century onwards, dormers were frequently inserted into the roofs of cottages, as part of the conversion of the building from one to two storeys. In the case of the farmhouse, this alteration was often made to provide upstairs accommodation for servants, while in areas where cottage industries were practised the well-lit upper room served as a workshop. During the Georgian period, fashion demanded symmetry in the placing of windows, and a few village home-owners distorted the face of an older home in order to conform. In the nineteenth century, the Picturesque movement and then the Gothic Revival called for deliberate asymmetry in the placing of windows and in general composition; but their influence was far from universal.

The chimney provides more reliable guidance to the dating of a house. Until the sixteenth century, in all but the grander halls, smoke from the hearth, sometimes directed upwards by a centrally placed hood and flue, found its own way out of a house, filtering away between the rafters or escaping through a smokehole in the top of the gable. The first chimneys, substantial creations of brick or stone rubble, were built on the ends of existing houses during the sixteenth and seventeenth centuries, and can be recognized by their massive proportions. In spite of their dominating appearance, these early structures served only one hearth, and when later generations demanded a higher standard of comfort and warmth, additional chimneys were built to serve other rooms in the house; so in seeking to date a village house, one should always look for the

86 Stone mullions, transoms and dripstones give an archaic air to these cottages at Kettlewell in Yorkshire, which may be as late as about 1700. There are niches for doves beneath the eaves.

oldest chimney, which may have been part of the original house, or added to it at an early date. The most ornate and imposing feature of the larger seventeenth-century village house is likely to be the chimney, and it was in the construction of twists, panels and spirals in its brickwork that the craftsman chose to display his skills. In an age when the warm and cosy parlour was still a novel feature, it is not surprising that the chimney was a focus for pride and attention. As warmth without smoke became expected as a matter of course, so the chimney became less embellished and more functional in appearance, with chimneypots being introduced at the start of the nineteenth century to increase the efficiency of the flue.

The down-to-earth countryman has usually put comfort before appearances, and cottage interiors have generally undergone more practical modifications than have the exteriors. Although differences in the wealth and position of village households make it difficult to generalize, the typical village home until well into the eighteenth century was a narrow one-storey building which, in the poorer homes, consisted of a single room. This was a living room in every sense, being used for sleeping, eating and sitting. In the older buildings, this room was open to the roof and heated by a central hearth. Any adjoining rooms or outbuildings would be used for storage or livestock. In the poorer and more remote farming country of the north and west the one-room farmstead remained common even during the eighteenth century, with a loft overhanging the living room sometimes providing sleeping quarters, and grew by extension lengthways with the addition of barns and byres. Examples of these longhouses are still to be seen, often serving as barns beside the newer two-storey eighteenth-century farmhouse. (A photograph taken in 1897 in the Isle of Man shows a windowless sod-walled and turf-roofed cottage of prehistoric design still in active occupation, and in the 'black house' of the Scottish highlands the one-roomed house with a central hearth and no chimney survived into the twentieth century.) By the sixteenth century, however, many farming families had two or even three rooms, and the living room might be flanked by a parlour to one side and a small kitchen to the other.

87 *Above left* A smokehole can be seen in the gable of the king-post roof of this fourteenth-century yeoman's house. (Re-erected at the Stowmarket Museum of East Anglian Life, it provided the setting for the schoolroom in the film *Akenfield*.)

88 The interior of a Hebridean 'black house', photographed in 1905, suggests the unfurnished gloom of old English peasant dwellings. There is no chimney, only a central open hearth. A spinning wheel stands nearby.

89 The gentleman who failed to keep within the compass might fall into the various fates displayed at the corners of this engraving of 1785. Several stepped outside the compass and lost their homes and estates as a result.

Each old house has its own particular history: this is what makes the study of village buildings so fascinating, and generalization so difficult. Let us imagine nonetheless the evolution of a house owned by a family which generation by generation rises from the normal village condition of poverty to mild prosperity. The original sixteenth-century timber-framed home consists of two rooms side by side. To the left is the hall or living room, and to the right the parlour, which also serves as the main bedroom. Sleeping arrangements are fairly informal, and the rooms contain both tables and mattresses. During the seventeenth century, a number of refinements are added, not least of which is a brick chimney, which is built on to the end wall of the hall, and though the rooms are still open to the roof it is now possible to see the rafters, no longer blurred by a swirling haze of woodsmoke. The builders who built the chimney also provide two new rooms, a kitchen and a buttery, which are added to the hall at right angles, giving an L-shaped plan (ill. 71). The kitchen is particularly welcome: previously cooking was carried out in the parlour. The buttery becomes the jealous preserve and workplace of the mistress of the house; it also contains the pails, barrels and copper used for home brewing, and, to the great annoyance of the mistress, her husband's gardening equipment. This problem is resolved a few years later, when a wing containing a barn, stable and dairy is built on to the parlour to run parallel with the kitchen and buttery wing.

As the fortunes of the farming family continue to rise in the later years of the seventeenth century, two labourers and a maid are employed. In order to accommodate them, a new storey is created by using the empty roof space to provide two 'chambers', a sleeping room for the men, and a small bedroom at the top of the stairs for the maid. For more than a century, the household consisting of the master's family and his employees exists as a homely unit, sharing the same hall dining table, and eating the same food. Increasing prosperity and changing social customs may, however, induce the master to move his labourers out of the household and into a pair of cottages, out of sight of the farmhouse and the fashionable garden which the mistress is creating.

As the eighteenth century advances, both master and mistress are falling prey to rather grand ideas, and the mistress finds herself spending less time doing domestic chores. A back'us boy from one of the poor village families is employed. He does all the most menial jobs about the house, working mainly in the 'back house' or kitchen, being always the first to rise, light the fires, and heat the washing water for the master, mistress and maid. A sleeping place is made for him in the hay above the dairy. Although the master and mistress no longer mix freely with the lesser folk of the village in the way that their grandparents did, the thought of building a bathroom never enters their heads, and is never even considered by the squire, from whom they take their lead in most matters. They are not too grand to make their regular trips to the earth privy at the end of the garden.

The further history of the house will depend upon the fortunes of its inmates: with continuing rises in prosperity, it might be greatly improved and embellished and take on the appearance of a mansion; otherwise, it might retain its basic form until the early twentieth century, when the temptation of at least a bathroom and lavatory would be hard to resist.

Between the eighteenth and nineteenth centuries a great many solid yeoman families stumbled and fell in their pursuit of gentrification, and their venerable farmhouses changed hands. A wise Berkshire farmer described with rural

directness the process from self-sufficiency to appearance as a bankrupt in the *London Gazette*.

1743	*1843*
Man, to the plough.	Man, Tally Ho!
Wife, to the Cow.	Miss, piano.
Girl, to the Yarn	Wife, Silk and Satin.
Boy, to the Barn.	Boy, Greek and Latin.
And your Rent will be netted.	And you'll all be Gazetted.

It can be seen that the house was always flexible and freely adapted to meet the changing needs of its occupants. Many of the larger village houses consist of a rectangular hall to which wings have been added at different periods. Such a nucleus began as a single-storey living room which was open to the high roof. The later addition of cross wings can provide L-, E- or H-shaped ground-plans, with the need for storage and the accommodation of workers and domestic servants often having precedence over domestic comfort. Almost invariably, the hall was eventually subdivided to provide two storeys and the cow byre and other agricultural functions tended to be displaced into outbuildings as the rustic yeoman subscribed to a modicum of gentrification. Since the hall nucleus and its various additional wings have generally experienced uniform re-roofing and re-plastering it is normally difficult to deduce which element succeeded which without a thorough and expert scrutiny (ill. 71).

The labouring classes fared less well, and even in the nineteenth century cottages built for farmworkers often provided no more than a single downstairs living room, an understairs kitchen or pantry and one bedroom upstairs. With families of a dozen or more children being common, the congestion would have been almost unbearable. The less deprived nineteenth-century village family might live in a new two-storeyed cottage, or in an older cottage with an upper storey inserted into the roof space, and the two bedrooms upstairs and two rooms downstairs would be considered adequate by the standards of the community. Earlier in this century, my own two-bedroomed cottage is said to have accommodated the ten or eleven children of a gardener's family. While the estate villages of the eighteenth and nineteenth centuries provided better-built rural housing, the extremes of congestion were not always removed. When forty new cottages were built to form the model village of Milton Abbas in Dorset between 1773 and 1786, each cottage was partitioned into two halves and two families often shared a half. In some of the cottages as many as forty people will have lived and the over-crowding must have defied description.

In what might be regarded as a 'typical' cottage home, the front door would open on to a front sitting room, which, despite the pressures of a large family, might only be used on a Sunday, for relaxation and entertaining visiting relatives. In this room, the village housewife might have a dresser with her best Staffordshire dishes on display, a few pottery figures to stand upon the mantelpiece, and homemade rag rugs on the floor. Framed biblical texts and exhortations might decorate the walls, and, could the family afford one, pride of place would be given to an upright piano around which the family would gather for the singing of hymns.

The back sitting room was the real living room, and unless a lean-to kitchen was provided it would be dominated by a vast black cast-iron cooking range. A

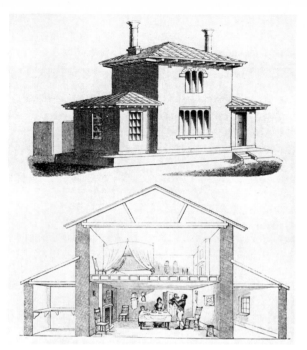

90 A model cottage, from Loudon's influential *Encyclopaedia of Cottage, Farm and Villa Architecture* (1833). The family have a living room, larder, scullery, and separate bedroom upstairs.

91 This photograph of an early eighteenth-century ironstone miner's cottage at Lightmoor, Shropshire, was taken in 1953. Many Victorian aspects remain: the hearth is used for cooking, candles and a paraffin lamp provide the illumination, and the knick-knacks are more for use than show.

cast-iron pump above the stone kitchen sink might save the inconvenience of hauling buckets from the village pump, but there was no escaping the chilling trips to the wooden or brick-built privy at the end of the garden.

Until the northern and midland factories made cheap Staffordshire pottery, cast-iron pans and calico curtains available to combine in the domestic scene with the pine tables and cupboards and elm chairs produced by village joiners and itinerant chair makers, village homes were but sparsely furnished. The household goods of a sixteenth- or seventeenth-century family might amount to no more than a rough-hewn table and stools, a mattress, a pewter basin, a couple of brass pans, a spit and gridiron, pothooks, wooden platters and spoons, mugs, a few worn knives and a chest. When widow Witham died at Barley in Hertfordshire her will, drawn up in 1637, revealed her worldly goods as consisting of a table and a bed, a flaxen table cloth, a brass pot, a sofa and several flaxen sheets. We can take it for granted that she also owned a few eating utensils, but very little else; and yet she was scarcely destitute by the standards of the time. While joiner-made bedsteads were prized possessions, separate bedrooms seem to have been considered inessential. Yeoman James Hawkes, a contemporary and neighbour of widow Witham, left to his three daughters his 'joined' bedsteads: one was standing in the parlour, one in the 'chamber over the parlour', and one in the buttery chamber.

Wills and inventories taken of the worldly goods of deceased villagers provide our clearest insights into the household goods of long dead folk. A number of seventeenth- and eighteenth-century Essex inventories have been collected by Francis Steer; they reveal the great variations in wealth between the prosperous yeomen, who had dozens of possessions, and the poor, whose total worldly goods could be listed on a postcard. Widow Mary May of Writtle lived in a cottage with a hall and a parlour downstairs and a bedroom above. When she died in April 1663 this is what she owned:

> IN YE HALL – One cubard, one Table, Tressells, and forme, one Setle & an old chair, 15s.
> IN YE PARLOR – One old Bedstead, one featherbed, two Boulstars, two pillowes, thre Blanckets, & one flock bed 3li. 10s.
> IN YE CHAMBER – Two Chairs, one old bedstead, Curtans, one Covering & a Blackit, 10s. 6d.; two Cobireons [andirons], one pair of tongs, one fire shovel, one Spitt, & one broken Warming pan, 8s. 6d.; one Wainscott Chair, two Stooles, two Wheeles, thre old pillowes, one table, and flaskitt, two Chists, & Severall other Small implements, 1li. 6s. 8d. Wearing a parell & redy Money 1li. 9s. 6d.
> Some Totall – 8li. 0s. 2d.

John Bridgman of Writtle was a gardener, and he died in November 1720. Most of his possessions seem to have been connected with drinking. (If one were to judge from the unusually free spelling, this hobby seems to have been shared by the writers of his inventory.)

> His waring cloes an poket mony, 15li.
> IN THE CHICHEN – on gun, an meterels [mattress?], 1li. 5s.; puter, 7s., too payer of cobioyrns [cobirons, i.e. andirons], 2s.
> IN THE BREWHOUS – On coper, too cettles, 5 tubes, 1li. 10s.
> IN THE PANTRY – 7 vesels, an beare stalle [stand for a barrel], an table, 15s.

IN THE SMALL BEARE BUTREY – A drinke stal, 1*s*.

IN HIS LOGIN ROUME – Too beeds [mattresses], an too beeds steds, a payer of toyngs, a shovel, 5*li*.

GOODS IN THE CHAMBER OVER THE BREWHOUS – 10*s*.

Hors, bridle, and sadle, 3*li*.

Trees and plants in the Croune Garden, 2*li*. 10*s*.; the stok in the hom garden, 5*li*.

92, 93 Change comes to Hale Barnes during its absorption by Greater Manchester, as the turn-of-the-century postcard and the photograph of 1979 show. Only the small house on the right survives; a war memorial has been added; is the new church on the left a superior building?

Most villages experienced periods of quite rapid growth and rebuilding, but most of the time growth was slow and piecemeal, barely keeping pace with the destruction and abandonment of houses. It would be quite exceptional to find a dwelling as old as the village itself in any long-established settlement. Neither can we necessarily expect to find the oldest houses standing on the longest-established dwelling sites. A well-built sixteenth-century house, for example, standing on the edge of the village as it then was, would be much more likely to survive than would a fourteenth-century dwelling in the centre of the village on the site of a Saxon hut. It is sometimes said that the oldest houses in the village stand end on to the main street or green. This seems unlikely, and such houses were probably built to fill in the narrow spaces left between other, older buildings which fronted onto the street or green.

With a few exceptions, the village is the product of centuries of rebuilding, improvement, demolition and disaster, with homes being pulled about, extended and freely adapted to changing needs, a room built for storing grain in the fifteenth century becoming a bedroom for the maids in the eighteenth century, and perhaps a study in the twentieth century. Even when one looks at Edwardian village photographs and compares them with the present village scene, a startling number of buildings are seen to have disappeared.

Over most of the country, the building and rebuilding took place at a pulsing rather than a steady rate, with the community responding to periods of affluence, population growth and rising expectations by creating new or better homes, while declines in their fortunes were expressed in desertions and dereliction. Some of the surges and declines in the village were local affairs connected with the fortunes of a local industry or the whims of a landlord. Others were national processes which can quite easily be dated, such as the plague which struck repeatedly between 1348 and the mid-seventeenth century, causing the abandonment of huts and of whole villages. Virtually the only dwellings with any hope of surviving from the fourteenth century to the present are manor houses, always desirable and worthy of being well maintained. The population gradually recovered, and during the sixteenth century undertook the reconstruction of villages on a massive scale. In his famous study of Foxton, Cambridgeshire, Rowland Parker estimates that between 1550 and 1620 the entire village was rebuilt, with more than fifty new houses, mostly well constructed of fresh timber and of such a quality that no less than twenty survive to the present day. In most of the north of England the age of rebuilding, like much else, came later, and in the Dales of Yorkshire and Lancashire the replacement of the ancient longhouse farmsteads and cruck-framed cottages with squarer stone-built homes of one-and-a-half or two storeys took place in the seventeenth and eighteenth centuries.

At a national level, the great ages of building and rebuilding in the English village were from around 1575 to 1725 and from about 1760 to 1860. Building based upon prosperity came first to some East Anglian and Cotswold towns and villages thriving on the medieval wool trade, while the greatest activity during the latter phase of the first rebuilding took place in the more remote western and northern parts of the country. The first age was in the main associated with the construction of superior buildings in the traditional timber and thatch, and the second with the renewal of buildings and the provision of new homes in brick and slate to increasingly standardized designs.

Village growth in the south and midlands slowed down in the seventeenth century, in many places amounting to no more than the replacement of worn-out buildings and the modification of sound ones. Under the Settlement Act of 1662, the Poor Rate was only available to destitute natives of a parish, and other poor souls could be shuffled along from one parish to the next, until at last, if they survived, they became a burden on the villagers and farmers of their native parish. Those villagers fortunate enough to own their homes did not want to bear the burden of the Poor Rate, and everything possible was done to keep it low. Landowners might demolish cottages rather than risk their occupation by unfortunates who might become destitute and a liability on the parish. There was a reluctance to build any but essential new houses, and during the late seventeenth and eighteenth centuries there was a considerable repartitioning of existing cottages to accommodate as many labourers as could be crammed in. Meanwhile, the worthies of the community made every effort to prevent the erection of squatter cottages on common or waste ground. Even so, growing rural populations and a general prosperity amongst the landlords brought renewed village expansion on a large scale until around 1725.

The eighteenth and nineteenth centuries saw the creation of a number of model villages, associated largely at first with the creation of great landscaped parks. The old manor house had often nestled cosily cheek-by-jowl with the homes of tenants: now the hall might move, but sometimes the whole village was swept away so as not to mar the contrived prospect, and rebuilt on the edge of the park – out of sight, if not out of mind. Generally the villagers had few reasons to complain (and since the squire was also the magistrate, much good might churlish complaint have done): the new cottages which they obtained were, if usually less picturesque to the modern eye, almost always more comfortable and easy to maintain than the ones abandoned.

While most estate villages and terraces of cottages that were built were replacements for dwellings swept away by emparking, others were needed to accommodate the bustling labour forces on vast rural estates, and a few were the result of genuine concern for the living standards of the families of agricultural labourers. The designers of many modern village housing estates could learn much about the planned integration of buildings and environment by taking a trip to an old model village like Chippenham in Cambridgeshire, set out by the emparking Lord Orford after 1696, where tile-roofed and colour-washed cottages are set back in generous gardens and the pleasant atmosphere is decidedly rustic (ill. 13). The remarkable village of Harewood in Yorkshire, outside the gates of the great house, was built about 1760 with Carr of York as the designer. Some of the terraced cottages echo vernacular styles of millstone grit architecture while others employ incongruous additions – extra storeys or half-storeys and arched surrounds for the upper row of windows (ill. 95).

While a certain air of northern austerity characterizes Harewood, Old Warden in Bedfordshire, built for Lord Ongley in the middle of the nineteenth century, positively exudes prettiness. Here the cottages with their bargeboards, arching thatched dormers and trellises for climbing plants present a distinctly contrived appearance which was heightened during the early years of the village when the cottagers were encouraged to provide a particular brand of local colour by wearing red cloaks and high hats! The merit of Old Warden concerns the sympathetic way in which the cottages have been placed in relation to the sloping terrain and the use of trees, shrubs and hedgerows which are introduced to punctuate the scene.

Easton, a picturesque estate village in Suffolk, was built in the same period for the Earls of Rochford and Dukes of Hamilton. Several extravagant varieties of the cottage orné can be seen there, while the model farmstead and dairy which were added in 1870 now form the nucleus of a fascinating working farm park where varieties of old English livestock breeds, including the formidable longhorn cattle, are preserved. Somerleyton in the same county, which dates from about 1850 (ill. 94), consists of twenty-eight ornate cottages for estate workers placed around a vast green. Its creator, Sir Morton Peto, amassed a considerable fortune as a builder of railways and some imposing buildings in the capital, such as the Reform Club, before falling victim to the collapse of the Overend and Gurney Bank in 1866. The cottages, built in a Picturesque elaboration of vernacular themes, with their exaggerated thatch and brick-and-timber-framing, were also intended to improve both the living standards and the morality of their occupants. They are full of interest, and at least the former objective will have been achieved.

In addition to highly ornamental designs in Picturesque, Gothic Revival and Neo-Georgian styles, many estate villages – and cottage terraces for estate workers inserted into existing villages – were built in down-to-earth manners based on both local vernacular and simple contemporary styles. At Barrow Bridge in Lancashire, a mill workers' village built in 1830, the only concession to ornamentation in the five rows of stolid stone and slate terraced cottages came from the provision of lozenge-shaped window paning. Baldersby St James in the North Riding of Yorkshire was constructed for Viscount Downe by William Butterfield about 1855; for their appeal the cottages rely not on exaggerated ornament but on good brick construction and on the bold geometry of their roofs and dormers.

Picturesque styles did not serve only for model villages: many of the more comfortably provided farmers fell prey to the Romantic Movement, adorning their sturdy old houses with buttresses, pilasters, curved roof tiles, or verandas,

94 *Opposite, above* A green features amongst a variety of fanciful cottages in the Suffolk village of Somerleyton, built about 1850 by John Thomas for Sir Morton Peto.

95 *Opposite, below* The estate village outside the park gates at Harewood in Yorkshire dates from around 1760; the terraces have an industrial air and a converted ribbon factory is part of this group.

depending upon whether it was a Gothic, Greek, Roman or Swiss ethos that they had set out to conjure. In the Victorian period, the mood of sentimentality became quite entrenched: the cottage orné had made its appearance in many rural settings, as an elaborate parody of the traditional cottage to be inhabited not only by estate workers but often by those members of the middle classes whose yearning for the rustic life did not quite extend to a life without servants in the genuine article; thatched 'Gothic' and magpie 'Tudor' were favourite designs. These cottages have had the scorn of contemporary writers such as Cobbett and Jane Austen and the sneers of more recent arbiters of taste heaped upon them, but we have learned to enjoy them – fortunately, because most were built so well that they will outlast much of the younger village architecture.

Houses that are joined to one another rather than freestanding, economizing on both side walls and land, are common in villages. Terraces of standard older houses are rare, and where they are found they usually either represent the efforts of a landlord to provide new accommodation for a whole group of tenant families or else they are almshouses. Almshouses, some of which date from the sixteenth century, are the oldest forms of unified terrace housing to be found in the village (pl. 13). They were built by both ecclesiastical and lay patrons, and bequests or revenues derived from the leasing of common lands continue to provide homes for the elderly in a number of villages.

Between 1860 and 1945 the village tended on the whole to stagnate or to decline. First the English farmer experienced fearsome competition from the exporters of the New World, then mechanization began to displace labour from the land, and the depleted agricultural labour forces were never really replenished following the carnage of the Great War.

During the nineteenth century, the surplus rural population emigrated to the industrial cities or abroad, and in the interwar period, when conservation was poorly served by ideas or legislation, many fine old unoccupied buildings crumbled or were demolished. The salvation, and in some ways the destruction, of the village came in the postwar age of the motorized commuter, and village houses which appeared destined for abandonment became valuable properties, often experiencing 'restoration' to an extent which would make them unrecognizable to past generations of occupants.

The study of old village buildings and vernacular architecture is fascinating, rewarding, but strewn with pitfalls: some styles, like the seventeenth-century importation of Dutch gables into the eastern counties, produce buildings which seem easily dated, but many cases will be found to tax the amateur historian to the limit. My own cottage, with its two-pitched pantiled mansard roof, hand-ground soft red bricks and many-paned 'Georgian' windows, appears typical of a style of building popular in the eastern counties in the eighteenth century. In fact it is but a century old, built as a gardener's cottage to a plan that almost certainly came from a Victorian architect's design book.

WHEN SEEN through the eyes of the modern town dweller, the village may appear as an island of stability, permanence and continuity – a communal refuge from the tension, competitive bustle and noise-polluted atmosphere of the city. In fact crisis has often come to knock on the door of the village household, and it is not the stability of the community that is to be admired so much as its persistence and its ability to absorb misfortune and stumble doggedly onward. Some villages – many, in fact – have been forced to give up an unequal struggle, and their only monuments may be a crumbling church or a few cottage-shaped hummocks in a pasture. Most of the villages which have survived have at some time or another been obliged to display the very qualities of tenacity and imperturbability wedded to resourcefulness which the English like to regard as the hallmarks of their national character.

Most villages were old, seasoned campaigners familiar with their adversaries of disease, fire and famine when they faced what was for many the cruellest onslaught of all: the plague, known then as 'the pestilence' or 'the great mortality', and today as the Black Death. It struck in 1348, delivering first a crippling blow and then a flurry of body punches which rocked the populations of the English regions for more than three centuries to follow.

The population of England in the middle of the thirteenth century was buoyant and increasing, and although we cannot be certain within a million, it probably numbered around five million. Prosperity too was increasing, and for many countryfolk there was at last a glimpse of a better life. Even so, what passed for villages were agglomerations of filthy hovels, whose inhabitants wore the same threadbare collections of rags for months on end, had bodies which crawled with vermin, who drank from the same streams that served their cattle and pigs, and whose huts were havens for rats, fleas and lice. Nine-tenths of the population lived thus, and most of the remainder lived in towns which at their biggest and worst were congested stinking deathtraps in which any disease worth its salt could spread quickly and disastrously. These people did not seek to live in filth, but they possessed neither the means to avoid it nor the knowledge of its consequences: they believed that mice appeared spontaneously in bags of flour, that cheese and not the fly gave birth to maggots and that disease could be caught by speaking its name. For living in conditions of squalor and ignorance, they paid a steady contribution to the graveyard, which they doubtless accepted with medieval resignation; but nothing could have prepared them psychologically for what was about to befall.

At least we now know, as the people who experienced it did not, the causes of the plague and the conditions in which it flourished. Bubonic plague seems to have had its heartland in northern India, and from time to time it spread rapidly outwards along land and sea trading routes to sweep across the Middle East and Europe. It was carried by the black or house rat, and was caused by an invasion of the human body by the bacterium *Pasteurella pestis*, an internal parasite of the rat, transmitted to man by rat contact and much more frequently by the rat flea, the stomach of which became 'blocked' by bacteria, causing the flea in a frenzy of hunger to attach itself to hosts other than the customary rat – including man. The plague could only achieve epidemic proportions in communities that supported a critically high population of rats. A severe epidemic ravaged England in AD 664, but it is unlikely that there were enough rats for this to have been bubonic plague, and it was possibly smallpox. By 1348, however, there were obviously sufficient rats, and also a sufficient movement of people and goods.

O ye London, thou paragon of this kingdome for beauty & braue | no doub: v. t God in his mercy will stay his beame wrath and indig- | The visage of the Country is so bare that at this present time that | bing the poore, and such as be shut up to be mercifully lokt vnto and
buildings, how art thou now vnuoiused of thy chiefest Inhabi- | nation, yet instised vpon vs. | a fathers house haue been shut vp for giuing his sonne but one nights | most fauourable comforted by our Magistrate.

Port towns were naturally the first to suffer; but 'blocked' fleas, travelling in the clothes of merchants, nobles and pilgrims or in trade goods, introduced the plague to villages whose immobile populations would otherwise have been spared. Once arrived in the agricultural village with a grain store and hovel dwellings supporting a seething rat population, the plague was fearfully effective. Most peasant rooms were open to the rafters, and from dead rats in the thatch fleas could drop freely onto the unsuspecting sleepers who huddled below. Many contemporary accounts tell how the disease took its fiercest toll of the poor; the lord in his stone castle or manor would certainly have been safer from rats, and hence from infection. Once infected the sufferer could expect a swift but painful death. In its usual form, the disease caused swelling and haemorrhaging around the lymph glands, and had a 70 per cent mortality rate. The pneumonic form of the plague was passed directly from man to man by air, and brought death within four days of infection, with a 100 per cent mortality rate. Other epidemics paled by comparison, and the plague was held in special fear even by a population that was familiar with smallpox and diphtheria.

The disease seems to have entered England from the Continent via Weymouth or Southampton, spreading to Bristol, Oxford and London during the mild winter of 1348–49, which failed to induce the normal dormancy in the rat flea. From London it probably passed by coastal shipping to the East Anglian ports. From the rat-infested towns it spread to the village farming communities, making rapid progress where the closely grouped villages of the grainlands provided convenient stepping stones, but making little headway in the more thinly populated areas of the north and west where grain stores and rats were fewer, and where empty tracts of forest, marsh and moorland shielded many communities from infection.

Estimates of the level of mortality in the intitial plague years of 1348–50 vary widely, from the traditionally accepted figure of one-third to one-half of the population to a recent estimate that only one-twentieth of the population of England as a whole was killed. We will never know the true answer, but perhaps death by the plague came to one in five. J. F. D. Shrewsbury, the author of a monumental work on the plague, estimates that the disease only achieved the traditional mortality figure of one-third in the crowded ports and cities, and within certain unfortunate villages of the south-eastern agricultural lowlands. Even in the heart of the plague-struck area, some villages emerged unscathed: my own village of Great Shelford in the rural plague heartland between Norfolk and Bedfordshire escaped the plague in 1348–50, only to suffer severely in the epidemic of 1360–62.

96 This woodcut comes from a broadsheet of 1603 urging the country folk to show pity on townspeople who fled amongst them from the plague-stricken centres.

While very few villages can have been permanently extinguished by the plague, the records show that many manors were stripped of their workforces. In parts of Dorset the pestilence was so severe that, a contemporary document tells us, 'the lands there lie untilled and other profits are lost'; in 1349, King Edward III pardoned the parishioners of a Bristol suburb for acquiring without his licence half an acre 'for the enlargement of the churchyard which had been filled up by bodies buried in the last pestilence'. Two years later, he remitted the taxes of Roger de Elmrugge who held lands in Staffordshire, as 'on account of the deadly pestilence lately in those parts the lands are so much deteriorated in value that he will not be able to answer the whole farm without great loss'. At Wyville in Lincolnshire – which was destined to be a lost village – contemporary records tell that 'the land is poor and stony, and lies uncultivated for want of tenants after the pestilence'. After the plague had made its initial assault on the Diocese of Bath and Wells, exemption from confession was granted as 'no priests are found who are willing either in zeal of devotion or for any stipend to accept the pastoral care . . . or to visit the sick and minister the church sacraments to them, perchance by reason of the infection and the horror of contagion: therefore many folk died without the sacraments'.

At the manor court of Birdbrook in Essex, which was held in July 1349, 37 tenants out of a number that cannot have been much more than 45 were presented as dead. New tenants were found for all but six of the vacant holdings, which may suggest a countryside that was over-peopled before the calamity.

After this first onslaught, a brief respite was granted to the weakened population of the grief-stricken land, until the plague struck again, particularly in the north, in 1360–62. It erupted periodically, coming again with violence in 1405 and reappearing in different English regions during the next two and a half centuries: the West Country, for instance, was devastated again in 1592–93. Finally, after a particularly disastrous outbreak in 1665, bubonic plague disappeared from England, for reasons that are still not certain: the black or house rat was replaced by the brown or field rat, which sought less intimate contact with man; more buildings were being built of stone or brick, less hospitable to vermin than lathe and thatch; and at the same time the disease itself may have mutated into a less virulent form which conferred immunity. Nevertheless, fear of the plague remained deeply engraved upon the national consciousness, producing an unfounded panic in east Suffolk at the beginning of this century. A house in the Fenland village of Landbeach is still known as 'Plague House' more than four hundred years after two occupants returning from London brought plague to the community.

While the mention of the Black Death is still sufficient to inspire horror, it is difficult to imagine its impact upon the heart and mind of a villager who might see the painful deaths of whole households of neighbours, stricken and dead within a matter of days, walk through fields where generous crops stood rotting in strip after strip, or feel the sudden loss of half the people who had been friends since childhood. Samuel Pepys, who stayed on in London during the Great Plague of 1665, when the court and a large part of the population had taken to its heels to seek safety in the country, exclaimed in his diary, 'But lord! what a sad time it is to see no boats upon the River; and grass grows all up and down White Hall court, and nobody but poor wretches in the streets!'

The chronicler Vincent, who recorded his recollections in the following year, wrote:

Now there is a dismal solitude in London streets . . . in many houses half the family is swept away; and in some the whole, from the eldest to the youngest; few escape with the death of but one or two; never did so many husbands and wives die together; never did so many parents carry their children with them to the grave.

Although four centuries have elapsed, one is still touched by stories of how the sole survivor of a family in Eyam singlehandedly buried all her offspring and relatives, and one wonders what life still offered to someone who was so swiftly stripped of all that was loved and gave a meaning to existence. Fathers who had laboured for years to provide their children with sound foundations were bereft of heirs; starving animals paced and bellowed in anticipation of the return of masters who were dead and cold; nettles and brambles seeded the neglected strips while the widows learned to handle the harness and flail.

The terror of the pestilence was heightened because both cause and cure were unknown: in some communities men were appointed to kill all domestic pets found roaming the streets; many believed that the disease was caught only by inhaling polluted air, and some tried to eliminate it by burning wood, gunpowder, leather or horn. In 1603, the reaction of the London authorities was 'to kill the dogs and mark the houses by fastening upon them a great printed paper with these words "Lord have mercy upon us" '. To hosts of people, some nobles and some peasants, the pestilence was a divine retribution: Vincent wrote, 'Now those who did not believe an unseen God, are afraid of unseen arrows.' Even so, attempts were made to escape and patent tonics abounded, ranging from infusions of herbs and candy sugar in the fifteenth century to tobacco in the seventeenth.

Although the 'pestilence' was specially feared, death was never far from the medieval village, and for most villagers life was short and full of hardship, and death painful. Other diseases ravaged the land: typhus often came on the heels of plague, while smallpox, pneumonia, tuberculosis and dysentery each claimed countless victims. The frequency of multiple epidemics is described in a manuscript in the Bodleian Library, Oxford, which tells how, after 1475,

> there fell a great disease in England called the 'stych' from which much people died suddenly. Also another disease reigned after that, called the 'fflyx' [flux], that never was seen in England before, and people died hugely of it for three successive years, in one place or another. And after that there bred a raven on Charing Cross in London; and never had one seen breed there before. And after that came a great death of pestilence, that lasted three years; and people died mightily in every place, man, woman, and child.

The plague was a great test of courage: in some places priests and surgeons deserted their charges but in others they tended the sick until they perished themselves. The most celebrated example of communal heroism is the Derbyshire village of Eyam, which gave up three-quarters of its folk in the final epidemic of 1665. The fleas that introduced the plague to this isolated Peak District community arrived in a box of old clothes brought from London. The fleas attached themselves to rat and human hosts, taking 6 souls in September, 29 in October and then but 16 in November and December. As infection declined during the long cold spring, the people of Eyam believed that their tribulations were at an end, when warmer weather reactivated the dormant fleas and 19 villagers perished in the June of 1666.

The Rector of Eyam, the Rev. W. Mompesson, then persuaded the people to isolate themselves to prevent the spread of the disease to neighbouring communities. The church and churchyard were closed and the services held in the open air. The survivors buried their dead, one woman digging the graves of her husband and six children all within a week. By November, 267 villagers from 76 families lay beneath the sod; 9 families were completely exterminated, and the few survivors set to burning the goods of the dead. While we cannot but admire the heroism of the Eyam villagers' self-imposed isolation, Professor Shrewsbury has pointed out that the disease was provided with exactly the conditions in which it could make its deepest inroads: had the villagers taken the normal course and dispersed, most of them would have survived.

Eyam did not die, and it demonstrates the point that while a village might lose the bulk of its population it was almost always re-occupied and survived. The Black Death has provided a convenient scapegoat for the thousands of lost villages which lie entombed beneath the countryside of England, but contrary to popular belief, of the villages that disappeared in the Middle Ages few died as a result of the plague alone. In the chapter on the medieval village we saw that population grew rapidly in the centuries following the Conquest. During a period which some experts date from 1450 to 1850, Western Europe was in the grip of the 'Little Ice Age', when temperatures were on average 1–3°C below those of today. The onset of these conditions was felt during the fourteenth century, and the populations which faced the Black Death were already debilitated by poor weather, storm surges and flooding and disastrous harvests. The villages which did not survive were likely to be those which had been pushed too far into the unrewarding marginal farmlands, where life was already a struggle and the pestilence was merely the last straw. Such was probably the case at Dunsthorpe in Lincolnshire, where in 1437 the Rector informed his Bishop that the parish was unable to support him because of 'the fewness of peasants, the low wages, the bareness of the lands, the lack of cultivation, the pestilence and epidemics with which the Lord afflicts his people for their sins'. M. W. Beresford, who has produced a national survey of lost villages, names Standelf and Tilgarsley in Oxfordshire as settlements whose disappearance was due specifically to the destruction of their populations by the pestilence; we can add Bolton, in Yorkshire, Hale in Northamptonshire and Tusmore in Oxfordshire as other examples. In the unlikely event of the whole community of a prosperous village being wiped out, the well-endowed site would almost certainly be re-occupied, sometimes by the sons of tenants from nearby manors who moved in to take over the better holdings. There was little cause, on the other hand, to recolonize the borderline villages where decline had already set in before the plague dealt the death blow. A. E. Levett has shown that on the estates of St Albans Abbey 491 new lettings of land were available after the pestilence struck, and because the lands were attractive they were taken: 168 lettings were made to children and teenagers and many to strangers from outside the village. In some areas, as we have seen (p. 70), the surviving peasants were actually better off, able to expect higher returns for their scarce labour.

The culprit responsible for the destruction of far more villages than the plague was not a creature so detestable as the rat or the flea, but that most gentle of beasts and symbol of peace, the sheep. In the absence in some places of tenants to farm the poorer ploughlands many landlords in the fourteenth century turned to sheep; and the monks of the great Cistercian abbeys in the north and midlands,

who had earlier moved villages in the interests of rational farming, now demonstrated to all who cared to look how profitable sheep rearing could be.

The real troubles for the late medieval peasant came when the landlord, flushed with the success of the woollen enterprise on the lands he controlled directly, his demesne, began to cast greedy eyes upon the lands which supported the village community, as so often he did in the fifteenth and sixteenth centuries. Bitter voices were raised, but the fact remained that sheep offered higher profits than the taking of rents from ploughmen: there was a brisk market in both England and the Low Countries for the long-fibred fleece of the English sheep, while government policy kept the price of grain artificially low. As a sixteenth-century pamphleteer wrote, 'who will maintain husbandry which is the nurse of every County as long as sheep bring so great a gain . . . make cheese, carry it to market when one poor soul may by keeping sheep get him a greater profit . . . who will not be contented for to pull down houses of husbandry so that he may stuff his bags full of money?'

Underlying the smash-and-grab of villages and village lands there was a great change in attitudes and values taking place as England emerged from the Middle Ages. In the Age of Chivalry, the noble landowner was much more than just a landlord: he was also the father and protector of the community of loyal vassals who would rally to his banner when the call to arms was sounded. Though feudalism was also a cover for the gross exploitation of the people of the village, it was founded on a sense of obligation and duty which cast the lord as the guardian of the community which owed him rent, service, and, if need be, warriors. During the late fifteenth and sixteenth centuries, the relative peace which the Tudor monarchs imposed devalued the peasant as a fighting man, while the increased value attached to wealth rather than nobility or armed

98 Sheep, so innocently portrayed in this fifteenth-century manuscript, were shortly to result in the dispossession of thousands of peasant families.

manpower transformed the lord into little more than a rent-collector and exactor of fines. Money called the tune and the landlord and villager danced; they were often out of step and it was the peasant's toes that were trampled.

Some landlords turned to rackrenting, some to sheep, and some to a bit of both. The decay of ancient customs on the manor left many peasants without rights or privileges, and while the law protected the freeholding tenants from eviction, the leaseholders could be squeezed for their last penny. Some copyholders (see p. 72) were protected by the law, but most presented little obstacle to the landlord who was determined to be rid of them: they could be fined impossible sums, persecuted through loopholes in the law or pressurized to convert their copies into leases. Some lords were content to sort out the strips of their demesne from the patchwork of the open field holdings to create for themselves a compact sheep run. Others looked hungrily to the common grazings of the waste, where only the free tenants of the village had their rights protected by the law. Others still had the influence and power to ignore the legal rights of all the villagers and cast them from the land, like the lord of Wootton Bassett in Wiltshire, who took 2,000 acres of peasant land and then impoverished the deprived freeholders with costly lawsuits when they tried to assert their rights.

While the government did not approve of the excess of the sheep enclosure movement, as we shall see in the case of Wormleighton, it was unable to do very much to stem the tide of evictions. The very Justices of the Peace who were entrusted with the protection of tenant rights were likely to be either themselves evicting landlords or the friends of such men, and when the village of Steeton in West Yorkshire was depopulated the guilty landlord, Sir Guy Fairfax, was Justice of the King's Bench.

Up and down the country, peasants were singing the bitter ballad called 'Now-a-dayes':

> Commons to close and kepe
> Poor folk for bred to cry and wepe;
> Towns pulled down to pasture shepe;
> This is the new gyse [fashion].

During the Tudor period, whole villages were torn down. Their evicted inhabitants were unwelcome in the towns, where the established artisans and craftsmen saw in them the threat of cut-priced labour. Later, the Statutes of Inmates of 1589 and 1593 forbade more than one family to occupy a house, preventing many displaced villagers from finding lodgings in the town. Yet when the ejected peasants took to the roads they could be condemned as vagabonds and sentenced to slavery or death. As the villagers could not write, we can only imagine the bitterness that must have torn at the heart of the peasant whose grandfather had been lured to take over a plague-stricken holding and who had worked hard and well to pay his dues and improve the land, and yet woke one morning to find the landlord's agents pushing over his cottage and barn. A farmer one day, and a tramp the next, treading the lanes for mile after mile with a starving family in tow and nowhere to go. The outcast might retrace his steps to his old village and see nothing but a shepherd's hut where homes once stood, and nothing but nodding stupid sheep where strips were once bright with beans, wheat and barley.

The roads of the kingdom swarmed with the broken remnants of the class which had furnished the medieval state with its formidable archers and pikemen, and the men's discontent erupted in the Pilgrimage of Grace in 1536 (see p. 69) and Kett's Rising in 1549. In June 1549 an enclosure riot broke out at Attleborough in Norfolk and the illegal fences erected by Squire Greene were torn down; three weeks later crowds gathered for the annual feast at Wymondham and hackles were still high. There were speeches and shouting and the following morning an angry mob fell upon the unlawful fences which a man named Flowerdew had erected around the common lands. Robert Kett was a yeoman farmer who had himself enclosed some land; he faced the mob, listened to their grievances and not only accepted their complaints but provided them with a stirring leader. A long manifesto was composed, which told how

> The lands which in the memory of our fathers were common, those are ditched and hedged and made several; the pastures are enclosed and we are shut out . . . they seek from all places all the things for their desire and the provocation of lust. While we in the meantime eat herbs and roots, and languish with continual labour, and

99 This photograph was taken in Northampton-shire in 1978 but it shows a scene that was depressingly familiar in Tudor England, as sheep graze the overgrown ridge-and-furrow of the lost village fields.

yet are envied that we live, breathe, and enjoy common air! Shall they, as they have brought hedges about common pasture, enclose with their intolerable lusts also all the commodities and pleasure of this life, which Nature, the parent of us all, would have common, and bringeth forth every day, for us, as well as for them?

Under Robert Kett's leadership, a peasant army of 20,000 bitter men controlled Norfolk and swam the Wensum to take Norwich. They treated the vanquished with great propriety, but when they themselves were defeated by government forces of artillery and German mercenaries, they fought to the death knowing that the proffered pardons were worthless. Robert Kett rotted in chains on the walls of Norwich Castle, and his brother William met a similar fate on a tower of Wymondham Abbey.

The rate of enclosure and eviction only subsided when some of the prohibitions on the export of grain were removed during the reign of Elizabeth, and in the latter part of the sixteenth century peasant wheat-growing was able to compete successfully with sheep-rearing in the battle for land control. In the meantime many villages had disappeared beneath sheepwalks and lay silent except for the lonesome bleating of sheep whose sharp little hooves pressed the fragments of mud daub walls back into the ground from which they had come.

Wormleighton in Warwickshire was such a village; its troubles began with the Spencers. They were a free tenant farming family until they grew prosperous by buying up abandoned ploughlands and converting them into sheep grazings; they married well, hauling themselves into the ranks of the lesser gentry. Old John Spencer married his daughter Joan to William Cope, who did very well for himself, being made Cofferer to the Household of King Henry VII. William rented some lands from John Spencer at Wormleighton – land which had passed to the Crown when the old Wormleighton family of Peche had become extinct and their heir by marriage was sentenced for treason. The King must have liked William, because he granted the whole of the manor of Wormleighton directly to him in 1498.

William then set about buying up the holdings of all the lesser landlords, and when he had bought the whole parish the proud new owner set about destroying a dozen farms and some cottages and put his sixty peasants out on the road. Wormleighton had already had a bitter taste of enclosure: before another landowner, Sir Edward Raleigh, sold out to William he had destroyed six farms that stood in the way of his sheep. Wormleighton originally had a long narrow green flanked by two rows of thatched cottages. The green terminated in a fine chain of fishponds, and further on there was a cluster of cottages facing the church. Overlooking the village was the crumbling moated manor house which had stood silent since the extinction of the Peche family had given the village to uncaring strangers (see ill. 37).

John Spencer, cousin of William's wife Joan, became very rich by renting and then buying land for sheep grazing, and in 1506 he bought the Wormleighton lands from William and added them to a Spencer empire of sheepruns that formed a chain across four Midland counties. Eviction and enclosure troubled the government at the start of the sixteenth century: in 1517 Cardinal Wolsey set up a Commission of Inquiry in an attempt to end illegal enclosure, and in due course its gaze came to rest on John. He denied responsibility for the destruction of Wormleighton, naming the now dead William as the guilty party. He claimed that he had set up a new village beside the ruins of the old, and so he had – a

village to house the shepherds and drovers that were the citizens of his empire of depopulated manors. The plea of rebuilding was just enough to get John off the hook. Between his pleading and his death in 1522, he was knighted.

In the peasant-stripped parish which might only accommodate the household of the lord and his shepherd, there was plenty of room for the great park of the manor, where deer provided the grace and sheep the profit. In other parishes, emparking alone provided sufficient motive for destruction, and in Professor Beresford's phrase, 'Many a lost village stands in the shadow of a Great House.' Some emparking took place even before Tudor times: Widerton in Nottinghamshire was emparked in the mid-fifteenth century, while Fulbrook in Warwickshire met a similar fate at the hands of the Duke of Bedford early in the following century.

The movement to enlarge the manor park and create fashionably landscaped vistas reached its peak during the eighteenth century. By then the age when a lord could ride roughshod over the property rights of a cowering tenantry was long passed, and the uprooted villagers could at least expect to be rehoused.

100 Deserted medieval villages rarely show any upstanding masonry, but at Pickworth in Rutland, which had disappeared by 1491, an arch of the church still stands, near a holloway marking a lost street. The decaying farmstead is probably of the seventeenth century.

Emparking was most easily achieved when the lord controlled a large and undivided estate: sometimes the villagers were transferred into neighbouring villages, as happened when Stowe in Buckinghamshire made way for a great park. Other communities were given homes in a new village erected outside the park, with, as we have seen (p. 120), usually few material reasons for complaint.

For the victims of Tudor emparking, there was little prospect of compensation and but few cases to suggest that the dispossessed villagers were capable of much resistance. Wilstrop in west Yorkshire was an exception; there the landlord, Miles Wilstrop, who had a taste both for emparking and for sheep clearance, seems to have been an unmitigated tyrant even by the standards of his class and time. On one occasion he incited an assault on a priest during morning service, having already destroyed the poor man's corn and tormented his sheep.

Towards the end of the fifteenth century, Miles destroyed the village from which he took his name and set up a park, planting fruit and walnut trees and surrounding his creation with a solid fence. In 1497 a dozen villagers pulled the fence down; the following year, four hundred were present to see the re-erected fence come down again and the young orchard be uprooted. Then Miles found his mill pond drained and his rabbit warren dug up. The next year, the fence was down again, and had Miles been at home when the mob ran though his house, he would probably have been hanged. It is tempting to see here a case of the people of the village getting their own back, but these villagers were encouraged by a powerful patron in Sir William Gascoigne, Abbot of Fountains, who had a long-standing feud with the Wilstrops.

The seventeenth century saw the waning both of the pestilence and of clearance for sheep. In the centuries which followed, while the prospects for survival for any particular village were more secure, forces were at work to erode the very classes which provided the community with its core and strength: the village-dwelling yeomen and tenant farmers. Whereas plague and clearances had struck like apoplexy at a minority of villages, the decline of the small farmer was a wasting disease which affected almost all, eventually transforming them by the nineteenth century into communities of cowtowing labourers and tradesmen. The village that emerged from feudalism was still dominated by manorial lords, but it included many sturdy and independent farming families. Gradually their lands were to be absorbed by the few large farms of the neighbourhood.

Small fish tend to be devoured by the bigger fish: this was figuratively as true on land as in the sea, and during the seventeenth and eighteenth centuries armies of small farmers were forced to abandon an unequal struggle against rising rents and costs and fluctuating prices. In 1727, Edward Laurence, a large landowner, gave instructions to his steward: he was to buy out all the freeholders without delay, 'convert copyholds for lives into leaseholds for lives . . . get rid of Farms of £8 or £10 *per annum*, lay all the small Farms let to poor indigent People, to the great ones'. What Edward was attempting was known as 'engrossment'. It was not popular, but it happened throughout England, creating large landowners and large tenants, and leaving little room for smaller men. In 1795, one 'Suffolk gentleman' bemoaned the disappearance of

> a race of Men in the Country besides the Gentlemen and Husbandmen, called Yeomanry, Men who cultivated their own property . . . the Pride of the Nation in War and Peace . . . hardy, brave, and of good morals . . . by the influx of riches and a change of manners, they were nearly annihilated in the year 1750.

Thus although the Parliamentary Enclosure movement of the late eighteenth and early nineteenth centuries has been blamed for the ruination of the small farmer, the destruction of the peasant community and, in the eyes of some commentators, the death of the traditional village, the trouble had started long before. The enclosure of the village open fields was not new to England: as far back as the fifteenth century tenants in various villages were willingly exchanging strips of land in order to create compact hedge-enclosed fields. The Tudor period saw the iniquitous sheep enclosures, and sufficient enclosure took place during the seventeenth century to ignite the Levellers' rising of 1647 and to fan the flames of the agrarian communists who supported Gerard Winstanley and were dispersed by troops in 1649 during their attempt to colonize St George's Hill in Surrey. Yet even though power had passed from a monarchy which often attempted to safeguard the small farmer to a Parliament of landowners, many seventeenth-century enclosures were the result of agreements between landlord and tenant and between tenant and tenant, all parties being concerned with the more efficient production of grain.

101 Surveyors are at work in this detail from the enclosure award map of Henlow in Bedfordshire, 1798. The fellow on the right is using a simple surveying instrument called a 'cross head'. His colleagues hold markers and knotted string lies on the ground.

Towards the end of the eighteenth century what changed was the scale and pace of enclosure, which was no longer a piecemeal affair but an irresistible tide of change that swept village communities into the world of commercial farming and created the classic English countryside of hedgerows and rectangular fields. In one parish after another the landowners petitioned Parliament to pass a Private Enclosure Act, after which commissioners were appointed to survey the village fields and produce a complete redivision of the ploughland and common land, replacing the scattered strips and common pasture with a series of compact and consolidated holdings. The farmer who could establish title to a series of arable strips scattered amongst the open fields and who consequently exercised rights in the common grazings could expect to receive in the enclosure award a compact block of ploughland equivalent in value to his scattered strips, and an allotment which was supposed to equal his common pasture rights.

Enclosure may have paved the way for more efficient farming, but it weakened the village in two ways. Firstly, the farmers whose share entitled them to a substantial farm after enclosure often chose to desert their old home for a new farmhouse set up in the middle of their new holding. Time spent in travel

102, 103 'A Common Improved in Yorkshire', from Repton's *Fragments on the Theory and Practice of Landscape Gardening*, 1816. We do not know what the commoners thought of the proposed improvement: their cottages have been tastefully screened by trees and a classical folly.

was time wasted, and whereas when land was held in scattered strips there was no better place to live than in the village, at the centre of the lands and in the heart of the community, after enclosure it often made more sense to move out of the village. A great many isolated English farmhouses can clearly be seen to date from the period immediately after Parliamentary Enclosure. Secondly, enclosure brought crisis to hosts of people lower down the scale. The first to go were those who lacked a permanent title to the strips which they rented: landlords were in no way obliged to offer them new holdings within the compacted fields, and usually chose to let lands to a single tenant of substance. Cottagers who rented cottages which by ancient custom carried rights to the common grazings usually went uncompensated when the commons were enclosed. Squatter families who had long been settled around the fringes of the commons and wastes without establishing a title to their lands, eking out a bare living often supplemented by craftwork and casual labour, were faced with eviction. The village farmer whose holdings were small, and who consequently received only a small share in the enclosure award, did not generally hang on for long. Sometimes he was unjustly treated by the award; more often, though fairly treated he found himself much worse off than before. He immediately faced a bill for the cost of producing the enclosure award, and another for the fencing of his new holding, but most serious was his loss of access to the common and waste.

The survival of ancient manorial customs on the common and waste had provided a basis for peasant self-sufficiency. These rights, established in the early

Middle Ages, included *estover*, the right to collect wood; *firebote*, the right to take gorse, heath and tree loppings for fuel; *heybote*, the right to timber for gates and fencing; *housebote*, the right to timber for house building; *piscary*, the right to fish; *plowbote*, the right to wood to repair ploughs and carts; and *turbary*, the right to dig peat for fuel.

Now all the little essentials which supported a way of life based on independent subsistence were gone – the ferns from the common for litter in the pigsty, the turf for smoking bacon, a run for the chicken and geese, the raw materials for cottage craftwork, and many other items that allowed the villager to stand apart from the world of commerce. While these rights to timber, fish and fuel were often valuable, most serious was the loss of common pasture rights: unable to support so many beasts as before, the small farmer was deprived of milk, fresh meat, and the farm muck which was an essential fertilizer for his arable crops. Now he must buy milk and fuel and go to the baker for the bread that was formerly baked at home in an oven fired by gorse and furze faggots gathered on the waste. Vanished were all the petty tasks which filled the idle hours of winter, as too were the incentives for a life of toil. The small farmer needed cash to pay for all the goods which he now had to buy, and when the ploughlands failed to produce sufficient profit, he had only one thing left to sell – his labour. He might sell up his farm and depart with his capital to one of the growing industrial towns or, deep in debt, beg for work at the farmhouse door of one of his neighbours.

Although he supported enclosure, the late Georgian agricultural theorist Arthur Young recognized the problems which were being created when he penned his famous lines:

> Go to an ale-house kitchen of an enclosed county and there you will see the origin of poverty and the poor rates.

For, Young says, the peasant there might ask,

> If I am diligent shall I have leave to build a cottage? If I am sober, shall I have land for a cow? If I am frugal, shall I have an acre of potatoes? You offer no motives; you have nothing but a parish officer and a workhouse. Bring me another pot.

George Bourne, who wrote in 1912 about change in the Surrey village from which he took his *nom de plume*, talked to villagers who were able to remember the enclosure of the village lands and found that 'The older folk talk about things that happened "before the common was enclosed" much as they might say "before the flood", and occasionally they discuss the history of some allotment or other made under the award.' Although not everybody appreciated it at the time, Bourne believed that

> To the enclosure of the common more than to any other cause may be traced all the changes that have subsequently passed over the village. It was like knocking the keystone out of an arch . . . the old thrift – the peasant thrift – which the people understood thoroughly had to be abandoned in favour of a modern thrift – commercial thrift – which they understood but vaguely . . . it struck at the very heart of the peasant system.

At the start of the nineteenth century, when enclosure was at its height, village populations were growing rapidly at rates which could outstrip the migration of families to the factory towns or abroad, until a peak village population was achieved in most parts of England around 1850. The years which followed were to witness a great exodus from the village. This desertion was due partly to the fall in farming employment, which pushed the villager from the countryside, and partly to the pull of higher wages and better housing offered in the factory and the town. Other more adventurous families deserted the slavish labour, subsistence wages and cramped cottage squalor which was the lot of the average farmworker for the beckoning opportunities of the New World. In 1861 the English countryside provided work for almost two million farmers and labourers; by 1901 this was halved.

The fall in the number of jobs was partly caused by the seasonal nature of farm work: rather than employ a large labour force of workers who would often be idle during the winter months, farmers discovered the profits to be made by reducing the permanent workforce to a minimum. During the busy weeks of summer the extra hands were recruited from Irish harvest gangs who migrated to England for haymaking and harvest, from the women of the village and from the village children.

Mechanization also began its relentless erosion of the village workforce. Attempts to build reaping machines produced various outlandish and incompetent devices during the late eighteenth and early nineteenth centuries, but by 1870 improved machines were in general use. By the 1880s the ungainly

ancestors of all recent harvest machines except the combine harvester were to be seen in the English countryside. The mechanical reaper-binder not only replaced the swishing scythe of the casual farmworker: it did away with the tying of sheaves which had employed his wife and children, and its efficiency put an end to the gleaning of the harvest field which had enriched the family grain store. Other eighteenth-century inventions that were developed further included horse-drawn seed drills for sowing the crops, hoes, and muck-spreaders. In the 1860s steam engines were introduced for ploughing and for powering the cumbersome threshing machines. These might do in a day the work which had busied the village labourers on winter days when there was little else but hedging and ditching to keep them in work, their hand flails beating a steady tattoo on the threshing floor.

The steam traction engine did not achieve a total victory over the horse and the village horseman, but waiting in the wings there was the petrol-powered tractor: described in 1917 as 'the least reliable of all ploughing instruments', after improvements it vanquished both the horse and the steam engine a decade or so later. Although hand reaping was not completely overtaken until after the turn of the century, the advance in mechanization and the fall in farm employment was such that, in the words of one villager at Britwell Salome in Oxfordshire, 'you didn't dare say a word as big as a clover seed or you might lose your job.' Some farmers were needlessly callous in their handling of the village workers and on occasions the villagers attempted to sabotage the machines. One particularly

104 A mechanical belt from the nearby traction engine powers this threshing machine, photographed at Gipps Farm, Newick, Sussex about 1900. The machine seems to us now quite antediluvian, but it will have cost several men their work in the threshing barn.

ruthless farmer in 1830 who heard the news of attacks on machinery on a neighbouring Kentish farm said of the distressed labourers, 'I should be well pleased if a plague were to break out among them, and then I should have their carcasses as manure, and right good stuff it would make for my hops'.

As well as the losses in permanent and casual farmwork, the second half of the nineteenth century saw the rapid collapse of dozens of rural craft industries in the face of overwhelming competition from the mass products of the factory. Village tailors, shoemakers and maltsters found themselves bankrupted, while even wheelwrights, joiners and blacksmiths found factory-made wheel hubs, cupboards and ploughs making inroads into their trade. In many localities village industries had provided seasonal or permanent jobs for landsmen and their wives. There was button-making in the villages around Blandford in Dorset, dye-making from woad in East Anglia, garden pots were made at Broxley and gloves in the villages around Worcester. Looms were to be found in thousands of cottages: some cottage industries specialized in flannels or worsteds, some in linen, some in sailcloth; at Witney in Oxfordshire blankets were made, and at Oakingham, hat bands.

The collapse of cottage industries and the depletion of the farm workforce often left village shopkeepers, innkeepers and craftsmen without a sufficient custom to support their trade, and they too headed for the city or the port. Everywhere, labour was streaming from the land and villages, leaving behind poverty and hopelessness, groping for opportunities which the countryside could not provide, but in many cases exchanging rural penury for urban squalor.

The farm-owner has often been cast as the villain of the piece. He was sometimes mean and ruthless, but he could be no less than thrifty in order to survive. After 1862 the agricultural river of plenty slowed to a trickle, and in 1875–84 and again in 1891–99 English agriculture was on the brink of collapse in the face of overseas competition, shortages of capital and climatic disasters. In 1875 and 1876, cold springs and rainy summers produced small mildewed crops of wheat, and with wheat from the New World granaries flowing in, scarcity no longer meant high prices for the English farmer. In 1877 the potato crop failed and there was an outbreak of cattle plague. Sleet in the summer of 1879 brought crop failure, pleuro-pneumonia in the cattle and liver rot in sheep. The two cold summers of 1891 and 1892 were followed by drought in 1893, while farmers worked their land into exhaustion in trying to make good their losses.

The novelist Rider Haggard made a tour of England to study the causes of agricultural depression, and of northern Hertfordshire he wrote,

> It was a melancholy sight that met the eye of the traveller between Baldock and Ashwell in the drought stricken season of 1901. He saw stretched before him huge flat fields, some of them sown with barley, half hidden in the yellow blooms of charlock, their scanty stunted corn ravaged by wireworm, and some with wheat for the most part of a faded, sickly hue.

With wheat prices at rockbottom, the farmer who was not prepared to shed his labour force and abandon some of his labour-demanding arable farming might expect to go under. Looking back in 1912, Lord Ernle recalled,

> this was the great lesson that was being learned, how to get the work done on the arable land with less labour. What with the turnover of arable land to grass . . . and economy in methods, something like a third of the labouring population left the

land in the last quarter of the nineteenth century. There were other occupations to absorb the men, but none the less the forced exodus left a bitterness against farmers and landlords among the working classes that has not yet wholly disappeared.

The theme of mechanization against a background of farming depression was to be repeated during the 1920s, but in the meantime something more sinister than the factory and the steamer was to beckon the village labourer, and villages were to be depopulated more swiftly and fatally. Europe had gone mad and men were needed to fight in the Great War.

For many years the villages of England had supplied the forces with a steady stream of volunteers, men and boys lured by the promise of adventure, travel, and, most enticingly, by the offer of three square meals a day. When the call came for volunteers in 1914 some men were moved by patriotism, while for others, buoyantly optimistic in the invincibility of the British fleets and armies, war was not a threat but a welcome relief, an interlude in a life of drudgery and humiliation. The spirit was echoed by one of the Suffolk villagers interviewed by Ronald Blythe and quoted in *Akenfield*:

> When the farmer stopped my pay because it was raining and we couldn't thrash, I said to my seventeen-year-old mate 'B – – – – – him. We'll go off and join the army.'

105 The beauties of the countryside, always a source of comfort, mask the full anguish of *The Emigrant's Last Sight of Home* in this painting by Richard Redgrave, 1858.

141

He went on to recall that

> In my four months' training with the regiment I put on nearly a stone of weight and got a bit taller. They said it was the food but it was really because for the first time in my life there had been no strenuous work. I want to say this simply as a fact, that village people in Suffolk in my day were worked to death.

Most of those who marched jauntily away with their comrades to the music of the local band and the approving smiles of the village were to meet deeper mud, fatter rats and hardships more gruelling than any that even they could have imagined. The sons of squires and middle-class villagers who rushed to enlist often became junior officers, the grade among whom there were to be proportionally the highest casualties. Although the villages of England made no greater contributions than the towns, in a close and compact community the yawning war-torn gaps were to be more starkly obvious and perhaps more deeply sensed. Some English villages furnished the army with all of their menfolk who were fit to serve and several who were not. Reginald Pound, the biographer of the 'lost generation', records that Buckland in Berkshire provided 79 recruits from a total population of only 302. Hever in Kent furnished 74 men from a population of 366, and Wroxall in the Isle of Wight, with 460 inhabitants, produced 70 men; while 61 houses in Chapel Street at Altrincham in Cheshire yielded up 82 soldiers, and Cosgrove in Buckinghamshire gave up all its 35 eligible men.

The parish of Barley in Hertfordshire, including Barley village with a population of about 500, made a contribution that was not abnormal: it furnished 141 service men, and a further 39 men who were Barley-born also served. Of these 180, 77 – almost half – were to be recorded on the village roll of honour, including nine members of the Scripps family, seven Days, four Daytons and four Slaters.

The comradeship that came from recruitment on a local and regional basis buttressed the British armies against the torments of the shell-battered trenches; it also served to shame the man who ran. Childhood comrades fought side by side in the county regiments, and for this comradeship many communities paid a desperate price: the annihilation of a company could mean the instant extinction of two generations of a village's manhood. From the Dales and the fells of the North Riding of Yorkshire four men out of every ten went marching to war with the famous 'Green Howards'. The second battalion of the regiment entered the first battle of Ypres 1,000 strong and came out of action with but 250 survivors. In the futile attack on Auben Ridge in May 1915, 11,000 British soldiers died: only 70 men survived from the Leicestershire Yeomanry; the Northamptonshire lost 560; the 2nd Sussex, 551; the York and Lancasters, 425, and the 2nd East Yorkshires, 383. At Loos in September 1915 the 2nd Royal Warwickshires went into battle with 667 soldiers and at the end of the day there were no officers and only 140 men still alive. The first four weeks of the Battle of the Somme in 1916 provided *The Times* with 68 closely printed columns listing the names of dead private soldiers.

E. P. Brand, living in the Norfolk Fens, remembered:

> all good horses were commandeered. Grandfather's horse – a fine chestnut – was taken. They came and said 'We want so many horses'. Then there were the

Volunteers, who were trained locally. When war was declared 150 to 200 left the village to go off and fight, and from then on those that did not volunteer were called up, and others as they became eighteen, and there were a lot who went when they were only seventeen. As you know they were slaughtered in the Battles of the Somme, Hill 60 and Vimy Ridge, and every week there was sad news for some family. I recall two families who lost two sons, and the total of those from Warboys who lost their lives was fifty-two, many more than in the Second War.

After the church, the most common village landmark is not the green, the pump or the mill, but the war memorial.

Poets, writers and artists have eulogized the lost generations, but perhaps the memorial which the countrymen would best appreciate was composed in the medium that was their own favourite mode of expression. Written long after the events, to the traditional tune of 'The False Bride', 'Dancing at Whitsun' tells of a village where only the women survive to dance at Whitsun. An aging war widow left with only her memories walks through a deserted countryside, where

> *The fields they stand empty, the hedges grow free,*
> *No young men to tend them or pastures go see,*
> *They are gone where the forests of oak trees before*
> *Have gone to be wasted in battle.*

> *Down from the green farmlands and from their loved ones*
> *Marched husbands and brothers and fathers and sons.*
> *There's a fine roll of honour where the maypole once stood*
> *And the ladies go dancing at Whitsun.*

During the war, while the arguments between the agricultural departments and the War Office (which was ready to accept men without asking questions) rumbled on, the farmer had been compelled to use women, children and machines to replace the men and the requisitioned farm horses. After the war, there were fewer jobs and fewer men to fill them. War service had broadened the horizons of the village survivors and many were reluctant to return to a life on the land. Two more decades of mechanization, farm crisis and rural unemployment brought the village to its knees. In most parts of England the farm depression between 1922 and 1936 was the worst within living memory, and farm wages which had climbed to £3 per week by the end of the war fell to £1 16s. Cottages stood empty, hand tools rusted on their hooks, and for the first time in its history, the English village had lost its role; it was depopulated, weak and bewildered. It did not die, as we shall see in the final chapter. The destruction of the peasant community which had begun with enclosure and the flight of the small farmer ran its course, and the modern village which emerged from the ashes of the old is more prosperous, more comfortable and more secure, but it has lost its ancient role and lives in bondage to the town.

The outstanding feature in the saga of recurring village crisis is the pitiful weakness of the people. Because they lived in crowded hovels, the villagers suffered more when plague stalked the land. When their homes were torn down to clear the way for sheepruns, the villagers did not rise up and fight, they crept away. Later they did not rally and stand to protect their common lands, they muttered and suffered; and when the guilty politicians and warlords stretched an inferno of mud and death across Europe, the villagers marched in – no more blindly than the townsfolk, but in their small communities their deaths left disastrous gaps.

On the rare occasions when, starving and humiliated, country people rose up in anger, their attempts at revolution were pitifully uncoordinated and unconvincing and they did not seize the power that was theirs for the taking in a country of peasants. But then the peasant was not a radical: left to himself he was as conservative as could be. All he and his family asked for was to be left alone, to work a little land of their own in a time-honoured manner. This simple goal remained beyond the reach of most.

When then was the Golden Age of the English village? Indeed, was there ever such an age? It might have been glimpsed in the Saxon period; it might even have been grasped but for the sapping wars with the Danes. Perhaps the village farmers were preparing for the Golden Age when they undertook the Great Rebuilding, although plague still threatened, the sheep still advanced and the fall of the small farmers was not many generations away. There never really was a Golden Age: it was adversity, poverty and mutual dependence that moulded the communities of the English village. For what did the fortunate villager do when enclosure provided him with a compact productive holding and set the seal on his prosperity? Did he care for the less fortunate friends of his childhood, the men whose grandfathers had toiled shoulder to shoulder with his own? He did not. He moved out of the village to a smart new farmstead and set about buying out his weaker neighbours.

It was hardship and the lack of opportunity that brought the villagers together, taught them how to pool their meagre resources and find pleasure in the free communal arts of conversation, music and dancing. Prosperity for some brought the community little but rack-renting, clearances and slavery.

106 This memorial at Sledmere in Yorkshire was erected by Sir Mark Sykes in 1919 to commemorate the company of wagoners which he had raised from local men. Note the emotive caricature of the Germans and the blithe imperturbability of the English faces.

6 · The good old days?

THE ENGLISH VILLAGE of the century which preceded the Great War was as different from the modern rural settlement as it was from the village of open fields and peasant farming which had gone before it. It was, on the whole, the home of the families of hard working and low-paid farmworkers and of the tradesmen who provided them with goods and services, a parochial and thrifty community which still retained a measure of the communal spirit that had existed in the days before enclosure. It is of special interest and more easily recreated because there is still today a handful of old villagers who can recall vividly what the good old days or the bad old days – opinions vary – were like. The Victorian and Edwardian village strikes a chord of romance in the minds of those who decry the modern world with its unwholesome food and unfriendly suburbs and who envy the simple sufficiency of the country household with its stone-ground flour, family pig and vegetable plot. At the same time, it is remembered by some, who can recall the dictatorship of the landowner and hardships of child labour, with bitterness. A word of caution, however: these 'survivors', whether speaking today or recorded in books like *Lark Rise to Candleford* and *Akenfield*, are, as John Hunter (a countryside officer with Essex County Council) points out, 'witnesses describing a countryside in the throes of deep depression. It is the landscape of the landless labourer, rural poverty and the lonely trek to the workhouse. This gives a false impression of the rural economy before the arrival of North American grain and New Zealand lamb.' The village of a century ago possessed both the qualities which the romantics admire and the poverty and suffering which affront the upholders of social justice.

As we have seen, enclosure and the decline of the small farmer undermined many of those self-sufficient and independent-spirited members of the community, reducing most villages to reservoirs of labour for the prosperous farmers of the parish. For a while there was a considerable demand for the labour of the fallen yeoman, the broken smallholder and the squatter displaced from the common, but as the years rolled by, the community offered more labour than farming could absorb, particularly as falling profits forced the farmer to pare down his workforce, substitute the seasonal labour of women, children and itinerant gangs for the fully-employed worker, and cast an appraising eye over the new-fangled contraptions of mechanized farming. With an over-supply of cheap, un-unionized labour on offer to a farming industry which faced its own problems of fearsome foreign competition and a blustery climate, it is not surprising that the essence of much Victorian village life was to be found in poverty and servitude. These however did not produce a drab existence; rather, they encouraged the villager to find his delights not in material possessions and the comforts of home but in the enjoyment of the company of others, in song and dance, craft and workmanship and the beauties of the countryside. They reinforced the family spirit in the over-large cottage households where every member had to contribute a share to the slender family budget. Home brewing and home baking, the breathless excitement of midnight poaching, the coddling of the family pig, rug-making and patchwork, in fact all the pursuits which have captured the imagination of the romantic were the products not of choice or an unhurried existence, but of necessity.

Power in the land, power over the lives of the people of the village, lay with the farmers, as employers, the squires, as employers and as magistrates, and the parsons, as representatives of God – and too often of the squire and establishment as well. Not every village had a squire, some had more than one,

107 'Parish Relief', a caricature of 1833: the snuff-taking woman is reproved for her extravagance by the snuff-taking magistrate.

and some squires had more than one village. They were lords of their little kingdoms, and in the words of the late eighteenth-century writer John Scott, 'Happy is the parish that has a good king.'

The governors of the countryside for much of the period were the Justices of the Peace: usually squires and large landowners, they were selected by the Lord Lieutenant of the county acting on the advice of the grander gentry of the shire. They wielded a formidable array of powers, including justice (which was sometimes dispensed in the country home of the squire magistrate), they were responsible for the upkeep of roads, bridges, workhouses and prisons, and they levied the rate. Until the Local Government Act of 1888 created county councils to supersede the old system with its blending of despotism and unpaid public service, the villages experienced a form of government which was cheap but tailored to the outlook of the prosperous squire. Until 1834, when a national system of Poor Law Guardians was set up, the Justices also administered relief to the poor. The Boards of Guardians were to prove severe, however (see below, p. 160): it is significant that one argument for their creation had been that squires were too generous to the destitute souls of the village.

Government at local level was carried out by the Vestry (so called because it originally met in the church vestry), which was the ancestor of the elected parish council, eventually instituted in 1894. Only ratepayers had a voice at meetings, and some villages had a Select Vestry with a more restricted membership. The Vestry was dominated by the partnership between the squire and the parson; below them came the parish officers – two churchwardens, often substantial local farmers who kept a close watch on the village and its follies, a couple of constables, the Overseer of the Poor (who until 1834 was responsible for the employment and support of the poor and would attempt to keep out or eject

108 *Left* Thomas Nuthall, shown in this eighteenth-century portrait by Nathaniel Dance-Holland, looks like a masterful squire with typical interests.

109, 110 *Left and above* The poacher's world. A mantrap design of the early nineteenth century is described as 'humane', because it lacks the bone-gripping spikes of other designs. James Campbell's painting of 1858, *The Poacher's Wife*, shows the strain of poverty on a family. In both cases the poachers have been caught with hares.

Humane Man Traps

non-native paupers), and finally the Surveyor of the Highways who had powers to exact six days' labour per man per year on road maintenance from a reluctant population. Often one man held more than one office, and there was not always great competition for service in a role which exposed the holder to the grumbles and resentment of his fellow villagers.

A modern civil police force was organized by Sir Robert Peel in the capital in 1829, but it was not until 1856 that such a force became universal, and up till then law enforcement was a matter for the amateur, unpaid constables. The constable was often a fearsome character: armed with a short staff and with the stocks and the poky village lock-up at his disposal, he dealt rough justice to those who had caused offence to the law or to the squire. However, if he was wise he brought discretion to work, for he was appointed on a yearly basis and was a man of the parish. Some of the healthy respect with which the villagers regarded their constables rubbed off on the village policeman when he made his appearance after the mid-century.

For a spirited account of what a villager might think of Vestry rule we can turn to the 1893 reminiscences of the radical Warwickshire parson, the Rev. F. W. Tuckwell: 'He hates, with a bitterness sometimes personal, always official, employer, magistrate, guardian, parson; he craves with passionate earnestness emancipation from his tyrant and control of his affairs.' But other villagers, while they hated the farmer who was tight-fisted and bullying, revered tradition and noble birth; and whatever else the squire may have been, at least he was a gentleman.

The problem for the people of the village was that they depended so much upon the character and attitude of their little king, and if they had a rogue or an ardent sportsman in the hall there was little they could do about it. If hunting was

111 The mistress of Cusworth Hall in Yorkshire, with her staff, ready to entertain the local regiment to tea in 1911.

his fancy then heaven help the growing crops when the hounds were in full cry, and if shooting was his sport – and it usually was – then there was little hope for the poacher who faced him across the courtroom. On some of the larger estates the gamekeepers formed small armies, complete with livery and arms. On smaller estates the gamekeeper was an isolated figure, in some ways as pathetic as the villagers that he persecuted. The nature of his work placed him outside the community both physically and socially. He was the upholder of game laws which half the village flouted – at considerable personal risk – and nobody respected. With reason or not, the villagers took pleasure in believing that the keeper was the biggest and greediest poacher of all, a traitor both to his village and to his master. When he passed by, gossiping groups of men would fall suddenly silent and follow his passing with sullen eyes. The agent was much more despised than the master: the keeper had often been born into the village community but had become a spy on his fellows, the instrument of a harsh and unjust code. It is estimated that between 1833 and 1844 no less than 42 gamekeepers were killed. The culprits were chiefly gangs of poachers from the towns who were quite prepared for a shoot-out; but since the keeper himself was often prepared to shoot, and since capture could mean transportation, some village poachers would in desperation turn to murder.

Few landowners ever attempted to understand the simple causes that drove men to risk their all by poaching, and the squire who had dropped a brace of rabbits outside a cottage door in the morning might think nothing of having his keepers set lethal mantraps in the afternoon. In his almost paranoid obsession with game, the squire had an ally in the law. After 1816 the harmless poaching of a mere rabbit could result in transportation for seven years for the villager caught carrying nets at night. Mantraps and spring-guns that were as likely to kill a child gathering berries as a hungry poacher were legal until 1827, and only the squire and his eldest son were allowed to kill game under any circumstances until 1831. Some rural benches even today seem to have more concern for the battered pheasant than for the battered wife.

The iniquity of a system which so favoured the squire over his tenants was bitterly attacked by the reforming parson Sydney Smith (1771–1845): could there be such a mockery of justice, he asked, as an Act of Parliament 'pretending to protect property, sending a poor hedge-breaker to gaol, and specially exempting from its operation the accusing and judging squire, who, at the tail of his hounds, has that very morning, perhaps, ruined as much wheat as would purchase fuel for a whole year for a whole village?'

On the credit side, however, it should be remembered that before the nineteenth-century reforms of local government, the countryside would not have been administered without the voluntary and unpaid efforts of the squirearchy, whose members were sometimes intensely committed to public service, giving generously of their time to service as Justices of the Peace, inspecting schools, prisons and workhouses, administering lunatic asylums and generally accomplishing hosts of unexciting and burdensome tasks which would otherwise have gone undone. There were many squires who performed willingly a wider and more genuine range of tasks than noble duty had expected of their feudal forbears. While some grander squires chose only the company of their equals, there were others who played a leading and charitable role in village affairs, organizing festivities, providing generous prizes for the victors of hurly-burly village games like pig catching and barrel rolling. Patronizing the squire

112 This engraving of 1843 satirizes the discomforts and secular atmosphere of a sermon in the unreformed Anglican Church. The vicar or rector, royal arms above his head, preaches from a three-decker pulpit to a congregation some of whom have to turn their backs to him. The medieval font has degenerated into a hat stand.

almost invariably was, but without their patron many villages would long have lacked schools, been without church bells or wells, sports, and many of the small gifts which gave substance to a festival.

A stereotyped image of the country squire would be misleading. Some, unlike the fictional Sir Roger de Coverley, were more interested in land and stock improvement than in fox-hunting, and others, like Mr Bennet in *Pride and Prejudice*, were more bookish than countryfied. The squire was by no means a fixture in the English landscape; and the small farmer squire had almost disappeared by the nineteenth century, along with many other small farmers. Contrasts in attitude existed within the squirearchy: Squire Frampton of Moreton Hall in Dorset, as we shall see, led the magistrates who hounded the Tolpuddle labourers into transportation in 1833, but in 1846 Richard Sheridan, his heir by marriage, wrote to *The Times* to state his sympathy for the lowly-paid farmworkers of the county. Describing his visit to a cottage, he wrote,

> when I found that the meal they were about to partake of consisted merely of a small quantity of horse beans and turnip-tops boiled in water I asked the wife of one of the men what she intended to prepare for her husband's supper when he returned home from his hard day's work, and her answer was, in the most cheerful tone, 'Why, bless you, Sir, horse-beans and turnip-tops'.

The role of the Church of England parson in the affairs of the community was one which caused a number of incumbents to question and to attempt to redefine their positions. It was also one which caused hosts of villagers to forsake the church of the establishment for the Nonconformist chapel. The parson should have been an impartial figure, ever ready to offer comfort and encouragement to the village household in times of distress. Too often he was so securely rooted within the ranks of the privileged that he lived the same life, espoused the same causes and expected of the village the same tokens of deference as did the squire himself.

The hierarchy of the Anglican Church in the early nineteenth century still made no great attempt to dissociate itself from the abuses of privilege; the extreme example of the Bishop of Ely must have cost the Church dearly in humble adherents. In 1816 enclosure had brought starvation to the unemployed farmworkers of the bountiful Fen farmlands, and starving families stood by as barges removed the grain harvest for sale in London at five guineas a quarter. In a hamfisted demonstration of frustration the unemployed Fenmen mounted punt guns on a farm wagon and marched on Ely carrying scythes, spades and billhooks; after a great deal of shouting they marched back home and only a few windows were damaged. The army was called into the Fenlands to scour the district and eventually eighty men were ferreted out. In the final exercise of a temporal power that predated the feudal era, the Bishop of Ely appointed judges, with the result that seventy men were sentenced to long terms of imprisonment, five were transported for life and five were publicly hanged. So deep was the breach that the Bishop had made between himself and his flock that he had great difficulty in finding anyone prepared to lend a cart to transport the poor victims to their fate. The Bishop then processed to the cathedral behind his ceremonial sword to the singing of 'Why do the Heathen Rage'. The local Christians raged too, wondering no doubt how a church of Christ could have so lost sight of its most basic principles, and the village of Littleport was remembered not for its convicts but for its 'Littleport Martyrs'.

The Christian who felt that the Anglican Church had lost touch with its mission and the poor had a choice between Nonconformism and the reform of the Established Church from within. John Wesley had for long attempted to 'live and die a member of the Church of England', but the split could not be avoided. During the eighteenth and nineteenth centuries a great many village congregations became polarized between the church and the chapel, the one building a symbol of deep medieval devotion, the other, more austere, a symbol of a loss of trust in the establishment. Methodism often attracted the more independent spirits of the working community, who were not afraid to display their disillusion with the established order and Vestry government.

Villagers still choose between church and chapel; but while the visit of John Wesley to a village is still faithfully recalled, and the sermons of the Wesleys and Whitefield retain a freshness for many Methodists, the social connotations of church and chapel have largely disappeared. Whereas in the past the Nonconformists could see the sentiments of the Church of England summed up in the lines

God bless the squire and his relations
And keep us in our proper stations

the modern choice is a purely personal one – whether, as they say in Yorkshire, you prefer to get your religion at the pub (the church) or the off-licence (the chapel).

The hungry village family was not always without a sympathizer in the vicarage. We have met two parsons with social consciences, F. W. Tuckwell and Sydney Smith; another was Charles Kingsley, best known as the author of *The Water Babies*, but first and foremost, in his own mind, the rector of Eversley in Hampshire. He managed to proclaim socialist beliefs and campaign for farmworkers' education, science and improved village sanitation without alienating himself from the powers in the community, for when he died in 1875 his funeral was attended by labourers, gypsies, Nonconformists – and the squire and the Master of the Foxhounds. The Rev. Tuckwell also rejected the notion that the mission of the Church was to teach the poor to be content with their lot and in 1886, in spite of his Bishop's displeasure, he did something practical to improve the situation of his flock and divided his 200-acre (81-hectare) glebe farm into twenty smallholdings.

The members of the Vestry government did not always present an entirely united front, for the issue of tithes sometimes drove a wedge between landowners and tenants large and small and the Church. In the medieval period some parsons used the fearsome bludgeon of excommunication against the tithe defaulter, and most parsons remained diligent in the pursuit of their lawful tenth. Some of the sting was taken out of the conflict by the Tithe Commutation Act of 1836 which substituted a rent charge for payment in kind, and after 1891 the charge fell only on owners and not on tenants. Tithe wars erupted again in this century, when several farmers with uncharacteristic radicalism attempted to barricade their farms against the takers of tithes. In 1925 the levy was stabilized; in 1936 it was abolished, and former tithe payers now contribute to redemption annuities which will cease in 1996. Sentiments as old as Anglo-Saxon England are expressed in the words of the traditional harvest song introduced into Purcell's *King Arthur* (1691):

> *We've cheated the parson, we'll cheat him again,*
> *For why should a blockhead have one in ten?*

The ordinary villager was long denied any role in the political affairs of his country or community. Although urban workers received the Parliamentary vote in 1867, the agricultural worker was not enfranchised until 1884. Four years later, as we have seen, the creation of elected county councils left the hitherto omnipotent squire Justices as simple magistrates, although the Vestry survived until 1894. In the General Election of 1885 villagers defied squire and parson by voting Liberal. In so doing, some faced dire consequences: a number of farmers had forced their employees to sign a pledge that they would vote for the Tory candidate. A cottager at Alderminster in Warwickshire was given notice to quit in 1895 because he had offended the squire by offering himself as a council candidate.

Trade unions, concerned less with political rights than with the fundamental need for a living wage, were never very successful among farm workers, and they got off to a tragic start, with the case of the 'Tolpuddle Martyrs'. In 1833 progressive sentiments were taking root in England: this was the year in which slavery was abolished in the British possessions and the Oxford Movement was established to attempt the reform of the Anglican Church. But what amounted to slavery was not entirely abolished in the English countryside, and the farmworkers of Dorset were amongst the most enslaved, receiving a weekly wage of 7s., which was 3s. below the normal minimum agricultural wage in the south.

Attempts by the Tolpuddle labourer and Methodist lay-preacher George Loveless to obtain a higher wage for his fellow workers by bargaining in an open meeting which was presided over by the local squire and Justice James Frampton failed to produce an answer. Loveless prevailed upon the vicar, Dr Warren, to visit local farmers and speak for a minimum farm wage of 10s.; this the Rev. Warren did, but when the promises were dishonoured he refused to pursue the matter further. Loveless appealed to the trade union movement for help. Two delegates visited the village, and in 1833 the Grand Lodge of Tolpuddle of the Agricultural Labourers' Friendly Society was formed, with members swearing the customary oaths of loyalty to the union and to each other and following the normal code of secrecy. As the Tolpuddle union gained in membership disquiet grew amongst the local landowners: having collected the names of suspected members, they approached the local magistrates – who, as landowners themselves, were scarcely impartial in the matter. Squire Frampton had already crossed swords with the Dorset workforce, swearing in special constables during agitations for higher wages in 1830, when his hall was only saved from burning by constant patrols of the Dorset militia.

Squire Frampton made his concern known to Lord Digby, the Lord Lieutenant of Dorset, who communicated with the Whig Home Secretary, Lord Melbourne. He received in reply a hint that legislation concerning secret oath-taking might be invoked against the union members. Armed with this information, the Dorset magistrates placed a proclamation in the county newspaper and posted notices around Tolpuddle. The gist of it was that the oath-

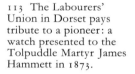

113 The Labourers' Union in Dorset pays tribute to a pioneer: a watch presented to the Tolpuddle Martyr James Hammett in 1873.

takers were liable to transportation for seven years unless they came forward and declared their full knowledge of the union and its doings to the authorities within four days. Before the four days had fully elapsed six members received an early morning visit from the Dorchester constable and were marched off to gaol. Not surprisingly, the magistrates, who could not impose heavy sentences themselves, sent them for trial at Dorchester Assizes.

The Act under which the labourers were tried had been passed in 1797 to deal specifically with the mutiny of the *Nore* and had remained on the statute books by an oversight. If it was applicable to the Tolpuddle labourers, then by implication not only were all trade unions illegal but so too were societies like the Freemasons and Oddfellows which also included secret oaths within their rituals. The Judge was a prominent Whig sympathizer and friend of Lord Melbourne and he delivered what must have been among the most partisan of summings-up ever heard in an English court; when the obedient jury returned a 'guilty' verdict, Judge Williams sentenced the farmworkers with the remarkable words, 'I am not sentencing you for any crime you have committed or that it could be proved that you were about to commit, but as an example to the working-classes of this country.' The sentence was seven years transportation.

Three years later the 'Tolpuddle Martyrs' received the King's pardon, by which time half a million people had signed a petition for their release, and around 40,000 demonstrators had marched in London and 10,000 on Newcastle Moor. On their return from Australia, after brief stays in Essex five of the Martyrs emigrated to Canada; only James Hammett went back to Tolpuddle, where he died a blind man in the workhouse. The case of the Tolpuddle Martyrs aroused national feelings against the injustices of village society, exposed the unsavoury behaviour of the landowners and magistrates and also focused attention on the role of religion in social matters, not least because five of the six Martyrs were Methodists, two of them lay-preachers.

Although the Tolpuddle labourers had attracted national interest to their cause, unions of farmworkers did not spring up throughout the country, and eventually the most successful of the nineteenth-century organizers, Joseph Arch, came to believe that the answers to the problems of the farmworker were more likely to be found in Parliament than in union organization. Arch, too, was a Methodist lay-preacher; he established a small union in his native Warwickshire and saw it expand very rapidly to become the National Agricultural Labourers' Union in 1872. By 1874 the union had 86,000 members, but then the membership fell away as rapidly as it had grown and at the turn of the century the union disappeared. When Free Trade and falling prices brought the near collapse of English farming in the late nineteenth century, there was little than anyone could do to turn the tide in favour of the village farmhand.

At various times during the century, desperation drove small bands of villagers into futile gestures such as rick-burning and the smashing of farm machinery. These night marauders were never the equal of the forces of special constables and militia which were swiftly mobilized when real trouble threatened, and they had neither clear aims nor organization. Mysterious midnight raiders also emerged like latter-day Robin Hoods, threatening much but accomplishing little. The most notorious of these was 'Captain Swing', whose supposed exploits were reported throughout the country. He was never caught; perhaps there were several self-appointed Captains Swing, pretenders to a title which struck real fear in the hearts of some squires and farmers. Lawful and

114 Starving workers, bullying squire, burning ricks: woodcut from a pamphlet purporting to be *The Life and History of Swing, the Kent Rick Burner, Written by Himself.*

just or illegal, none of the efforts of the village workers did very much to raise standards of living, and at the end of the century the choice for most villagers was between poverty and emigration.

Questions of working conditions, education and freedom were secondary to the central issue of wages, for it was income that determined whether a village household would prosper or starve. The wages of a nineteenth-century village labourer can only be judged in relation to their purchasing power, and fortunately a few household budgets have survived. Neither wages nor most prices rose drastically during the century. A glimpse of conditions on the eve of the nineteenth century was provided by the Rector of Barkham, who calculated a typical budget for a Dorset village family of six in 1795. This was the year in which the Berkshire Justices, meeting at Speenhamland, resolved to pay to labourers in addition to their wages an allowance that was linked to the price of bread and varied with the size of the family concerned, a system that was widely copied throughout the country. We are not told the income of the Dorset family concerned, but with child wages at around 3*d.* a day, it might be less than 10*s.* a week.

	s.	d.
bread and flour	6	0
yeast and salt		2
bacon and other meat		8
tea, sugar, butter, cream		10
cheese		3
beer		2
soap, starch, blue		1
candles		2½
thread, etc.		0¾
potatoes and barley		2
	8	7¼

As well as showing the slender nature of the family budget, where luxuries had no place, an account such as this helps us to recreate a picture of cottage life, with the housewife using yeast and flour – and presumably faggots gathered in the countryside – for home-baking, and darning the family garments by candle light. As for these garments, the Rector tells us that 'Clothes they get as they can, and the children go nearly naked.'

More precise information on conditions at the end of the nineteenth century is provided in the reports of the Labour Commissioners for 1893–94. The example of a village family at Letcombe Regis in Berkshire is fairly typical. There are seven children in the family, and one of them is at work earning 5s. a week, while the father earns a weekly wage of 10s. It is clear that with the regular weekly shopping complete, only 7½d. remains to be saved towards the periodical purchase of essentials such as clothing and shoes. The basic family diet remains unchanged, and the only luxury is the husband's tobacco – probably of the chewing variety. The house is lit by oil lamps and the family is obliged to pay for its fuel. Here is their account:

	s.	d.
bread and flour	6	0
butter	1	0
cheese		7
bacon	1	3½
sugar		6
tea		5½
salt and pepper		1½
lard		8
firing and oil	1	6
rent	1	6
tobacco		3
soap, soda, starch, blue		6
	14	4½

The family may not have revealed all their secrets to the Commissioners, and with such a slender budget it is difficult to imagine that some of the six remaining children would not have been frequently absent from school, earning pennies by working in the fields.

There can be little doubt that at least when English agriculture reached the peak of its prosperity, around 1870, the farmers could have afforded to pay higher wages. At that time farmers in the West Riding of Yorkshire, who had to compete for their labour with the mill and the pit, were offering wages of 14s. a week, while those in the richer farmlands of Suffolk and Wiltshire were paying only half that wage.

Although we know that the average village family survived on very slender means, the calculation of household income is not as easy as it may appear to be. Even the fully employed farmworker did not normally receive a regular reliable wage. When the weather was bad, he might be sent home without pay; and some workers were hired by the week and transferred to piece work at harvest when their bargaining power was high, so that their incomes rose accordingly. Almost every village had families which did not rely on farm wages entirely, and in many cases it was difficult to say what the main occupation of the father was. Once the harvest was in and work on the land became scarce, many Norfolk labourers would enlist for the winter in the Yarmouth herring fleet. After the meadows had been stripped and the hay stacked, the worker in the Broads might turn to reed-cutting, then eel-catching and duck hunting; when the Broads froze he would gather ice to sell at the fishing ports; and spring might find him collecting the eggs of marshland birds to sell to naturalists. The thatcher might turn harvest labourer in the summer, taking advantage of the higher farm wages at a time when his rick was low and his straw old, while the farmworker might turn to thatching, ditching or hurdle-making in the winter.

Labourers' incomes were often at their lowest in counties like Suffolk where the land was richest and farmed to the full, while in the less valuable forest and heathlands the local environment often offered attractive opportunities for part-time and winter work, G. E. B. Eyre, writing in 1883, documented the rare case of a New Forest farm labourer who made the remarkable transition from employee to farmer. By early morning and evening work at hurdle-making and bark-stripping for the local tanners he had managed to save £100 before he married. He then worked as a woodman and underkeeper, saving nothing but keeping his nest egg and interest intact while his wife took in washing. At forty-five, with his children now independent, he rented $2\frac{3}{4}$ acres (about 1 hectare) of meadow and vegetable garden and bought a cow and pigs. By landwork, jobbing and the sale of his calves he was able to buy a second cow and more pigs and to take on another $5\frac{1}{2}$ acres (about 2.2 hectares). He then used his original savings to rent a 35-acre (14-hectare) farm, and in three years he had a small dairy herd, a horse and foal and two sows, and was earning £16 per annum from the sale of pigs. He was clearly an unusually gifted and energetic man, but even so his endeavour was only made possible by the wide range of part-time occupations that the New Forest made available.

115 A Norfolk couple setting traps for eels in the Broads in 1886.

116 A family gathering faggots on the waste in the late eighteenth century (watercolour by Paul Sandby).

117 Charcoal burning in the New Forest.

The village worker with several strings to his bow clearly had more independence than his neighbour. His work might take him away from home for weeks on end: in the 1860s six or eight villagers from Filkins in Oxfordshire would leave for the summer haymaking in the rich meadows of Middlesex; then they would work their way homewards doing hoeing for market gardeners, arriving in Wantage for the early autumn grain harvest. The majority of village workmen, however, were bound to particular masters and were pleased to be busy from dawn till dusk and beyond, unpaid lay-offs being greatly feared. There was little time left for casual jobbing, and the bit of extra income that might be crucial to family welfare was contributed by the poorly paid labour of wife and children.

Few families could afford to support a shirker, and most cramped cottages contained a close-knit unit bound together for collective survival. Poverty was the enemy that could break a family, consigning its members to separation in the workhouse. In 1838 the writer William Howitt expressed his forebodings:

> the poor have their objects of admiration and attraction; their domestic affections and their family ties, out of which spring a thousand simple and substantial pleasures ... Yet our New Poor Laws have aimed a deadly blow at this blessed security ... every poor man's family is liable, on the occurrence of some chance stroke of destitution, to have to their misfortune, bitter enough in itself, added the tenfold aggravation of being torn asunder and immured in the separate wards of a Poverty Prison.

Neither the powerful nor the powerless in rural communities could afford to do without child labour. The children were given not the easiest tasks, but those which did not merit even the low wages paid to the adult worker. On the eve of the Education Act of 1870 a report was compiled for the Agricultural Employment Commissioners on the nature of child labour in Norfolk, Essex, Sussex and Gloucestershire. It showed that in January the children in wooded areas could be found shaving hop poles and cutting sticks; in February there was widespread work in stone picking and setting beans and peas; in March they were out bird scaring and setting potatoes; April and May found them bird scaring and weeding the corn; in June there was haymaking and the backbreaking task of singling or thinning out turnip seedlings, which continued into July when children were used to scare the birds from the ripening corn, cut thistles and pick peas. In August every available hand was needed for the corn harvest, while September saw the children watching over sheep and pigs on the stubbles. The potato harvest of October demanded so much child labour that until quite recently a school holiday was granted. In November the children were out in the bleak fields scaring birds from the winter wheat or gathering acorns for pig food, while December was a time for stone picking, muck spreading, topping and tailing turnips and ditching. There are no tasks in farming more exhausting than stone picking, potato setting and turnip-singling.

Anyone at the turn of the century taking a walk across a February Norfolk landscape in the icy blast of a north-east gale would have seen plenty of pathetic little figures crouched in the mud from which they picked stones, or dashing from the shelter of hedgerows to whirl clackers at largely uninterested rooks. Edith Mary Sargent, born in Essex in 1880, attended school half time and worked the rest, she recalls:

we had to stone pick that was to pick the stones from the stetches and make heaps of them and then they would be carted in a tumble [tumbril or cart] marked with chalk and we had to pick a load for 1/6 and then we picked up acorns and sold them at 1/- a bushal and oh it did take a lot of them to make a bushal then we had to glean in the corn fields . . .

Stone picking, which could only be done in winter and spring when the crops were too short to be damaged, was the least pleasant task of all. It was of little if any agricultural value, but the stones provided material for repairing the parish roads and the pennies that were earned were often spent on new shoes for the children. George Ewart Evans reports that around the village of Blaxhall in Suffolk farmers would allocate a field to one family, and some children would have to pick two or three buckets of stones before going to school in the morning; in the words of an old villager, 'You had to pick stoons at that time o' day if you wanted to keep the children tidy. Some of the children today don't know they're alive – they don't pick stoons or nawthen.'

Parents can scarcely be blamed for sending children to work in the fields when without their earnings there would have been insufficient in the family purse to pay for their food or clothing, even if as a result some children whose ragged coats could not keep out the March winds died of pneumonia and pleurisy, and others were crushed by carts and hooves. A Blaxhall farmer recalled,

you would sometimes see a sight which would make your blood run cold . . . a great lumbering tumbril, weighing a ton or two with two wheels nearly six feet [1.8 metres] high, loaded with manure, drawn by a great Suffolk cart horse as big as an elephant; and conducted by a tiny thing of a boy who can hardly reach the horse's nose to take hold of the rein.

Although in 1880 farmers complained to a Royal Commission that the loss of child labour due to schooling was having an adverse effect on farming, school log books of the late Victorian and Edwardian periods are filled with complaints like the following collected by Jennie Kitteringham:

Henny, Essex, October 1870 There have been few children at School since the Acorns began to fall.

Yalding, Kent, October 1873 Opened School today after the Hopping Holiday. Attendance rather small, children not quite ready to come. Some are waiting to buy shoes.

Roxwell, Essex, September 1880 Attempted to open school but found it impossible to do so for the girls were out gleaning and hop picking.

She points out that 'Where schooling tipped the balance from subsistence to starvation, school was easier to give up than food', and quotes from the log of an understanding schoolmaster of Ermington, Devon, who thought it 'hard to snatch a few pence from a parent's weekly income' by enforcing attendance.

Readers of Hardy's *Tess of the D'Urbervilles* (1891) will be aware of the important role that village women as well as children played in working the Victorian countryside. Trudging across a lowland landscape in October the rambler in 1900 might see a row of Irishwomen down on their knees in the mud gathering potatoes for a shilling a day; returning a month later, he might see a tattered windbreak set up in the corner of the hedge and behind it a solitary

village widow trimming the mud from a heap of frozen swedes. The spring
rambler would meet mothers weeding hedgerows, while in August and
September it was all hands to the harvest, male and female, young and old.

David H. Morgan quotes the wife of a Sussex shepherd who told of life in the
1870s:

> After an early breakfast, I used to start with my children for one of the Hall fields
> . . . Even the toddlers could help by twisting the straw into bands and also by
> helping me tie up my sheaves . . . Many is the time that my husband came round to
> us when his own day's work was done, and we worked together setting up the
> shocks [groups of sheaves set up for drying] by moonlight.

Reminiscences such as this recreate a picture of a landscape which was alive
with human activity in the days before machines, herbicides and pesticides
brought a drab stillness to so much of the rural scene. The rambler of today,

tramping across an eastern landscape of factory fields, grubbed-out hedgerows and barren lanes, may hear nothing but the chugging of a distant tractor and so easily forget that within living memory the countryside teemed with labouring souls. The walker seventy years earlier might have seen instead the members of an itinerant gang strung out stooping across a field, carts and wagons rumbling along the rutted lanes, the master riding out to review his land army, while children with cloth-covered baskets and billycans scamper along bringing lunch to sweating fathers whose purposeful movements are accomplished with an eye for the approach of their master and ears alerted for the lunchtime chimes of the church clock. Turning around he might see the ant-like figures of women and children relieved of sheaf-making to glean amongst the stubble. From the village below comes the tap of the wheelwright's mallet, while up on the skyline the shepherd and his lad plot the downfall of a hare, safe from the eyes of keepers setting snares for weasel and rabbit in a distant coppice.

119 Reapers and overseer (the squire?) in 1784. Stubbs shows work without dirt and sweat; but his workers are dignified individuals, not quaint rustics.

120 Child gleaners at Pinchbeck, Lincolnshire, 1890s. Note the long tufty hand-cut stubble.

121 Mowing team at Wenham Grange, Suffolk, about 1880.

122 Little but time and an improved iron plough separate this ploughman of about 1880 from his medieval counterparts. The photograph conveys some of the pleasures of work in an unspoiled countryside.

Each farmer was the colonel of a regiment of disciplined workers; his lieutenants were the leading carters, cow men and ploughmen, while his wife presided over a small force of dairymaids and servants with the back'us boy the butt of the ridicule and banter that are the lot of those at the bottom of the pecking order. Rowland Parker's study of Foxton in Cambridgeshire shows that in 1901 the 8 farmers of the village employed 45 farmworkers and kept 35 workhorses, while in 1974 there were 6 farmers, only 6 farmworkers, and of course no horses; their places were taken by 19 tractors and 6 combine harvesters. It can be calculated that during the Victorian era, a large farm of 750 acres (303 hectares) would employ a fleet of around three farm wagons and a dozen carts, with a light market cart for shopping and a trap or governess cart, for the farmer's country jaunts or social visits, completing the wheeled armada. With some of the horses doubling between cart work and ploughing there would be around twenty horses in the stables with a large force of carters, ploughmen and horsemen in attendance.

The crowded village fields were never so full of bustling souls as at the time of harvest; this is the time village survivors remember above all, and their abundant recollections allow a clear reconstruction of the scene in the early morning as the gate swings open on a modest 10-acre (4-hectare) wheat field in the reign of Victoria. Ten men of the harvest company enter, reaping hooks in hand, and behind them step their families. The men form a huddle around their chosen leader, the 'Lord of the Harvest', who, often after hours of haggling, would have concluded the 'harvest bargain' with the farmer. Together they debate whether to cut with the grain of the plough or across it; then the men draw lots to determine the strips that each will reap, each hoping to work the headlands where the wheat grows more thinly. Now the work commences: the reapers advance upon the ripened grain, each man sweeps his blade around a clump of stalks and, gripping the clustered ears of grain in his left hand, severs the stalks and bunches them under his left arm, where a sheaf swiftly grows. The sheaf drops and his wife in close pursuit falls upon it; the children twist ties from the yellow stalks, passing them to their mother who binds each sheaf in its golden bond and then stacks it against its fellows to form a shock of drying grain. As the morning wears on and the small birds seek shade in the shortening shadows, the lengthening lines of shocks chart the progress of the reaper families.

Diverted from his toil by panting neighbours and a dulling blade, the Lord calls a halt and stones rasp along the curved reaping hooks, grinding them back to a wicked sharpness. This is the time for a swig of home-brewed ale from the harvest allowance, brewed in advance by the head horseman and waiting in a shady hedgerow. It sparkles and splashes from the keg into the ancient drinking horns which the men favour over glasses and mugs: they say they give the ale a cooler, sweeter taste. Back at work, the stooping men glance swiftly upwards, seeking the arrival of children with the midday lunch. There is no singing and little chatter over lunch, for the men are on piecework and the harvest cannot wait.

As the afternoon draws on, the sun reddens arms and necks, burning over the scratches of the prickly straw. Streaming sweat forms channels through the caking dust and speckling husks that cover the heaving chests, and older men drive themselves to the brink of exhaustion, envying the younger men the vigorous wives who help them. Upward glances reveal a field that is nearly cut, and the patch of upstanding corn quivers with the movement of dashing, quaking rabbits. The field explodes in a flurry of fur, boots, sticks and shouts and before the gutted rabbit corpses have stiffened in the hedgerow, the field is cut. The harvest company, triumphant, marches to the next field, leaving the women to finish shocking the sheaves in the gathering dusk.

In the field nearby, the regular farmhands have been carting and stacking the sun-dried sheaves of the earlier reaping. The carter arrives with an empty wagon and hands it over to the charge of a 'half-man' (a lad on half pay), and two of the older, weaker but wiser men clamber aboard, taking stances on the stud-scraped boards in the middle of the wagon. Two strong young pitchers toss up sheaves, and the older men stack them fore and aft with clockwork motions while growling at the lack of expert timing from the pitchers. The old men rise with the heightening stack, filling the centre space last and then slithering down from the swaying load while the carter heads off towards the rickyard, to return to the field again after another gang have unloaded the sheaves. As evening falls, some men roll stiffly homeward but others return to the fields to help their wives complete the shocks before stumbling silently down towards the village, too numb to avoid the brambles and branches which reach out from the black hedgerows, and too scratched to care.

The harvest ends when the last sun-scorched sheaf from the last field is pitched atop the waiting wagon. Then the horse is off-harnessed and roped to the branch of an oak; a heave and a crack and down crashes the harvest bough, soon to be perched above the shaggy load. A rousing toast from a dozen parched throats to the harvest bough and another to the last sheaf and the harvest is over. Now at last there is time to absorb the mellow early autumn landscape as the basking crowded fields begin to slumber.

The fields are not yet at rest, for as the sun rises the next morning a throng of women and children are waiting at their gates poised for the toll of the gleaning bell before bursting into the fields to scour for fallen ears with stubble-scarred hands. Throughout the country gleaners or 'leazers' enacted the scene described by Flora Thompson at 'Lark Rise', the Oxfordshire hamlet where she grew up during the agricultural depression of the late nineteenth century:

> up and down and over and over the stubble they hurried, backs bent, eyes on the ground, one hand outstretched to pick up the ears, the other resting on the small of the back with the 'handful'. When this had been completed, it was bound round with a wisp of straw and erected with others in a double rank, like the harvesters erected their sheaves in shocks, beside the leazer's water-can and dinner basket. It was hard work, from as soon as possible after daybreak until nightfall, with only two short breaks for refreshment; but the single ears mounted, and a woman with four or five strong well-disciplined children would carry a good load home on her head every night.

Gleaning was an age-old custom which conservatively-minded villagers pursued, sometimes in defiance of the wishes of the farmers. There was no objection to the gleaning of wheat, but barley and beans were a different matter: a free supply of these encouraged the villager to keep livestock, and when the gleaned fodder stocks were exhausted there was always the risk of furtive pillaging of the farm granary. Usually, however, the most a farmer could do was to regularize the custom. By a widespread convention, he would leave a shock standing until he was satisfied that further raking of the stubble was not worthwhile. Then, between five and seven in the morning, a bell would be rung to admit the gleaners to the field. At the end of the day, another bell sounded to exclude them before dusk, lest they be tempted to 'glean' standing corn. Gleaned wheat could supply a winter's reserve of flour, and with bread and flour often accounting for a third to half the family budget gleaning was a crucial task. Little boys whose exploits had incurred the farmer's wrath might be brought to the stubble field disguised in female clothing; and in a few villages, to ensure that the benefits of gleaning should be shared, a 'Queen of the Gleaners' was appointed to enforce the code.

The harvest thanksgiving service had its secular equivalent in the harvest home supper, or in East Anglia the Horkey or Largesse Spending. This occasion for merrymaking, song and fellowship had a long history, and was celebrated by Tusser in the sixteenth century:

> *In harvest-time, harvest-folk, servants and all*
> *Should make all together good cheer in the hall;*
> *And fill out the black bowl of blythe to their song,*
> *And let them be merry all harvest-time long.*

The communal harvest supper paid for by the landowner was gradually replaced in most areas during the 1860s by a cash payment; but a Dorset version was immortalized by Thomas Hardy in *Far from the Madding Crowd* (1874), and the custom, in modified form, survived longer in the south-east. At Hill Farm near Saffron Walden in Essex, one autumn evening at the beginning of this century, the workers organized their own celebration at the Fox Inn, 'where the landlord and the butcher next door contributed meat and ale to add to dishes brought by wives for the big night'.

In the days of the crowded fields, harvest was the closest that the villagers came to a time of plenty, and a farmhand earning 10s. a week might make as much as £4 extra over the harvest period. Overnight the status of the men, led by the Lord of the Harvest, changed from that of servile labourers, jobbers and small tradesmen to that of powerful merchants, free to bargain with the farmer and demand special rates for difficult fields. The bargain was sealed with horns of beer and the gift of a shilling to each man in the company, which often occasioned a pre-harvest frolic in the local inn.

Rates of pay varied from job to job and farm to farm, but at harvest time the casual harvester doing piecework usually came out ahead of the envied regular farmworkers. The reaping and shocking was done in the main by the harvest company men and their families, while the regular carters, cow men and shepherds worked on overtime or enhanced day rates and fitted the carting and the stacking of the harvest around their day-to-day duties. Some tradesmen and jobbers downed tools during the summer months to join harvest companies: leaving their village to cut the early hay, they moved from farm to farm, often earning pennies singing, fiddling and performing morris dances on distant village greens before returning home for the grain harvest. A member of a well-organized and hard-bargaining company might earn in a day what a regular farmworker earned in a week.

Armed with his harvest earnings, the village farmhand might make his one annual visit to the town. At Ashdon in Essex, Ketteridge and Mays record,

Horkey was always celebrated on a Saturday night. With the harvest bonus many

123 *Below* This old butcher's shop, photographed in Robin Hood's Bay, Yorkshire, about 1900, has many similarities with shops of the Middle Ages.

124 Several village shops have retained their Victorian and Edwardian frontages almost intact. Note the painted window blind in this example from Great Coggeshall in Essex.

families went out for the day to Cambridge, Saffron Walden or Haverhill to buy new clothing for the winter. There was never enough money for luxuries but the trip to town was a treat in itself. They trudged to Bartlow station in great excitement for the twelve-mile ride behind the puffing engine.

Heading the shopping list would be a pair of boots for the farmhand: hand-sewn, expensive and strong, they must give good service until the next harvest payment. The horseman would buy a handsome pair of whipcord breeches, the proud hallmark of his trade. If the harvest was a good one, there might be a new coat for the wife, clothes and even sweetmeats for the children. But such forays were rare and exciting and most of the family income was spent on the mundane necessities – flour, cheese, candles and salt – which the village shop provided.

When enclosure stripped away the self-sufficiency of the peasant family and the commons-scouring cottar became a wage-earning farmhand, as we have seen, village stores sprang up to provide the essentials which must now be bought. In the days before village trading was swamped by factory products and

125 A village smithy at Essendon in Hertfordshire, about 1866–70. The business seems to be diversifying by repairing iron fencing and farm machinery.

126 The occupation of the deceased in this grave at Harpley in Norfolk is in no doubt.

then supermarket goods, most communities supported a small company of craftsmen and traders, shopkeepers, blacksmiths, wheelwrights, joiners, cobblers and even tailors. Their trade was essentially local, and it was largely their monopoly until the arrival of cheap public transport and car-based mobility. Pubs and ale-houses were abundant, many of them seedy and but minutely profitable; the now dry Fenland village of Landbeach once supported seven such establishments and Cottenham nearby had over a dozen.

In an age when horsepower came on four legs, the work of the village blacksmith or farrier was indispensable to the farming community. Through his power over fire and metals, the smith has always been a symbol of strength: mythological masters of hammer and iron included Hephaestus, son of Zeus, the Roman Vulcan and the Viking god Thor. In England, smiths of one kind or another are as old as the working of metal itself. Domesday Book mentions 64 village blacksmiths; there were probably many more, along with a host of itinerant smiths, during the early Middle Ages when the blacksmith was a toolmaker, a forger of ploughshares, a maker and mender of weapons and armour and even a maker of locks. As the guild system developed, the specialist branches of the smith's trade were hived off to separate exclusive societies, each with its own mystique, rules and skills.

Although the work of the later village smith revolved around the horse and its needs, he was still much more than a shoer of horses: he made hinges, nails, spits, the handtools of the farmworker and pans for his wife, and provided the wheelwright with metal fittings and iron tyres for his carts and wagons. In the Victorian era, when the bulk of farmwork was done by hand labour, the village blacksmith provided custom-built tools tailored to the whims and the physical characteristics of the particular villager and the local countryside. Landworkers were very particular to use tools which felt right and gave efficient service, and the blacksmith made left-handed scythes, billhooks of specified weights and shapes and spades and ditching tools adapted to the local soil. Each horse received a specially fitted set of shoes, so that a smith finding a shoe might be able to tell from which foot of which horse it had come, and as winter approached horses were sometimes fitted with frost nails to give extra purchase on icy roads. The smithy was often a meeting place for the village menfolk, especially the out-of-work, infirm and elderly who sheltered from the cold around the warm blast of the forge.

Factory-made tools and the demise of the farm horse put paid to most village smithies: in 1851 there were some 112,000 smiths; now perhaps 1,000 survive, shoeing hunters and ponies, repairing farm machinery, and making fancy wrought-iron work, gates and fire-baskets for cottage 'restorers'. While once every village of any size supported a smith, now the epitaph of Thomas Garner, of Houghton in Huntingdonshire, could almost serve for the whole craft that gave England its most common surname:

> *My sledge and hammer lie declined,*
> *My bellows too have lost their wind,*
> *My fires extinct, my forge decay'd,*
> *My vice is in the dust all laid,*
> *My coal is spent my iron gone,*
> *My nails are drove my work is done,*
> *My fire dried corpse here lies at rest,*
> *My soul smoke-like soars to be blest.*

If the blacksmith was the magician, Hercules and fire king of the village craftsmen, the wheelwright or cartwright was certainly the master, for it was in the products of his shop that village craftsmanship reached the summit of its achievement. Forgetting the elegant panel work and chamfered struts of the wagon body, the title of Master of Craftsmen would belong to the wheelwright for the wheel alone, its hub or 'nave' turned from a solid block of elm with spokes of oak connecting it to the 'felloes' of ash, beech or oak which formed the outer rim, each piece meeting in a precision mortice and tenon joint. Wheels were the products not of plans but of a practised eye guided only by a handful of wooden templates. Workmanship and ingenuity blended in the perfection of the wagon wheel: it was not flat, but dished with the spokes sloping inward towards the nave, protecting it from buffeting against gateposts, throwing the rim clear of the wagon sides and countering the sideways stresses caused by the swaying motion of the horse.

In hundreds of English villages, generations of wheelwrights developed cart and wagon designs which embodied local needs and regional preferences. In East Anglia, where an efficient wagon design arrived through sixteenth-century contacts with Holland, the original box-like design was retained and a class of massive wagons capable of moving the heavy grain harvest evolved, permitted by the gentle eastern terrain. The more undulating landscape of the western counties demanded lighter, more manoeuvrable wagons, and there the stylish bow wagon with its shallower body and sweeping curves was developed. Even within a single county village wheelwrights designed wagons to suit local conditions – narrow wheels for the lighter soils, less bulky bodies for the hilly ground. Most counties even had their preferred colour scheme: the wheelwrights of Rutland mixed orange pigments, those of Somerset chose yellow or blue, yellow bodies and red wheels gave striking contrasts in Oxfordshire, while even pink was chosen for many Lincolnshire wagons.

Early in the nineteenth century, village wheelwrights were producing elegant wagons, objects of great functional beauty with sweeping sides and curving outraves to gather a spreading load, each strut finely chamfered to remove every ounce of extra weight. Later in the century, factory-built barge and boat wagons with slab-like bolted sides and iron hubs appeared and the village craftsman was forced to dispense with frills and mimic their cost-cutting designs. Many wheelwrights survived to compete with the factory products until the tractor and the pneumatic type put all wagon builders out of business.

In the smaller village workshops there was insufficient custom to allow the wheelwright to concentrate solely on his main craft, and many took in general carpentry, like the wheelwright of Ashdon in Essex remembered by Christopher Kitteridge:

> Plump, pompous Charles Cooper, part builder, part wheelwright, also functioned as village undertaker, making sturdy coffins of elm and oak which his son Chalky boasted were 'guaranteed to larst a bloody lifetime'. But his main work was the making and repairing of tumbrils, dog-carts, wagons, wheelbarrows; combining carpentry, building, smithing, paint-making and painting.

The village shoemaker and cobbler followed a less prestigious and less profitable trade, reflected in an anonymous twentieth-century curse on a cobbler

128 The beauties of this bow wagon speak for themselves. It stands in the Abbey Barn at Glastonbury, Somerset, of about 1400, under a cruck-framed roof – a demonstration of craftsmanship in wood that spans more than four centuries. The collection is that of the Somerset Rural Life Museum.

which systematically damns the man together with all his tools and materials and includes the lines:

Damn his pinchers and his knife
Damn his half-starved kids and wife.

In the days before the rubber Wellington boot, the farmworkers relied upon good, heavy footwear to keep their feet dry during winter ploughing and ditching, and when they could afford to, they chose the products of the village shoemaker, hand-stitched with waxed thread, above the factory-made boot. Few boots were sold between the annual payments of extra harvest wages, so shoemakers relied on repair work to boots and harness to tide them over. Some were more dependent upon obtaining harvest work than the farmworkers themselves. In some western districts of England there was a preference for wooden-soled clogs with leather uppers, and the clogmakers scoured the countryside for likely sycamores and alders which provided wood that was durable but easily worked.

The range of craftsmen that a village supported depended upon the size of the community and of the area that was served. Where there was a large catchment of consumers one might find specialist farriers, wheelwrights, cobblers, saddlers and thatchers. Where the community was small, wheelwrights became general joiners and undertakers, thatchers doubled as builders or farm labourers, cobblers eked out a living by harness-making and odd jobs, and combinations of jobs abounded. As well as accommodating their own craftsmen, villages were visited by itinerant tradesmen including gangs of chairmakers and solitary tinkers, knife-grinders and hurdle-makers.

Most village craftsmen abandoned the unequal struggle against the factory product decades ago, and the disappearance of the heavy horse put hosts of smiths, saddlers, harness-makers and wheelwrights out of work. The number of English harness-makers rose to a peak in 1904, and then immediately the trade fell into a slump from which it will never recover; by 1939 there were only 1,800

129 An itinerant tinker, 1815. Note the peculiar mobile furnace, items for repair or scrap and the scattered tools. The craft of itinerant metalworking is one that goes back to the second millennium BC.

TINKER

saddlers in England and Wales, and that number was halved by 1960. The village market for hand-made boots and gaiters has long disappeared, few farmers will pay for a hand-made gate or hurdle, and any ham-fisted welder can make a serviceable trailer to follow the tractor at speeds impossible for the horse-drawn wagon. There is still work for the skilled thatcher, but other village craftsmen have been obliged to adapt or go down: many blacksmiths became mechanics, and their sons, garage proprietors; joiners became handymen or undertakers; other craftsmen became bicycle mechanics or electrical repairmen. With the passing of the village craftsman a whole outlook on work, a sympathy for materials and a pride in accumulated skill passed too.

The village craftsman's pride in accomplishment derived not from his being superior as a person to the modern factory worker, but from the nature of his work. The assembly-line worker in a modern vehicle factory may perform the same mindless assembly of a couple of components day in and day out, knowing nothing of the origin of the materials and little of their destination, but the work of, say, a wheelwright was completely different. Apart from four tyres and a few fittings forged by his friend and neighbour the blacksmith, the wheelwright made an entire wagon within his workshop. He was intimate with the materials from which it was made because he had scoured the countryside to obtain them. For the ash which made the felloes he would scorn the lush trees of the meadow, seeking a tougher roadside tree grown hardy from the search for water. He would scan the branches for a suitable shaft-shaped bough, then buy the tree, fell it and season it himself. Each cart or wagon was made to meet the specification of a known farmer, carter or higgler (a travelling dealer), and after it left the workshop the eyes of the village would be on it for the next fifty years; its strengths or weaknesses would be known and talked about, and if the wagon was a good one it would still be seen when the wheelwright was dead and his grandson in his place.

We have met the village womenfolk at work in the harvest fields, but the housewife was much more than a casual farmhand and gleaner. As she had been since time immemorial, she was a mother, cook, baker, brewer, seamstress, and the organizing force in a household which might include a dozen children. She was as hard-working as her husband, and although her work was sometimes warmer and more varied, it was similarly attuned to the changing seasons, with the pre-Christmas brewing, the spring stone-picking, the August harvesting and gleaning followed by the shopping expedition, jam-making and the pig-killing.

The modern abundance of labour-saving gadgets makes it easy to forget the tedious toil that the most routine of chores once involved. As cottager Sylvia Warner recalls, 'Only those who have had to carry water into the house and out can appreciate the beatitude of a tap, and a run away.' On washing day the housewife would begin by hauling pails of water from the outdoors water butt, or the village well or pump, to fill the iron boiling pot which hung from a pot hook up in the chimney. Often this was the same pot that was used to cook the family dinner. If the children were out at school or working in the fields then she herself would be obliged to gather twigs, gorse or turf to light the fire. The fire lit and the water boiling, the clothes were put in the pot and the lid swiftly replaced before soot falling from the chimney could ruin the wash and renew the quest for water. Then while the clothes were drying on the line the housewife turned to other chores, and when they were dry she ironed them using a flat-iron or box-iron heated in the embers.

130 *Left* Stacked turves at a farmstead near Whitby in Yorkshire around 1900.

131 *Below* Peeling osiers for basket-making in Norfolk about 1888, one of many small-scale village industries which still flourished at the time.

Opposite
132 Feeding the chickens at Stainton Hall Farm, east Yorkshire, about 1900. Only a slender fragment of the haystack remains.

133 Gathering and binding the wheat which the men have cut in Norfolk around 1900. All the women favour aprons of coarse sacking, while the hoods which shield their necks from the sun give them an almost medieval appearance.

The woman was tailor and dressmaker to her family. She knitted long, warm socks for her husband, made her own dresses, hessian apron and red flannel petticoat, and used tough unbleached calico to make underclothes for her family, softening the material by hanging it out in the frost. Kate Mary Edwards, a housewife of Ramsey in Cambridgeshire, recalls:

> Women expected to work hard, and I dare say they were just as happy as folks with too much time on their hands. They were forever making and mending and washing and ironing, and took a pride in doing it. They knowed very well what they cou'n't or di'n't conjure up out o' bits and pieces, their families cou'n't have. So sewing and mending took up any spare time they might have had . . . Most women made their husband's shirts. They ha'n't much shape about 'em – just the width o' the material, with the neck cut out and gussets under the sleeves to keep them from tearing. The backs were left with a good long tail to tuck in their trousers, and the bit cut from the shirt front was used for the collar, bands and cuffs, gussets, etc.

Although most proud village families had a tolerably smart outfit for Sunday wear, no piece of material was discarded before it was utterly threadbare: old sheets became napkins and father's old shirt, an apron, while the younger children seldom wore anything but the older children's hand-me-downs. Characteristic village pride and respect for ritual ensured that while few families could afford sufficient clothes to keep out the workday cold, a set of black garments for funeral attire and a corpse outfit of clean white sheets, garments and stockings were kept on hand for a sad occasion. (Shepherds – whose solitary life placed them somewhat on the edge of the village community – were often buried in their smocks, with a tuft of wool in the coffin to show their profession and thus justify the fact that they had worked on Sundays.)

In spite of being sparsely furnished, overcrowded, usually in need of repair and having the under-bed spaces packed with potatoes, turnips and fruit, most village cottages were kept clean. The floor, which might only be of beaten earth given a hard black lustre with ox blood in the older cottages, or otherwise floored with bricks, was often brushed and where possible scrubbed every day. Of carpets there were usually none; where they did exist, they were regularly cleaned by dragging them across the green. The most common floor coverings were home-made rag rugs, where pieces of material perhaps several times re-used came to rest at last. Feather beds were a luxury which only the husband and wife

134 Killing the family pig, 1805.

might enjoy; and the straw-, hay- or oat-flight-filled palliases upon which the children slept needed to have the stuffing constantly replaced to rid them of vermin. In the battle against pests, the walls and ceilings were regularly whitewashed, while the hearth was often swept twice each day and treated with red ochre every week.

The housewife fed her family, and it was no fault of hers that the diet was monotonous and often inadequate. Thousands of Victorian village families existed for years on end on home-baked bread, horse beans, home-made cheese, turnips and swedes, with meat, potatoes and tea as occasional luxuries. However, most cottages had a plot of land or 'yard' attached, and on this bit of land fragments of the old peasant self-sufficiency survived, the fresh vegetables providing a nutritious addition to the family diet. It was the ambition of most families to keep a pig; when one was kept, it was the cornerstone of the cottage economy and the one reliable source of protein. Its health and progress were subjects for anxious discussion, and it was the destination of the few household leftovers and whatever windfall apples, acorns, roots and greens that could be gathered. Breeding and feeding ensured that the pig grew to grosser proportions than the modern streamlined beast, for, unlike today, the choice was for fatty bacon that would 'stick to the chest' in cold weather: one cottage pig killed in Cheshire was over nine feet (2.75 metres) long. A dozen different regional

135 The children in this cottage interior scene by James Collinson, of 1850, are *Answering the Emigrant's Letter*. Not all village children obtained sufficient schooling to master the art of writing. Note the sparse furnishings, the range, the ornaments on the mantel.

179

varieties were kept; the large black of Cornwall, the red Tamworth of the Midlands, the spotted Gloucester and the white banded saddleback of Wessex were bloated monsters compared with the modern landrace pig which supplies the lean cuts demanded today.

The killing of the family pig was a landmark in the cottage year, and while the beast was still alive and well, a proportion of its meat was often mortgaged to tradesmen. Some choice cuts fell to the pigkiller, and then, as the saying was, use could be made of every bit except the squeak. Salted, and hung in the larder, the pig provided the family with whatever meat it might expect to consume for months to come. Except, that is, for the fruits of poaching.

As part of their harvest allowance, some village farmhands might expect to receive a comb of wheat, three bushels of malt and a joint of mutton. The malt was destined for home brewing: most housewives were adept at making the weak ale which was safer to drink than water and the main village family beverage until the Great War. Essential cottage equipment included a brewing tub and 10-gallon (45-litre) copper. Two brewing sessions, at harvest and Christmas, each produced around 20 gallons (90 litres) of ale. The housewife carefully arranged a supply of the yeast which circulated around the village from house to house and from brew to brew, and the children were kept at home to help with the crucial day-long process. The progress of the brew was followed with anxiety, and only when the water, malt, hops and yeast had combined to produce a frothy surface could the housewife go to bed content in the success of her labours. A week later the ale was ready to drink.

Some larger villages supported a baker, in whose oven for a small charge the housewives were allowed to roast the mutton from the harvest allowance. A few, like Papworth St Agnes in Cambridgeshire, had a communal bakehouse, but most of the bread that the cottage family consumed was baked at home in a brick fireside oven using flour which if it was not bought would come from wheat grown in the cottage yard, gleaned, or given as part of the harvest allowance. The homebaked loaf, flecked with charcoal and made from stoneground flour, was more filling than its limp modern counterpart, and so it needed to be, for a hunk of bread and a wedge of cheese sustained the village worker from dawn to dusk.

Cheese was made in many households and also sold locally from the dairies attached to the larger farms. It varied in character according to the local pasture and cheese-making tradition; some places like Stilton, Cheddar, Wensleydale and Derby gave their names to renowned cheeses, while others produced less memorable products, like the Suffolk 'bang', of iron consistency, made from skimmed milk which had had the cream removed for butter-making.

Poverty fell hardest upon the children of the village, particularly when the family was large and the cottage and income small. Kate Mary Edwards remembers that

> Most o' the cottages only had two rooms, so when a couple 'ad as many as ten child'en, you can see how packed in they'd be, though of course there weren't likely to be a time when they were all at home together. As soon as the oldest girls got to eleven or twelve, they'd be packed off to service, and out of a family like that, they'd nearly allus be one or two drowned, or die o' diptheria or something.

Frequently, there were no chairs or stools for the children, who would stand

136 This factory-like building on the little green at Papworth St Agnes in Cambridgeshire is a communal bakehouse, dating from about the middle of the last century.

around the table or squat in corners to eat their meal, while sleeping arrangements were dreadfully cramped. Droves of small children could sometimes only be accommodated by making their bed sideways, while the taller children slept top to tail in another bed. At least one houseproud Fenland mother kept her children in a shed, only allowing them to tiptoe in to bed at night.

While most people today would only resort to an earth closet in extremes of desperation, the backyard privy was often a luxury which only the adults could use with safety, and the children resorted to the garden. Here is Mrs Edwards again:

> There were one family I knowed where there were a 'whull hustle' of little child'en, and in the morning afore they set out for school, they'd all go round to the house end together. If you went past just at that time, there'd be a row o' little white bottoms all sticking up.

Victorian middle-class notions about the importance of personal cleanliness were unable to make great progress in the village, for of course the heating of water was a major operation. Families tended to bath but once a week, if then, and some men often slept in their workclothes.

In concentrating upon the 'typical' village – the community of farmworkers and tradesmen – we have so far overlooked two other kinds, the industrial village and the fishing village. In the century before the Great War, the former was tending to spring up as the personal creation of the industrial magnate, while the latter was in decline. In the years which followed the Industrial Revolution (1760 is the popular timemark for its beginning), purpose-built industrial villages were mushrooming in the north of England, while some older villages provided nuclei for industrial growth. There was nothing new about the presence of manufacturing in a rural setting: village industries were as old as the day when the first potter set up his kiln within a hut stockade. East Anglia is for many the epitome of rural England, but during the medieval period it was England's leading industrial region, and many of its churches and villages grew fat upon the golden fleece of the cloth trade. Thaxted in Essex supported a thriving guild of cutlers; Dedham, which so inspired Constable, had its fulling mills; textile workers abounded in the glorious Suffolk villages of Kersey, Long Melford and Clare. In Derbyshire generations of villagers supplemented their farming by mining, in Cornwall the china clay industry brought greater affluence and independence to several villages, and flax mills offered an alternative to meagre pastoralism in isolated Nidderdale. Across the northern fells farmsteads were built with light and airy upper-storey spinning galleries. There was peat-cutting in several Fenland villages, quarrying at Headington in Oxfordshire, weaving at Aldbourne in Wiltshire, pottery at Beaminster and glove-making at Cerne Abbas in Dorset; the cottages of stocking-makers lined village streets in the valley of the Trent, and dozens of other places had local industrial specialities.

During the late eighteenth and nineteenth centuries, as mechanized factories produced a widening range of products with economies of scale which undercut the goods of the cottage workshops, a number of purpose-built industrial villages were being created by the prosperous mill and coal owners. Sheltered beneath the black pall of industrial success and warmed in the glow of the furnace, some of these villages were destined to grow into towns while others became fossilized, their soot-streaked streets patrolled by the unemployed.

The modern conception of the towns and villages of the Industrial Revolution is one of 'dark, satanic mills', slavish working conditions and blackened terrace barracks. It is easy to forget that the horrors of industrial life were accepted and indeed welcomed by the many farmworkers whose families starved on agricultural wages of 7s. a week and shivered together in poky, decaying cottages, by those who toppled with the decline of cottage industries, were evicted from the commons, or by self-employed industrial workers like the hand-loom weavers of Fixby in West Yorkshire who earned less than 5s. a week working fourteen hours a day and carrying their materials a nine-mile (fourteen kilometre) journey home.

The model industrial village was, for people like these, a progressive haven with luxurious amenities. In Yorkshire there were the textile settlements of Akroydon near Halifax, founded by Sir Edward Akroyd, and Saltaire, Sir Titus Salt's Airedale creation with its library, institute, infirmary, school, almshouses and public park (pl. 15). Bromborough Pool in the Wirral, built by Price's Patent Candle Company, was considered most spacious and advanced by the standards of the time. The Merseyside site had a creek in which the necessary imported oils could be unloaded and from which the by-products of candle making could be exported for use in the nearby textile factories. Since there was

no housing nearby it was provided by the industry, and in 1857, three years after the commencement of work, a community of 460 people was accommodated alongside the factory in the brick and slate cottages of a 'garden village' with only four homes to a terrace, gardens front and rear, a green, school, and an isolation hospital for the anticipated victims of cholera and typhoid.

Not many modern country dwellers would choose to live in what is now the industrial wasteland between Birkenhead and Ellesmere Port, and it is not easy to imagine how, a little over a century ago, the new villagers of Bromborough Pool must have thanked their stars to leave a ramshackle cottage for a house which had no less than three small bedrooms – only two or three members of a family to a room – and a scullery as well as a kitchen. The *Illustrated London News* was interested, proclaiming that 'The fresh air, open space and cottages give the new factory at Birkenhead a great advantage over the parent works.'

Fishing villages clung to the coastline wherever there was a sheltered harbour, and often where there was not. Some were primarily agricultural settlements in which only a minority lived by fishing, or some fished sometimes, and others depended entirely upon the net, pot and line. The coastline of England is seldom at rest and there are many declined fishing villages which nature has deprived of a living. Walberswick in Suffolk is such a place: it rose during the fourteenth century when the harbour of Dunwich lying not far to the south (and destined to topple into the sea) became choked by sand. Walberswick took over some of the trade and fishing, but in due course it too lost its accessibility and in the seventeenth century the shrunken community petitioned to have the greater part of the massive church – which had become but a monument to former prosperity – closed down.

137 *Above left* A Buckinghamshire lace-maker at work.

138 *Above* Spinning galleries like this were commonly found in northern farmsteads where they provided well-lit but sheltered working conditions. This example is in the Lake District village of Troutbeck.

139 Weighing fish at the Cornish village of Polperro in 1893.

In the many small villages which clung to the sides of narrow inlets, fishing was like a cottage industry, fated to collapse in the face of competition from bigger, better organized and better connected brethren. The industry became centralized in a handful of larger ports which harboured the distant-water fleets, had bigger markets, handling and processing facilities and attracted the bigger buyers – and, above all, had gained the attentions of the railway companies. For centuries women from small fishing settlements had peddled fish in nearby towns and villages while their menfolk braved the treacherous sea, but the railways permitted the nationwide distribution of the catch from the large successful ports, killed a hundred little fishing industries and saved a thousand lives.

Other villages flourished as bustling little trading ports with harbours able to handle what one might call the handcarts of the age of sail, but proved unable to cope with the juggernauts of modern shipping: Overy Staithe in Norfolk was one such port, and nearby Thornham another.

As the railway network expanded and the Victorians promoted the benefits of sea bathing, the railways restored the prosperity of a number of fishing villages. In their new roles as tourist resorts many places have, in a sense, never looked back: though some villages continue a small trade in shellfish, shrimps and lobsters, the most profitable catch for most local fishermen is the fare-paying angler.

The decline of the hazardous lifestyle of the open-boat fisherman who sailed from a harbour that might be impenetrable across rock-strewn waters during a storm is not to be mourned. The industry has left behind a legacy of village gems which stud the English coastlines – places like Robin Hood's Bay in Yorkshire, Clovelly in Devon, Polperro, Mevagissey and many more in Cornwall.

We have looked at many aspects of life in the old village and a picture of the villager of Victoria's day begins to emerge, although people were as varied then as they are today and eccentricities abounded. It is already clear that survival demanded a will to work and deep reserves of stamina, but what of the natures, beliefs and attitudes of the old countryfolk?

Firstly, most country folk were good-humoured and affable people, as the Surrey villager George Bourne recalled in 1912:

> In fact, if the folk were not habitually overworked they would be boisterous, jolly . . . The cheerfulness of the cottager rests largely upon a survival of the outlook and habits of the peasant days before the common was enclosed . . . My neighbours are not merely patient and loftily resigned to distress; they are still groping, dimly, for an enjoyment of life which they have not yet realized to be unattainable.

In describing the hardships and disasters that have afflicted the people of the village we are exposing but one side of the coin of rural existence. Nothing has been said of the pleasures of life amongst the beauties of the countryside, the fellowship that blossomed in the fields and village ale-house, or the satisfaction when all was safely gathered in and the free harvest beer sent the harvesters stumbling home through the naked fields, whooping and hollering in the age-old manner, their calls taken up and echoed by the men of the neighbouring villages. There are dozens of traditional songs which tell of days when

140 Artists painting on the beach at Appledore, north Devon, in 1890.

The roses are red and the leaves they are green,
All the bushes and briars are a pleasure to be seen,
And the small birds were singing and changing their notes
Down among the wild beasts in the forest.

and

It was pleasant and delightful on a midsummer morn
And the green fields and the meadows were all covered in corn
And the blackbirds and thrushes sang on every green spray
And the larks they sang melodious at the dawning of the day.

Throughout the villages of England there were musicians who could not read a note of music. With calloused work-gnarled fingers they played dance tunes that would challenge the professional violinist, on fiddles that were sometimes home-made, and they sang songs of love, of work and of sorrow, but few songs of bitterness.

For in spite of their bondage to squire and master, the villagers kept their pride and self-respect and restrained resentment or class hatred; rich men were welcomed in the village because their spending created work. The existence of rich and poor, industrious and idle was accepted with the resignation which was the villager's defence against misfortunes and a barrier to thought: Bourne observed, 'Being born to poverty and the labouring life they accept the position as if it were entirely natural.' The village worker would tend to grumble monotonously about the details of his servitude – an inopportune lay-off, an ungenerous harvest allowance or a missed lunch break – without attempting to attack the foundations of the system itself.

The villager was prone to donkey-like attitudes which undervalued his intelligence, but, like the donkey, he would kick if severely provoked and occasionally he was capable of forceful action. In 1914 the Agricultural and Rural Workers' Union made advances in many parts of England, and in north Essex, Christopher Kitteridge writes,

'Rough Music' at midnight and dawn, ringing of bells, blowing of whistles and thumping of tin cans, announced that the strike had started. About 400 men were defying the farmers. This was 95 per cent of the workforce of Ashdon, Birdbrook, Helions Bumpstead, Ridgewell, Steeple Bumpstead and Sturmer.

There then followed a scene which was completely uncharacteristic of the English village:

Suffragettes came from London to harangue the crowds gathered on Crown Hill; open-air concerts were staged in the meadow behind the Fox Inn where to the accompaniment of a tinny piano and a wheezy accordion the 'Red Flag' was sung time and time again, punctuated by frenzied wavings of red flags and loud cries of 'No Surrender'.

This turned out to be one of the rare occasions when the farmworkers got what they wanted, which was not revolution, but higher wages. It shows that villagers were capable of concerted action but it does not prove a widespread interest in politics, which did not exist.

A candidate for Parliament is not, in their eyes, a servant whom they may appoint to give voice to their own wishes; he is a 'gentleman' who, probably from motives of self-interest, comes to them as a sort of quack doctor, with occult remedies, which they may have if they will vote for him, and which might possibly do them good.

Attitudes to religion varied greatly within and between villages; in some, staunch Methodists were a majority; in others there was a large and devout Anglican flock; but there were plenty like Bourne in Surrey, where, George Bourne tells us, 'the majority of the labouring men appear to take no interest at all in religion'. If the mission of the unreformed Anglican Church was to preach the acceptance of one's lot in life, it was preaching to the converted and simply echoed the peasant sentiment. While attitudes ranged from boldly voiced cynicism to unquestioning belief, there was little depth to religious understanding and it was often reduced to axioms and platitudes like 'There'll come a great day for they to have their Judge, same as we poor people', and 'If the Good Lord meant us to drive around the country us 'ud been borned with wheels.'

This approach towards religion was characteristic of the poor capacity that the average villager had for abstract thought. He or she had as much innate intelligence as the next person and was a master of practical tasks, but tended to dismiss other sorts of problems with biblical platitudes or references to ancient lore. To quote George Bourne again, who wrote on the eve of the Great War and studied the outlooks of his fellow villagers, the countryman 'is entangled in a network of economic forces as wide as the nation; and yet, to hold his own in this new environment, he has no new guidance. Parochial customs and the traditions of the village make up the chief part of his equipment.'

The key to this rural mentality is found in village history: in the days of the open fields the village peasant was well served by the accumulated knowledge of generations of forbears. He could read the land, its beasts and the weather like a book, and communal survival was guided by a rich reserve of folklore. It was safer and wiser to fall back on this knowledge than to pursue an individual course, and in any case feudalism, the collapse of the yeoman and the rise of the landlord left little scope for individualism. But in changing times this reservoir of custom ran dry and the villager, unaccustomed to abstract thinking, was poorly fitted to cope with change. He did not like or trust it, and the experience of enclosure and mechanization and Free Trade gave him every justification. Wedded to the conservatism of his ancestors, he walked naked in the age of industry and technology. He was not adaptable and he fluttered between fatalism and ostrich-like postures. In truth, however, there was little that many villagers could do to improve their lot in the years which followed 1870 but pack up their bags and leave. The village farmhand was an indefatigable worker on land which he understood with a penetrating insight; he just could not understand a world which no longer valued these skills.

7 · Past, present and future

WE LEFT the village on its knees, rotting in the agricultural depression of the interwar years, stripped of its labour force by mechanization, farm bankruptcy and the legacy of the Great War. We know that the English village is now alive and well, but the place that arose from the ashes of war and depression was not the place that the old folk remember; the days of the land wage and cottage economy which had dawned with enclosure were done, and the village had lost all but the vestiges of its role as the home of the landworker. It did not discover a new role; rather, it was itself discovered. It became the rural refuge of the mobile urban worker, and in the process the ancient link between the village and its immediate country setting was broken. The severance was often painful, for the link had been forged before the arrival of the Saxon peasant farmer, beyond the age of the volatile Celt, further than the occupation by the thickset Bronze Age settlers in the misty era of the late Mesolithic hunter-herdsman or that of the Neolithic pioneers, who had begun to cultivate the land soon after their boats first grated on the shingle of an English shoreline more than six thousand years ago.

As the old gives way to the new, comparisons are invited; people want to know whether life was better in the days gone by. The answer will not be found in guidebooks which complain about telegraph poles and enthuse over stocks, for if the village is reduced to an object to be peered at then all its meaning will evaporate. The only people who are in a position to compare the villages of yesterday and today are the survivors who have lived in both – and they are hopelessly divided. No mathematician or cost/benefit analyst can quantify the delights of a harvest home supper or measure them against the advantages of a mobile library service, assess the merits of a thatched but oil-lit cottage against those of an anonymous but well-appointed council house, or compute the physical hardships of the ploughman against the mental anguish of the traffic-bound commuter.

If standard of living is to be our measure, then the modern villager is almost incomparably better off than the Victorian cottager. But if quality of life is our guide then we are thrown into confusion. There is no denying that life was excruciatingly hard for the average village family, with working hours almost double those of today and with wages scarcely stretching beyond the bare needs of subsistence. In the evening of a life of toil which had begun almost at walking age, a couple who had struggled to raise a dozen children and seen most of them through to maturity might face nothing better than the double and swiftly fatal tragedy of removal to a segregated workhouse.

Perhaps remarkably, though, we find that the survivors usually reserve their bitterness for individuals – a hard master, a gamekeeper or a policeman. They do not tell us with one voice that the old days were bad, and many chose to stay in the village when two days' labour on the railways would win a farmworker's weekly wage, in years when the most potent symbol that the army could hang outside its market town recruiting depots was a side of beef.

There was no meritocracy in yesterday's village: stations in life were accepted, and since the farmworker lacked opportunities for self-betterment, he accepted his lot however unjust it may have been; there was no rat race and none of the traumas which accompany the drive to succeed. Diagnoses were different and doctors expensive, but it seems that what little mental instability there was resulted more from village inbreeding than from psychological stress, and suicide was rare. Since high intelligence, even genius, was no sure passport to

wealth and fame, each village workforce contained people of great innate sensitivity and ability, gifts which can be traced in the direct but poetic and moving traditional music, and in the loving and precise work of the bygone village craftsmen.

The farmworker was exploited, exhausted and often underfed; at the same time, his work offered fulfilment and the highly prized respect of his workmates. Ploughmen with heavy feet strained their dulling senses to keep a straighter furrow than the mechanics of farming ever required, while the old and weakening members of a team of reapers drew on their last reserves of strength rather than fall behind in the relentless advance across the wheatfield.

Some of the best things that life had to offer lay in the very considerable wealth of experience and companionship that came from outdoor work in an unspoilt and living countryside in the company of childhood friends. There was scarcely a countryman who did not have an enthusiastic, intimate and expert knowledge of the ways of the weather, the habits of scores of birds and animals, the possibilities of different soils and the virtues and foibles of different beasts and crops. Entertainment was informal and homemade: humour was rustic, beery, repetitive and sometimes a little cruel, but storytelling was a practised art form with an established structure and was indulged whenever the men of the field had a few moments to spare. The themes were parochial and limited in range, concerning the personalities, vagaries and misfortunes of countrymen and country beasts. Tales that had been told a hundred times before were retold in deliberate and ritual fashion; the story was presented once, then again, with added detail, embellishment and exclamation, the key phrases underlined, and amid the swelling chuckles of approval that greeted an old favourite faithfully served, the punchline and highlights were repeated with increasing emphasis.

141 Staff outside the Post Office at Breamore, Hampshire, in the early 1930s. The postmistress and her mother are flanked by postmen with imposing bicycles.

189

There was no opting out of the cottage community. It gave the individual his role and status, entertainment and companionship; it tolerated most eccentricities, although it gossiped about them endlessly; and it shared the same oppressors. Well into the present century, the populations of dispersed Dales villages, hamlets and farmsteads would tramp across moonlit winter fields to dance in a barn or village hall to the music of local fiddlers and concertina players, returning sleepily through a freezing dawn to feed the stock and put out the chickens. The contemporary Yorkshire singer Bob Pegg evokes the old and new in his song 'Leaving the Dales':

> *My mother remembers the old village dances*
> *When uncle got out his squeezebox to play*
> *And the people would walk for miles in the darkness*
> *And dance through the night to the break of the day.*

> *   *   *

> *I'm leaving today, there's nothing to keep me –*
> *The doors they are bolted, the windows are nailed;*
> *I'm leaving a land that has nothing to offer,*
> *A land of a people who struggled and failed.*

> *Your children have taken the road to the city*
> *And strangers have come here with eyes open wide:*
> *Oh will you remember the life that we gave you*
> *When the last trueborn Dalesman has died?*

Community had more than just a social significance in the days when the safety net of social security was wide-meshed and flimsy. Many villages supported their own little friendly society, and some had several. Focusing on a particular pub, with the landlord as treasurer, these mutual benefit associations saved subscriptions to make donations to members afflicted with illness or misfortune, and every year, with brass emblems on poles to the fore, members of the society paraded through the village in a manifestation of their collective intent to face adversity and survive. Most of these small groups declined or were absorbed by national societies by 1900, but the survival of the communal spirit was demonstrated during the last war, when cost-spreading village pig-keeping associations spontaneously appeared in a number of places.

All the statistical evidence paints a picture in which even the average family would be considered desperately deprived by modern material standards; yet the memories of the survivors suggest that village life at the beginning of this century had positive qualities too, which have passed away or only survive in jaded, fragile form.

The ploughman of today, sheltered in the hood of his juddering tractor, cannot sniff the rain on the wind or listen to the skylark; he looks in vain for the corncrake or harrier, and the sterilized fields in which he works are unrelieved by the vivid splashes of the poppy and marguerite. There is no more storytelling in the threshing barn and stables, which now shelter soulless machines, and the ploughman has little rapport with his tractor: he cannot urge it, reward it or tell stories about its prowess in the pub at night. Away from the tractor's roar, the once crowded fields lie silent, more quiet than they have ever been before.

MEARE CLUB WALK

In the shelter of social security, the council estate, the modern school, the midweek surgery and the old age pension, the village too, after the departing rumble of the commuting cars, is quiet. There are fewer chances for women to chat around the pump or in the shop; the yeast no longer circulates, the water comes from a tap and the groceries in a supermarket box. And the old folk, the survivors, who were always on hand to advise on when to set and sow, how to poach a trout or get the bread to rise, to scare birds from the yard and lay out the dead have lost an audience and a role. The village is quieter now; cleaner, safer, but quieter. Good old days or bad old days? Who can tell?

One thing though is certain: the village of the survivors and crowded fields has gone forever; it cannot be recreated. It was built of poverty and hand labour and the generations which shared the crowded fields were often reunited in the workhouse. The days of the village pump were also the days of diphtheria, and the future of the village, for good or ill, is not to be found in its past.

The salvation of the village and, to a great extent, the destruction of the lingering remnants of the old community were largely the achievement of commuting. This resulted from the realization by increasing numbers of middle-class urban workers that although they must perforce seek their fortunes in the congestion and noise of the town, in the country they could enjoy the benefits of rural life (and buy a house more cheaply). The declined villages, whose gap-toothed streets showed the decay of farm employment and craft industries, were discovered; the old cottages became homes again, new houses were built and the communities began to grow once more. The village has never looked back, but salvation came at a price, although there are no 'goodies' or 'baddies' in this story.

142 The Meare Friendly Society in Somerset, photographed around 1910. Note the brass emblems of the Society which crown the poles.

Crowded and empty fields

143, 145 The Malvern Hills form the backdrop to this harvest scene, *above left*, painted by G. R. Lewis in 1815. Farming was enjoying an interlude of prosperity, due partly to the Napoleonic Wars. *Above* Two men do the work of dozens, and hundreds of miles of hedgerow are grubbed up to provide such combines with 'efficient units'.

144, 146 Prams and pushchairs are brought into the fields as women, doing traditional casual work, pick blackcurrants near Pembridge, Hereford-shire. But even here a machine can now take over, *right*, run by only a man and two youngsters.

In his trail-breaking academic study *Urbs in Rure*, R. E. Pahl chronicled the commuting process in Hertfordshire. He shows that London had long made its proximity felt: already in the eighteenth century merchants and bankers had been tempted to build country houses there, and a guidebook published in 1736 observes, 'The air of the county is esteemed so peculiarly clear, serene and healthful that it is the Residence of many Gentlemen; and it is an Adage founded in truth "He who buys a House in Hertfordshire, pays two Years purchase extraordinary for the Air of it".' Main railway lines arrived in 1840, 1850 and 1869 and branch lines connected many localities to the capital's arteries. Initially their effect was to benefit the county's farmers, and it was only in the 1870s and 1880s that the commuting potential of Hertfordshire was recognized. Henry Williams, historian of Watford, remarked:

> Many members of the great trading community of the metropolis, who at one time saw the country and breathed its pure air only on the occasion of their journeys on business or periodical holidays, have of later years deemed it necessary to the health of themselves and families to reside out of town, the head of the family going to London each morning to business, and returning to the country in the evening.

This movement was largely confined to towns lying along the railways; commuting did not make its full impact felt in the village until the motor car was developed and its ownership diffused downwards through society.

The postwar escalation of commuting in and out of London and the Hertfordshire new towns and overspill towns produced a situation where by the early 1960s over 78 per cent of the households in the parish of Tewin and almost 70 per cent of those in Hexton had moved in from elsewhere. Tewin received well over one-third of its newcomers from London; seven out of every ten households in the parish owned a car, and almost one-fifth of them had two cars.

194

In Tewin and neighbouring Watton about half the inhabitants were commuters (70 per cent of the newcomers), whereas only one in ten was a farmer or farmworker. In Britain as a whole today only three workers in a hundred work on the land.

This pattern, with local and regional variations, was echoed throughout England: the greater the proximity to a large town, the greater the commuter take-over was likely to be, while the more remote villages with cheaper property were scoured for weekend cottages and retirement homes.

Although commuting is a relatively recent process, it brings to mind the situation during the Saxon colonization when many villages would have contained two communities with different customs and different languages, the dominant Saxons and the disrupted indigenous British. Many of the twentieth-century village colonists were enjoying their first experience of country living; they were unfamiliar with country ways and codes of behaviour, and while the regulars in the public bar may have chuckled over the gaucheness and indiscretions of their new neighbours, they soon awoke to the realization that for the first time since the collapse of the yeoman their village contained a forceful and thrusting population.

The village in decline of the interwar period needed immigrants to provide the custom necessary to maintain its shops, schools, public services and transport. Paradoxically, however, the car, which encouraged the immigrants to come to the village, has served to insulate them somewhat from it. The indigenous population largely belong to the rural working class and, with lower car ownership, they depend on a rapidly contracting and increasingly expensive system of public transport. The largely middle-class commuter population, on the other hand, are highly mobile: they provide little of the support which is essential to revive the ailing public transport service, and their cars allow them to

148 Commuter housing beside the old green at Tewin in Hertfordshire.

shop cheaply at a supermarket in town, leaving the village-bound housewife to provide the main custom for the local store-cum-post office, paying the high prices that are necessary for its profitability.

In many villages a strange process of turn-about is taking place in housing, a process which in the end puts the newcomers in the old houses and the old inhabitants in the new. At the dawn of the age of commuting many country places abounded in cheap and decaying property, and the pioneer commuters took advantage of low house prices and low county rates. As the trickle swiftly increased to a stream and then to a flood, there was fierce competition for housing old and new, with the older, more picturesque property attracting the highest bidders. Soon it became impossible for the rural worker to afford anything in his native village: at 1979 prices, for instance, the cheapest house would be likely to cost double what he could afford. If he was unable to settle his family in a tied cottage or more recently built council house, he was squeezed out and had no choice but to move to town. Faced with rising costs and inconvenient cut-backs in public transport and services, an old village couple whose green-side period cottage has suddenly become highly desirable will be very tempted to sell up and depart for a convenient flat in town. If they have no house to sell, they may move into new cottages for old people built by the local council.

Although rightly or wrongly some middle-class families think their children will get a more progressive education in urban or public schools, the new villagers do often provide the additional children that are essential for the survival of the village school, that cornerstone of community life. Much publicity was recently gained by the inhabitants of Madingley near Cambridge, who bought the school which the authority had attempted to close and appointed their own staff. But Madingley was lucky in that most of its people are fairly well-off, and hundreds of less fortunate villages must stand by helpless as the school which kept the children in the community is extinguished.

149 At Madingley in Cambridgeshire, in 1978, parents refused to accept the closure of the village school: as the banner points out, such schools (which allow children to remain in the village) are the heart of the community.

We have seen time and again the weakness of the traditional villagers and their inability to defend their interests, and while the newcomers may pose something of an internal threat, at least they are a force which is well equipped to deal with threats that come from outside. They are more worldly-wise, articulate and self-assured, and they brook less interference: the immigrant lawyers, managers and executives are often the equal of the developers, road-builders and school-closers who hover threateningly over the community. They have also given the village a face lift, 'restoring' some homes to a degree that would render the cottages unrecognizable to any of their former occupants. (What a shock many of these Olde Worlde recreators would have if they could see the old village as it really was, with plaster masking the studwork, sparrow-tattered thatch, pathside dungheaps and muddy, rutted streets.)

The newcomers are great organizers: village societies flourish as never before, cricket pavilions are repainted and the teams replenished, dramatic societies are revived, the greens mowed and policed, and village conservation groups spring up. All this is almost entirely to the good, although the gaps in understanding between the old and the new populations often remain wide. It is not always appreciated that villages were never particularly tidy places, and that while the old villager's endeavours in backyard mower-mending, log-cutting or pig-keeping may be noisy, unsightly or smelly (and unknown to the planner or tax man), they may provide just sufficient extra income or interest for him to stay on.

The completeness of the change in role in many villages makes it easy to forget how much of the old pattern survived until quite recently, particularly in places removed from the first wave of commuter colonization. Birstwith in Nidderdale is today essentially a dormitory for Harrogate, Leeds and Bradford. From my

150 Village cricket on the green at Barrington, Cambridgeshire.

schooldays there in the late 1940s and early 1950s I can recall a village which was different, and quite withdrawn from the modern world. There were figures now departed like Mr Stott the cobbler, Mr Lewis the water bailiff, who kept live minnows for bait in his water butt, and Mr Martin, who was thought to be a merchant seaman and turned up each year on a mysterious walking marathon. There was, and still is, a blacksmith; and until his recent death Mr Byford had a small business mending bicycles and most other things when he was not serving as part-time chauffeur to the local worthies, and on winter evenings a group of old men and farmhands was sure to assemble around his stove as he worked into the night. School was interrupted by potato picking (tattie-scratting) each autumn, by a memorable trip to see the first combine harvester used in the village at work in the fields, and once by a solemn visit by the vicar to announce the death of King George VI. Stalin's death was revealed to us in a much lighter vein – though nobody was quite sure who he was – and we were instructed that President Eisenhower would make a good President because the Republican Party was the American attempt to emulate our Conservatives.

At the start of the 1950s, Birstwith was in some ways as much feudal as modern, and the Lady of the Hall, who owned it, sold it. This caused little hardship, and several cottagers bought their dwellings for one-hundredth or one-two-hundredth of the price that these gritstone dwellings would be worth today. The fishing rights on the River Nidd were owned, and still are owned (here as in other villages), by wealthy outsiders, although the only real effect of this was to increase the subtlety of the local fishermen.

The rusting cog wheels of an ancient cotton mill which found itself on the wrong side of the Pennines and a minute coal mine shaft represent the village's first industrial employment, and until the 1960s there was employment in a large

151 A familiar rural scene. Bridge in Kent was eventually lucky: it now has a bypass.

flour mill and a smaller dairy. The dairy has closed down, but the flour mill remains, now part of a large consortium. Like most other villages, Birstwith used to be more accessible to the non-car-owner than it is today; it was on the branch line from Harrowgate to Pateley Bridge and also enjoyed a cheap and regular bus service. The railway fell under Lord Beeching's axe and the bus service is no longer cheap and much less regular. The axeing of the railway came during the discovery of the village by commuters: houses and bungalows soon covered the abandoned railway yard and then spread to cover two meadows behind the Station Hotel.

The newcomers have caused little distress and their children help to keep the village school viable. The transformation of the sleepily detached world of the farmworker, estate cottage, mill hand, council manual worker and council house into a dormitory settlement of the world of commerce and conferences was accomplished in the space of half a dozen years or so. The Great House is now a private school.

152 Millstone grit cottages of former estate workers on the steep slopes below the Hall at Birstwith in Nidderdale. Occupants and their occupations change, but the village remains.

The future of the English village on the broad scale is assured. Since the introduction of the 1947 Town and Country Planning Act we can be fairly sure that death by vandalism rather than attrition will not be the threat that it was. Green Belt legislation and the hostile official attitude to ribbon development will save many villages from being engulfed in anonymous suburbia. But motorway developments, pounding by heavy goods lorries, school closure and decaying amenities remain a threat. From an aesthetic point of view the principal despoilers have been the same local authorities which use their planning powers to resist petty improvements and individual entrepreneurship but which, in village after village, have thrown up shabby, monotonous and badly sited council housing estates. These estates are essential if vital elements of the old community are to be retained, but the architecture employed is more often than not insulting to occupants and site alike, and in design eighteenth-century almshouses are by comparison palaces.

The need in the village is not for less planning, but for broader planning. In the south of Cambridgeshire where local schools are being squeezed out and narrow-minded planning regulations suffocate the initiative of the small tradesman, a monstrous motorway is being constructed which will shatter the peace of a dozen villages, nip the runway of the Duxford museum of historic aircraft and bring rumbling clamour within earshot of Grantchester Meadows and Byron's Pool. So long as local and national authorities fail to recognize that villages are communities which require an integrated development policy and continue to regard education, transport, conservation, planning and a host of other services in isolation then third-rate discordant policy is all that can be expected.

Most authorities at least are coming to take a more sympathetic view of rural industry. Only a minority of places can hope to attract industries, but where these do move in they provide the employment that gives new life to villagers of the old establishment, who must be retained in the community. In this field CoSIRA, the Council for Small Industries in Rural Areas, is doing an invaluable job of support and publicity. Industries which can be enticed into the village are of a particular kind: they must be small-scale and capable of accommodation in premises which will not detract from the setting, and they must be able to utilize the relatively unskilled rural labour forces. When they do, they can expect to be well served by the country worker's traditional readiness to 'muck in' and forget the rule book when an extra effort is needed. Unfortunately, the high cost of land and buildings resulting from the commuter boom can often price the village out of the small industry market.

Looking ahead, so far as one can tell (and who in 1340 would have foretold the pestilence, in 1820 foreseen the near collapse of English farming, or in 1914 predicted the destruction which the Great War caused?), the same economic and social patterns will continue. More villages will become commuter dormitories and the old community will have increased difficulty in maintaining a foothold, but there will be more voluntary conservation and, perhaps, broader-minded planning, and a return of industry to some places. The village will survive; it will evolve as it has always evolved; and, for the first time in a thousand years, it has a population which is ready and able to stand up for itself.

Some of my information has been gleaned from books which are long out of print and from articles in academic journals. The following list includes the most recent publications, and also older books, most of which are standard works which should be easy to obtain. A few titles will appeal mainly to the more dedicated student of the village: my comments will provide a guide.

F. ARCHER, *A Lad of Evesham Vale*, London (Hodder and Stoughton) 1972. One of many titles from this prolific writer on rural life in the West Midlands.

A. BARFOOT, *Homes in Britain*, London (Batsford) 1963. Covers the changing styles of the Englishman's home.

M. W. BERESFORD, *Lost Villages of England*, London (Lutterworth Press) 1954. Much more has been discovered since this pioneering study but it remains a compelling introduction.

M. W. BERESFORD and J. G. Hurst, eds., *Deserted Medieval Villages*, London (Lutterworth Press) 1971. New discoveries continue to outstrip attempts to produce an up-to-date guide.

R. BLYTHE, *Akenfield*, Harmondsworth (Penguin) 1969. A village and its people, based on interviews in more than one Suffolk community.

G. BOURNE (pseudonym of George Sturt), *Change in the Village*, London (Duckworth) 1912.

R. W. BRUNSKILL, *Illustrated Handbook of Vernacular Architecture*, London (Faber and Faber) 1978.

K. CAMERON, *English Place Names*, London (Batsford) 1961.

E. CARR, B. RUTHERFORD and G. STOREY, *People and Places: an East Anglian Miscellany*, Lavenham (Terence Dalton) 1973. A village, a hall and a wheelwright are subjects of detailed study.

A. CLIFTON-TAYLOR, *The Pattern of English Building*, London (Faber and Faber) 1972. Without equal as a communicator on matters architectural.

B. COPPER, *A Song for Every Season*, London (Heinemann) 1971. If you like the countryside and its folk you will love this account of life in a Sussex family famous for its singing of the traditional country ballads.

B. CUNLIFFE, *Iron Age Communities in Britain*, London (Routledge and Kegan Paul) 1974. An up-to-date and expert, if rather technical, account.

G. DARLEY, *Villages of Vision*, London (Architectural Press) 1975. A superb guide to the planned village.

E. EKWALL, *Concise Oxford Dictionary of English Place Names*, Oxford University Press 1936. Chances are it's in here.

G. E. EVANS, *The Horse in the Furrow*, London (Faber and Faber) 1960; and *Ask the Fellows who Cut the Hay*, London (Faber and Faber) 1965. Two from the list of works by a writer with legions of admirers. The author preserves the oral tradition of his beloved Suffolk neighbours.

JUNE FIELD, *Cottages and Conversions at home and abroad*, Edinburgh (Bartholomew) 1973. A well-illustrated guide.

M. M. FIRTH and A. W. HOPKINSON, *The Tolpuddle Martyrs*, Wakefield (EP Publishing Ltd) 1974.

P. J. FOWLER, ed., *Recent Work in Rural Archaeology*, Bradford-on-Avon (Moonraker Press) 1975. Scholarly papers, but not beyond the amateur historian.

J. L. and B. HAMMOND, *The Village Labourer*, London (Longman) 1978. Fifth edition of this study of village hard times and oppression.

W. G. HOSKINS, *The Making of the English Landscape*, London (Hodder and Stoughton) 1955, and Harmondsworth (Penguin) 1970. The Grand Master of landscape history would want now to modify some of his ideas; a great work for all that.

D. IREDALE, *Discovering Local History*, Princes Risborough (Shire) 1973. An easy guide to local documents and sources.

—*Discovering Your Old House*, Princes Risborough (Shire) 1977. How to interpret old houses.

GWYN JONES, *Rural Life*, London (Longman) 1973. Mainly for those with a fairly serious interest in the sociology of the countryside.

C. KETTERIDGE and C. W. MAYS, *Five Miles from Bunkum: A village and its crafts*, London (Eyre Methuen) 1972. Old country ways in East Anglia.

E. W. MACKIE, *Science and Society in Prehistoric Britain*, London (Paul Elek) 1977. Revolutionary ideas about British prehistory.

S. MARSHALL, *Fenland Chronicle*, Cambridge University Press 1967. A colourful glimpse of life in the Fenlands of old.

E. W. MARTIN, *The Book of the Village*, London (Phoenix House) 1962. An easy-to-read account of various aspects of village life.

D. R. MILLS, ed., *English Rural Communities*, London (Macmillan) 1977. Contains Prof. Thorpe's account of the destruction of Wormleighton and J. N. Tarn on the history of Bromborough Pool.

R. E. PAHL, *Urbs in Rure*, London (L.S.E. Geographical Papers, 2) 1965. Inspired thousands of student studies of commuting.

ROWLAND PARKER, *Cottage on the Green*, London (Research Publishing Co.) 1973. A brilliant reconstruction of the development of a cottage and the lives of generations of occupants.

—*The Common Stream*, London (Collins) 1975. Shows just how much the committed amateur historian can discover about a village though few professionals write so well.

J. and J. PENOYRE, *Houses in the Landscape*, London (Faber and Faber) 1978. A useful handbook for all those interested in the different regional styles of cottage building. More than 100 small colour illustrations.

P. H. REANEY, *The Origin of English Place Names*, London (Routledge and Kegan Paul) 1960. A readable approach to a complicated subject.

T. ROWLEY, *Villages in the Landscape*, London (Dent) 1978. Serious and up-to-date account of village development from the earliest times.

J. F. D. SHREWSBURY, *A History of Bubonic Plague in the British Isles*, Cambridge University Press 1970. Current medical insights combined with contemporary documents of disaster.

R. SAMUEL, ed., *Village Life and Labour*, London (Routledge and Kegan Paul) 1975. Designed for the student reader but contains some very detailed and readable sections on life in the days of the crowded fields.

F. W. STEER, ed., *Farm and Cottage Inventories 1635–1749*, Chichester (Phillimore) 1969. Absolutely fascinating: the possessions of countryfolk as revealed by their inventories.

TARN: see MILLS.

C. TAYLOR, *Fields in the Landscape*, London (Dent) 1975. A masterly interpretation of the development of fields. If you think that fields are dull, this book will prove you wrong.

THORPE: see MILLS.

Acknowledgments

Figures in **bold** type refer to colour plates.

Reproduced by Gracious Permission of Her Majesty Queen Elizabeth II 116; Aerofilms Ltd 12, 15, 39; Buckinghamshire County Museum, Aylesbury 137; Anthony Barton 17; Bedfordshire County Record Office 101; City Museum and Art Gallery, Birmingham 109; Birmingham Reference Library (Sir Benjamin Stone Collection of Photographs) 67, 139; British Tourist Authority 42; British Transport Hotels 2; British Travel Association 79; R. W. Brunskill, from his *Illustrated Handbook of Vernacular Architecture* (Faber and Faber, London, 1978) 72; *Cambridge Evening News* 149; University of Cambridge Collection, copyright reserved, 10, 11, 18, 19, 29, 30, 37, 38; courtesy M. J. Carpenter, Esq. 141; Peter Chèze-Brown **22**; Ruth Duthie **19**; University of Edinburgh, School of Scottish Studies 88; English Tourish Board 5, 55, 56; Essex County Record Office 35; courtesy Hale Civic Society, from their book *Hale and Around, Its Past in Pictures* (1976) 92; Hitchin Museum 125; Charles Kirk **2, 4**; Lucinda Lambton **3, 6, 7, 8, 17, 20**; Emily Lane **5, 9, 11, 15, 18**, 49, 94, 106, 124, 126; Anthony Levick 145; Museum of Lincolnshire Life, Lincoln (Parkinson Collection) 120; British Library, London 25, 26, 27, 28, 32, 33, 34, 36, 58, 60, 98; National Monuments Record, London 62, 81, 82, 97; Public Record Office, London 31; Tate Gallery, London 105, 108, 119, 143; Trades Union Congress Library, London 113; Victoria and Albert Museum, London 115, 118, 140; J. A. Longbottom 152; City of Manchester Art Galleries 135; Massey Ferguson Ltd 144; Richard Muir **1, 10, 13, 14, 21**, 13, 14, 21, 22, 23, 24, 40, 44, 45, 48, 50, 52, 57, 64, 69, 71, 73, 74, 75, 80, 83, 84, 87, 99, 100, 128, 138, 147, 150; Sarah Nichols 66, 70, 93; *Northern Echo* 95; Norwich County Library 78, 131, 133; Bodleian Library, Oxford 9; Pattenden Engineering Ltd 193; A. F. Palmer, *Kentish Gazette* 151; Museum of English Rural Life, University of Reading 105, 110, 117, 122; Sir Peter Roberts 16; F. Shuter 4; Edwin Smith 6, 46, 47, 54, 65, 68, 76, 77, 85, 86, 91; Suffolk Photographic Survey 121; Somerset County Museum, Taunton 142; Sutcliffe Gallery, Whitby, by agreement with Whitby Literary and Philosophical Gallery 123, 130, 132; Jeffery Whitelaw **12, 16**, 7, 8, 41, 53, 59, 61, 136, 148; Richard Whitmore 127; Reece Winstone 43, 53; courtesy Gordon Winter, from his book *A Country Camera* (Country Life, London, 1966; repub. Penguin, Harmondsworth, 1973) 111.

   Illustration 129 is taken from J. T. Smith, *Etchings of remarkable beggars, itinerant traders and other persons of notoriety in London and its environs* (London, 1815), and illustration 134 from W. H. Pyne, *Microcosm, or a picturesque delineation of the arts, agriculture, manufactures etc. of Great Britain* (London, 1803–06).

The lyrics of 'Dancing at Whitsun', on p. 143, are by A. J. Marshall (Shapiro Bernstein & Co. Ltd and Soundpost Publications); those of 'Leaving the Dales', on p. 190, are by Bob Pegg (Heathside Music).

Index